ABOUT THE AUTHOR

John Weinstein began his work with the Métis political movement in the 1970s and has since acted as advisor to successive Métis leaders, enabling him to participate in and document many of the events depicted in *Quiet Revolution West.* He accompanied the mercurial leader Harry Daniels to Parliament Hill on the day Métis were recognized in the constitution and later appeared as a witness for the fledgling Métis National Council in its lawsuit against Prime Minister Trudeau over the issue of representation in constitutional negotiations. He has contributed to a number of Royal Commissions and participated in work at the United Nations on the indigenous rights question.

Weinstein also worked in the venture capital industry in western Canada for fifteen years. He is an inveterate adventure traveler, having toured most of the world since the late 1960s. One of his most interesting journeys took him through the story behind *Quiet Revolution West,* "across a homeland in my own country that most people have no idea exists, that of the Métis Nation."

To contact the author, send emails to: johnweinstein@rogers.com

This book is dedicated to Howard Adams,
Harry Daniels, and Don McIvor, as well as to
Jim Sinclair and Clément Chartier, whose life-
long struggles, hardships, and achievements
inspired me to write this book

Quiet Revolution West

West

The Rebirth of Métis Nationalism

John Weinstein

FIFTH
HOUSE

Cover and interior design by Dean Pickup
Cover image: AR 301; Métis Sash, mid-twentieth century, wool, Native North American, Collection of Glenbow Museum, Calgary, Canada
Edited by Dallas Harrison
Copyedited by Ann Sullivan
Proofread by Liesbeth Leatherbarrow

The type in this book is set in Minion.

The publisher gratefully acknowledges the support of The Canada Council for the Arts and the Department of Canadian Heritage.

**Canada Council
for the Arts**

**Conseil des Arts
du Canada**

We acknowledge the financial support of the Government of Canada through the Book Publishing Industry Development Program (BPIDP) for our publishing activities.

Printed in Canada

2007 / 1

First published in the United States in 2008 by
Fitzhenry & Whiteside
311 Washington Street
Brighton, Massachusetts, 02135

Library and Archives Canada Cataloguing in Publication Data

Weinstein, John
    Quiet revolution west : the rebirth of Métis nationalism / John Weinstein.

Includes bibliographical references and index.
ISBN 978-1-897252-21-5

    1. Métis--Politics and government. 2. Canada, Western--History.
3. Métis--Land tenure. 4. Métis--History. 5. Métis--Government relations.
6. Métis--Legal status, laws, etc. I. Title.

FC109.W43 2007   323.1197'071   C2007-903484-5

Fifth House Ltd.
A Fitzhenry & Whiteside Company
1511, 1800-4 St. SW
Calgary, Alberta T2S 2S5

1-800-387-9776
www.fitzhenry.ca

CONTENTS

FOREWORD

The Right Honourable Paul Martin

Canada is a remarkable story. We are a nation of 33 million people with beginnings scattered throughout the globe and faiths spanning the entire spectrum, gathered here to live together and work together in the belief that we can build the most prosperous, peaceful, progressive, and fair country in the world.

We have done well by most standards, but any honest evaluation of our progress must include a forthright admission of where we have not succeeded. Ironically, many of our brothers and sisters in the Métis Nation, First Nations, and Inuit communities continue to endure a quality of life here similar to that which has caused so many of Canada's newer citizens to flee their homelands. That this situation has persisted is nothing short of shameful.

There is an unacceptable gap between the hopeful promise of youth and the experience of Aboriginal adulthood. It is a gap made even more unacceptable by the fact that Aboriginal youth represent the fastest-growing segment of Canadian youth. The Métis people form an integral part of this population.

We face a moral imperative. The descendents of the people who first occupied this land deserve an equal chance to work for and to enjoy the benefits of our collective prosperity. Today, the majority do not because of gaps in education and skills, in health care and housing, and because of limited opportunities for employment. Put simply, these gaps—between Aboriginal Canadians and other Canadians, and between Aboriginal men and women—are not acceptable in the twenty-first century. They never were acceptable. The gaps must be closed.

Building a shared understanding of the past is essential to achieving consensus on a plan to move forward. In publishing this book, John Weinstein has made a major contribution by bringing us much closer to a shared understanding.

Weinstein has given us a beautifully written history of the Métis Nation. His narrative, spanning three centuries, teaches us about its origins in what was then known as Rupert's Land, where in fact the union of the founding peoples of Canada—French, English, and Aboriginal—first took root. He further describes the Métis people's founding role in Confederation through the establishment of the province of Manitoba, where, we would all do well to remember, the Métis were, at the time, the majority population

Quiet Revolution West is a vivid tale of constant struggle and sacrifice. Nineteenth-century epic battles on the Prairies, endless examples of struggles to overcome terrible injustices, racism, dealing with the pain of forced assimilation, feelings of helplessness that come with confiscation of property and identity. These are indignities no Canadian should have to endure.

As Canada marched down the road to constitutional independence from Britain in 1982, the Métis leadership fought a long and testing campaign to have their rights enshrined in what would become our new Constitution. Weinstein captures this movement, its skirmishes and confrontations, victories and failures, in a gripping account of political intrigue and brinksmanship that no doubt will raise eyebrows in many quarters.

A significant portion of the development of the Métis Nation in Canada occurred in our courtrooms. We read of arduous marathon-like legal battles between governments at all levels and the Métis leadership. One can only marvel at the perseverance and determination of those who were out in front, wrestling with a much more powerful adversary who had unlimited resources. These are tense stories with consequences of great magnitude hanging in the balance. There are instances of triumph and occasions of defeat—all of which Weinstein portrays with striking clarity. In the chapter on Powley, one can almost feel first-hand, the jubilation experienced that day in 2003.

One of the most wonderful things about public life is the unrivalled opportunity to get to know so many outstanding people both here at home and around the world. I have had the distinct honour to know Clément Chartier, David Chartrand, and Audrey Poitras, and to call them my friends. They are passionate, accomplished, and professional and have worked body and soul for the cause of the Métis Nation. It is in no small part due to their hard work that the historic Kelowna Accord came into being.

Thanks to John Weinstein, you will have the good fortune to get to know them and others such as Tony Belcourt and Jim Sinclair—heroes to the Métis cause and people who want nothing but to build a better home for their people and a more prosperous Canada. Weinstein paints other compelling portraits of the champions and leaders of the Métis people, from Louis Riel to Harry Daniels, Elmer Ghostkeeper, Yvon Dumont, and many others. We don't do enough in this land to understand the people behind the story. Thankfully, this book greatly expands our awareness and understanding of a number of individuals for whom we should all have a deeper appreciation.

John Weinstein's chronicle of the Métis Nation would measure as a first-class, exciting political drama, were it not for the human suffering that is at its core. His account is a critical analysis of history that will no doubt stir a significant degree of controversy. One is of course free to disagree with Weinstein's analysis, yet it is without question that his contribution will not only enrich the public record, but it will also contribute to much needed discourse. This story needs to be told.

Over the course of our history we have heard the call for partnership from the Métis Nation, from the Inuit, and from all First Nations. Yet for too long we have been only negotiators, sitting across the table from one another. It's time we sit down on the same side of the table, as partners, time for all of us to take our rightful places and complete the task before us together.

This book will help us get there.

PREFACE

Quiet Revolution West was a work in progress for a long time, a contemporary political history written as the story unfolded, and, in fact, continues to unfold. As a student of political history, I had the good fortune to be involved in the Métis nationalist movement as a senior advisor to Métis leaders since the 1970s. In this capacity, I was able to participate in and observe much of what is described in the book and to interview most of the book's key actors while they were still leaders of the movement.

Quiet Revolution West explores various dimensions of the renaissance of the Métis Nation in western Canada. It also explains Métis nationalism and the Métis nationalist movement as a historical and contemporary force in Canadian politics. In paying particular attention to the interplay of this nationalist movement with Canada's constitutional initiatives starting with Pierre Elliott Trudeau, it is the story of how a people's historic struggle for nationhood within Canadian federalism has become an essential part of Canada's attempt to redefine itself since patriation.

The book was not meant as a thesis; it is intended to serve as a play-by-play (or blow-by-blow) account of what happened during the past three decades and hopefully point to the critical issues shaping future developments. Given the contemporary focus of the book, the historical background is not a definitive history of the Métis Nation but rather an overview of the origins of the key issues that remain outstanding today. The reader is advised to consult the maps and appendices for a better understanding of the early history of the Métis Nation.

Quiet Revolution West seeks to explain the internal dynamics of contemporary Métis political organizations and take the reader "behind the scenes" to get a feel for the "cut and thrust" of Métis politics. The situation, as can be imagined, has been very fluid, as attested to by the multiplicity of organizations, some short-lived, others that have evolved over time. For this reason, the reader is advised to refer to the list of abbreviations provided.

John Weinstein
August 2007

Abbreviations

AFN	Assembly of First Nations
AMNSIS	Association of Métis and Non-Status Indians of Saskatchewan
FMS	Federation of Métis Settlements
HBC	Hudson's Bay Company
IACHR	Inter-American Commission on Human Rights
ICNI	Inuit Committee on National Issues
IMHA	Interim Métis Harvesting Agreement
ITC	Inuit Tapirisat of Canada
MAA	Métis Association of Alberta
MCA	Métis Constitutional Alliance
MCC	Métis Constitutional Council
MHRDA	Métis Human Resources Development Agreement
MLA	Member of the Legislative Assembly
MMF	Manitoba Métis Federation
MNA	Métis Nation of Alberta
MNBC	Métis Nation British Columbia
MNC	Métis National Council
MNO	Métis Nation of Ontario
MNS	Métis Nation Saskatchewan
MP	Member of Parliament
MSGC	Métis Settlements General Council
MSS	Métis Society of Saskatchewan
NIB	National Indian Brotherhood
NCC	Native Council of Canada
NDP	New Democratic Party
NRTA	Natural Resources Transfer Agreements
NWC	North West Company
OACA	Office of Aboriginal Constitutional Affairs
OAS	Organization of American States
PQ	Parti Québécois
RCAP	Royal Commission on Aboriginal Peoples
UAS	Urban Aboriginal Strategy
UN	United Nations
WCIP	World Council of Indigenous Peoples
WGIP	Working Group on Indigenous Populations

Chapter 1

THE RISE AND FALL
OF THE NEW NATION

*I*n my childhood, I often stayed with my grandparents on the old scrip farm of Maxime Lepine at Batoche. I did not realize at the time that I was tramping in the footprints of a noble guerrilla warrior. Maxime's spirit was not there, not felt at all. Of the many games we halfbreed kids invented, not one was related to the struggle of 1885. This history was hidden from us because our grandparents and parents were defeated generations. We were a new generation, starting our lives of defeat, without hope, ashamed of ourselves as halfbreeds. Although our forefathers—Regnier, Boucher, Fiddler, McDougall, Parenteau, Ouellette, Short, Adams—had fought gloriously against the Ottawa regime, we were still the wretched of the earth.

—Howard Adams, *Prison of Grass:*
Canada from the Native Point of View [1]

FROM CONTACT TO CONFLICT

People of mixed ancestry appeared in eastern Canada soon after initial contact between Indians and Europeans. "Our young men will marry your daughters and we shall be one people,"[2] French explorer Samuel de Champlain told his Indian allies, and mixed unions became an integral part of state and church policy in the French settlements of New France and Acadia during the seventeenth century. The ultimate objective of this policy was to assimilate the Aboriginal people and boost the French population. This genetic mixing did contribute to the emergence of new and distinct peoples, the Acadians and the Québécois, though neither saw itself as an indigenous people.

It was on the isolated plains of west-central North America during the late eighteenth and early nineteenth centuries that people of mixed ancestry emerged as a new and distinct group that saw itself not only as an indigenous people but also as a new nation. The fur trade companies operating in this territory—the Hudson's Bay Company (HBC), which had exploited and administered the vast expanse of territory draining into Hudson Bay known as Rupert's Land under a royal charter granted in 1670; and its main competitor, the North West Company (NWC), the old Montreal-based French firm taken over by British and British-American merchants following the conquest of New France in 1763—had a common interest in resisting agricultural settlement. This resistance and the rugged barrier of the Precambrian Shield north of Lake Superior were among the factors that had blocked large-scale immigration onto the western plains from the British colonies to the east. Hence, the mixed offspring of French fur traders from the North West Company or Scottish fur traders from the Hudson's Bay Company and their Cree or Ojibway wives formed an ever-increasing proportion of the fur trade population.

They were first known as *metifs* or *bois brûlés* (burnt wood) if their fathers were French, or half-breeds and country-born if their fathers were Scottish or English. As their numbers grew and they married among themselves, they developed a new culture, which was neither European nor Indian but a fusion of the two. Their *michif patois* mixed the French, Cree, and Ojibway languages; their jigs combined the reels of Scotland with the intricate steps of Plains Indians dances. European observers were struck by the flamboyance of the mixed-blood traders they encountered, commenting on the bright colours of their dress, which was semi-European, semi-Indian in style but of European rather than western cut, and the decoration of their accessories with glass beads and quills.

With their mixed traditions and command of both European and Indian languages, people of mixed ancestry were logical intermediaries in the commercial relationship between the two civilizations. They adapted European technology to the wilderness through innovations such as the Red River cart and the York boat, which made possible the transport of large volumes of goods and supplies across the West to

Métis beaded jacket in Batoche Museum.
(Collection of Clément Chartier)

and from the far-flung outposts of the fur trade. The North West Company was less centralist in its operations than the Hudson's Bay Company, and the mixed offspring of its French employees enjoyed considerable economic and political autonomy, establishing separate communities on the open plains linked by economic interest to the Nor'Westers.

As provisioners to the NWC, the bois brûlés organized the commercial buffalo hunt. They left their permanent settlements periodically, electing a provisional government for each expedition to make and enforce the laws of the hunt. The political consciousness they acquired in organizing these hunts was heightened by the rivalry between the fur trade companies, and the Nor'Westers encouraged this nascent nationalism. It was among the bois brûlés that a sense of being a new nation first developed and led to conflict with the governing authorities.

In 1811, the Hudson's Bay Company made a land grant to Lord Selkirk of 116,000 square miles (300,440 square kilometres), including the Red River Valley (southern Manitoba), for an agricultural settlement and a source of provisions for the fur trade. The bois brûlés feared that an influx of Scottish settlers would disrupt their economy and displace them from territory they had rapidly filled with the decimation of the Indians by smallpox and other diseases. Efforts by the new colonists to restrict the hunting and trading practices of the bois brûlés eventually led to the colonists' defeat in 1816 at the Battle of Seven Oaks, where the victorious bois brûlés, led by Cuthbert Grant Jr., unfurled the flag of the Métis Nation.

In 1821, amalgamation of the Hudson's Bay Company and the North West Company closed many fur trade posts and caused many of their employees and families to move to the Red River Settlement. There the bois brûlés from the plains and NWC posts were joined by the half-breeds from HBC posts. The half-breeds had been raised in the hierarchical HBC society, which had denied them the autonomy of the bois brûlés. In the Red River Settlement, however, they became free people quite capable of concerted action with the bois brûlés to defend common interests against the governing Hudson's Bay Company. Ties between the two groups were reinforced by frequent intermarriage and common economic pursuits: supplying the fur trade with provisions such as pemmican (a mixture of dried meat, berries, and grains), transporting furs and supplies, interpreting, guiding, or farming. With greater concentration and marriage among and between themselves, the French Catholic bois brûlés and the English Protestant half-breeds developed a group consciousness as a Métis people[3] and a new nation that the HBC authorities had to take into account in their administration of the Red River Settlement. The *chanson* of Métis poet Pierre Falcon describing the Battle of Seven Oaks had warned of English interlopers coming "to rob our country" (see Appendix A), and so the HBC tolerated the division of some of the Métis parishes into long, narrow river lots as in Quebec as well as the Métis tradition of settling on these lots without formal legal title.

In trying to enforce its monopoly over trade, the Hudson's Bay Company had to contend with the demands of a Métis middle class. The Métis believed that as a people conceived on the western plains, they—along with the Indians—were its true owners and possessed certain rights that the HBC had not respected. They challenged the company's monopoly by engaging in the illicit free trade of furs; starting export industries; and opening up the route from Red River to Saint Paul, Minnesota, in order to gain access to the lucrative American market and a cheaper source of finished goods. In the process, they incurred the wrath of the Hudson's Bay Company, which retaliated with repressive measures.[4]

Métis free traders and merchants became the most articulate proponents of a growing Métis nationalism. In 1845, they petitioned the governor of the Red River Settlement for recognition of their special status. In 1849, they led an armed body of Métis horsemen, who surrounded a courthouse where fur trader Guillaume Sayer was being convicted for trafficking in furs, prompting his release before sentence could be passed and leading to a declaration of free trade ("*le commerce est libre*"). Among the leaders of the revolt was Louis Riel Sr., a businessman whose five-year-old son would go on to become the leader of the Métis Nation. In 1857, Alexander Isbister,[5] a Métis educator and lawyer who had taken up residence in London, presented the Métis case to the British Parliamentary Select Committee on the Hudson's Bay Company.

Half-breed traders with members of the North American Boundary Commission, ca. 1873.
(Library and Archives Canada, C-4164)

Red River served as an incubator of the new nation and Métis nationalism. In eastern Canada, large-scale immigration and agricultural settlement had caused the absorption of people of mixed ancestry into the settler or Indian population, but in the Red River Settlement between 1820 and 1870 the Métis absorbed Europeans and Indians. By 1869, the population of the Red River Settlement—one of the largest settlements on the plains of North America west of the Mississippi and north of the Missouri—consisted of 5,720 francophone Métis, 4,080 anglophone Métis, and 1,600 whites. This was the community that lay in the path of the new Dominion of Canada as it began its march from sea to sea.

Métis camp scene, Milk River, Alberta, July-August 1874.
(Library and Archives Canada, C-81787)

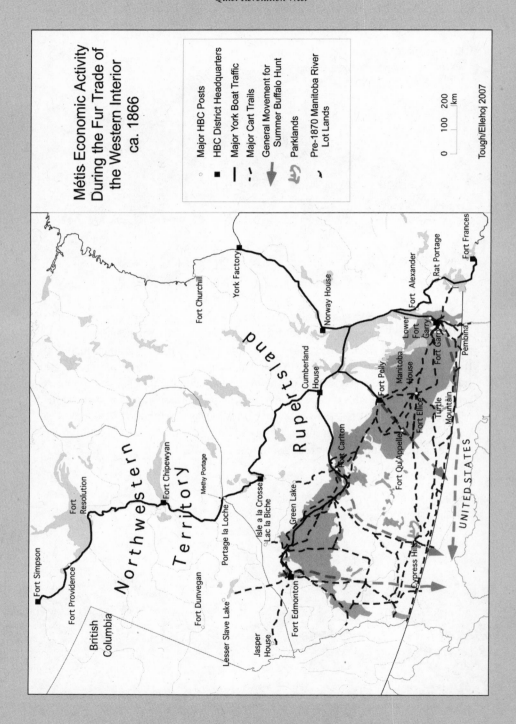

Métis Economic Activity
During the Fur Trade of
the Western Interior
ca. 1866

Major HBC Posts
HBC District Headquarters
Major York Boat Traffic
Major Cart Trails
General Movement for
Summer Buffalo Hunt
Parklands
Pre-1870 Manitoba River
Lot Lands

0   100   200
km

Tough/Ellehoj 2007

Métis Economic Activity During the Fur Trade of the Western Interior, ca. 1866

This map depicts the fur trade economy spanning the core area of the Métis Nation in 1866, just prior to the dramatic changes that came with the Hudson's Bay Company's (HBC) surrender of its charter rights in 1869. By engaging in trapping, fishing, commercial hunting, interpreting, freighting, and trading, Métis people held vital roles in this mercantile economy. In the prime fur-producing subarctic region, larger posts (known as District Headquarters) engaged or employed a significant numbers of Métis people. Today's large Métis community at Isle a la Crosse has its origin in the geography of the fur trade.

The commercial fur trade organized a transport system based on York boats that moved commodities such as pemmican between the grasslands, parklands, and the northern bush zones, and furs out for eventual export to the world market in London. York boat work was generally carried out by Métis tripmen, such as the famous Portage La Loche brigade. This particular work force was recruited from the Red River Settlement, and during the short open-water season they moved cargoes between the Red River Settlement, Portage La Loche (Methy Portage), Norway House, and York Factory before returning to Fort Garry. This map only depicts the main York boat routes.

The parklands was a resource-rich region and provided good shelter for both humans and the bison during the severe winters. Consequently, District Headquarters of Forts Edmonton, Pelly, and Garry, and important posts such as Forts Carlton and Ellice, were located in the parklands. Many Métis communities also developed in this region. The distinctive Red River Cart was well suited to the transport demands of the HBC and Métis buffalo hunting expeditions. These carts left an imprint on the land and later surveyors would map these trails. Like the York boats, Métis carts served to link distinct geographical regions by moving commodities between grasslands and parklands. The Carleton Trail, which connected Forts Garry and Edmonton via Fort Carleton, is well known, but this map depicts many more, but not all, of the trails developed by Métis hunters, freighters, and traders. Eventually, trails were pushed north thereby connecting Green Lake and Lac la Biche posts to the Carleton Trail. Starting in the 1860s, the HBC directed freighting activity from York boats to Red River Carts.

The largest concentration of Métis people was found at the Red River Settlement and it was here, under the leadership of Louis Riel, that a political resolve was forged and the colonial annexation of the Northwest by Canada was thwarted.

—Frank J. Tough

THE RED RIVER REBELLION
AND THE MANITOBA ACT

In 1869, the Hudson's Bay Company sold Rupert's Land to the Dominion of Canada for £300,000 and one-twentieth of the territory's fertile land. During the negotiation of the sale, no provision was made for the rights of the Métis majority in the Red River Settlement; it was expected to become part of a territory governed directly by Ottawa. In the words of historian W. L. Morton, "One of the greatest transfers of territory and sovereignty in history was conducted as a mere transaction in real estate."[6]

In advance of the formal transfer of authority, Prime Minister Sir John A. Macdonald sent a survey party to Red River. Its arrival at Fort Garry on 20 August 1869 caused great concern among the Métis, many of whom did not possess clear title to their land. They feared that the township system of survey preferred by the English Canadians, which laid out land in square lots, would disrupt their tradition of long, narrow river lots according to the seigneurial system of Quebec. By the end of the month, a young, educated, and bilingual Métis nationalist who had returned to Red River the previous year after studying for the priesthood and law in Montreal, was denouncing the survey party from the steps of the Saint-Boniface Cathedral.

On 28 September 1869, Prime Minister Macdonald appointed the minister of public works, William McDougall, as the lieutenant-governor-designate of the territory, with the transfer of authority set for 1 December. On 11 October, a group of Métis, including the emerging leader Louis Riel, disrupted the survey party. On 16 October, they formed a Métis National Committee. Riel then informed the HBC authorities that McDougall would be admitted into Red River only after Canada negotiated terms with the Métis and the general population of Red River. On 2 November, a Métis force under the command of Ambroise Lépine turned back McDougall's party near the American border while another group of up to 400 Métis, led by Riel, occupied Fort Garry without bloodshed.

On 1 December, McDougall proclaimed the transfer of authority over Rupert's Land from the HBC to the Dominion of Canada, but the Macdonald government had already postponed the transfer upon receiving news of the resistance in Red River. On 7 December, a group from Red River's pro-Canadian minority responding to McDougall's call to arms were forced to surrender to Riel's forces. The next day, in the absence of a clear authority, the Métis National Committee declared itself a provisional government.[7]

Early in 1870, a special committee of six Métis, three francophone and three anglophone, including the new president of the provisional government, Louis Riel, was appointed to draft a List of Rights for the Métis. This list, to undergo further

Louis Riel, 1844–85.
(Library and Archives Canada, C-052177)

amendment, would be carried to Ottawa by three delegates of the provisional government and would form the basis of negotiations with the Conservative government of Sir John A. Macdonald. Reflecting the three primary concerns of the Métis—political status, language, and land—the List of Rights called for the admission of their territory as a province into Confederation; for its representation in the Senate and the House of Commons; for the recognition of both English and French as the official languages of the new province; and for provincial control of public lands (see Appendix B).

By 15 February, the imprisoned members of the pro-Canadian party at Fort Garry had either escaped or been released by Riel after pledging not to engage in further agitation. Some of them remained intent on overthrowing the provisional government and were captured by Riel's forces as they approached Fort Garry on 17 February. One of the insurrectionists who was particularly contemptuous of the Métis and fought repeatedly with his guards, a fervent Orangeman named Thomas

Counselors of the Provisional Government of the Métis Nation, Manitoba, 1870. Front, L-R: Robert O'Lone, Paul Proulx. Centre, L-R: Pierre Poitras, John Bruce, Louis Riel, John O'Donoghue, François Dauphinais. Rear, L-R: Bonnet Tromage, Pierre de Lorme, Thomas Bunn, Xavier Page, Baptiste Beauchemin, Baptiste Tournond, Joseph (Thomas) Spence. (Library and Archives Canada, PA-012854)

Scott, was put on trial for defying the authority of the provisional government and threatening its president. He was condemned to death at a court martial presided over by Riel's associate, Ambroise Lépine, and was executed by firing squad on 4 March 1870. News of Scott's execution inflamed public opinion in Ontario, where Riel was reviled as Scott's "murderer" and a reward of $5,000 was offered for his arrest.

In April 1870, the delegates of the provisional government arrived in Ottawa for negotiations with Macdonald and his Quebec lieutenant, Sir George-Étienne Cartier. The parties agreed that the Red River Settlement would enter Confederation as the new Province of Manitoba (comprising a "postage stamp" of 11,000 square miles [28,490 square kilometres] in the southern part of today's province) with representation in the House of Commons and the Senate. As well, Manitoba's official languages would be English and French, and denominational schools would be safeguarded.

The main stumbling block in the talks was the demand for provincial control of public (crown) land. Although the Métis were seeking no more than what existing provinces enjoyed, Macdonald insisted on dominion control of Manitoba's public lands. At the same time, there was a need to compensate the Métis in order to annex the North-West peacefully and to assure Quebec that the francophone Catholic Métis of Manitoba would not be displaced, that Macdonald did not intend to transform the new province—as Archbishop Taché of St. Boniface had warned—into another Ontario.

Compensation would take the form of recognition of claims to land already occupied by Métis and for additional land allocations for their children. Furthermore, the Red River delegates and Cartier agreed that the new province (with its large Métis majority) would have control of land already occupied, including the river lots, and the distribution of land grants to the children of the Métis inhabitants. It was agreed that a local committee, to be established by the Red River population, would select these lands and divide them among the children of the Métis. On 2 May 1870, the Manitoba Act—including most of the demands in the Métis List of Rights—was introduced in the House of Commons. On 12 May, the act received royal assent. Section 31 conferred land rights on the "children of the half-breed heads of families" in the form of a 1.4-million-acre (560,000-hectare) land grant, while section 32 conferred land rights on all settlers in the province (the majority being Métis) who had interests in land (see Appendix B).

The rationale for the 1.4-million-acre land grant was to extinguish Indian title to the land in the new province prior to large-scale settlement, a practice originating in the British Royal Proclamation of 1763. This proclamation recognized an Aboriginal interest in the soil, a burden on the crown's title, and prohibited settlers from occupying Indian lands until the Crown, at a general assembly of the Indian occupants, extinguished Indian title through agreements providing for compensation. Canada, inheriting the principles of the proclamation, eventually concluded numbered treaties (Treaties One to Eleven) through which most Indians west of Quebec extinguished title to their land in return for reserves, hunting rights, annuities, and gifts.

Why the Macdonald government chose to deal with Métis claims on the basis of Indian title is not clear. Riel's List of Rights (the fourth and final draft of demands first issued in November 1869) did not claim land rights for Métis based on their share of Indian title;[8] its sole reference to Aboriginal rights provided for treaties to be signed by the Dominion of Canada and the Indian tribes in the new province. The Métis did see themselves as an indigenous people and co-owners of the land with the Indians, but they also saw themselves as a nation, not a tribe, and as such sought political equality with English Ontario and French Quebec in the form of provincial status and powers rather than the protection of the Crown offered to the Indians under the paternalistic and restrictive treaty and reserve system.[9]

The promise of a Métis land grant under the policy of extinguishment of Indian title was probably the most expedient method of removing the foremost obstacle to Canada's westward expansion. The recognition and extinguishment of

Métis rights would be concurrent. Ottawa would have control of the public lands of the West and would determine who would settle on these lands. Moreover, by invoking the need to extinguish Indian title, Macdonald could justify the land grant to the English Protestant Orangemen of Ontario, who demanded revenge for the execution of Thomas Scott.

On 24 June 1870, at a special session of the Legislative Assembly of Assiniboia at Fort Garry, the agreement reached between Cartier and Red River delegates in Ottawa and the Manitoba Act were ratified by the Métis provisional government. On 15 July, Manitoba became Canada's fifth province. In the words of historian G. F. G. Stanley, it was a "national achievement of the New Nation and the personal victory of Louis Riel."

It was to be a short-lived victory. Earlier in the rebellion, Macdonald had stated that "the impulsive half-breeds have got spoilt by their *émeute* [riot] and must be kept down by a strong hand until they are swamped by the influx of settlers."[10] The "strong hand" took the form of 1,200 troops dispatched to Fort Garry in May as a punitive mission. Troops and settlers arriving in the new province were hostile to the Métis, some of whom were killed or beaten. Métis landholders were harassed. Despite government assurance of amnesty to all participants in the Red River Rebellion, Riel was forced to flee for his life. Thrice elected to the House of Commons, he would be barred from ever taking his seat.

In keeping with the spirit of the accord between Ottawa and Red River, the first lieutenant-governor of Manitoba, Adams G. Archibald, suggested provincial legislation to secure Métis tenure of occupied river lots. He was overruled by Ottawa, with Secretary of State for the Provinces Joseph Howe arguing against "giving countenance to the wholesale appropriation of large tracts of country by half-breeds."[11] Section 30 of the Manitoba Act gave the dominion jurisdiction over "all ungranted or waste lands" in the province, but now Macdonald's regime considered all lands—including the river-lot farms occupied by Métis and the 1.4-million-acre Métis grant—to be ungranted or dominion lands. According to legal scholar Douglas Sanders, "the federal government—the government whose indifference had been a basic cause of the Red River rebellion—was in charge of the land grants which the Métis had won by their political actions."[12]

When Macdonald made a request to the British Parliament to amend the Constitution Act, 1867, to sanction what he had done in Manitoba, the subsequent amendment, the Constitution Act, 1871, confirmed the Manitoba Act but also—contrary to Macdonald's wishes—prohibited the Parliament of Canada from altering the provisions of the Manitoba Act by giving it constitutional force.[13] Accordingly, sections 31 and 32 of the Manitoba Act were immune from tampering by the federal government. Nevertheless, during the next decade, Parliament enacted a number of statutes, which, in the words of historian D. N. Sprague "either repealed portions of Sections 31 and 32 or set up qualifications and procedures which were so stringent or complicated that they robbed both Sections of their original meaning."[14]

One federal statute in 1873[15] restricted eligibility to share in the 1.4-million-acre land grant to children of Métis heads of families who weren't themselves also parents of children, disqualifying approximately 40 per cent of the people whom Lieutenant-Governor Archibald had considered entitled to allotments (i.e., the parents in a household with children, parents, and grandparents living together.) In addition to losing benefits under section 31, married children living with their parents were excluded from the benefit of section 32 because they were not owners of river lots. According to Sprague,[16] "The effect of the amendments was nearly total dispossession and dispersal of the original people of Manitoba. The pattern of loss varied enormously from family to family and not all people saw their claims defeated. About 15% of the claimants of allotments of the 1.4 million acres received and made use of their land and a similar percentage of river lot occupants obtained patents and remained on the land they occupied in 1870."

A process for distributing lands to the Métis in fulfillment of sections 31 and 32, originally envisaged by Archibald to take one or two years under local legislation, took more than a decade for the federal government to administer. Confronted by a mass influx of hostile Anglo-Ontarians frequently squatting on and gaining title to their traditional lands caught up in the red tape of Ottawa's chaotic land grant scheme, the Métis moved on; their proportion of Manitoba's population dropped from 83 per cent in 1870 to 7 per cent in 1886. Two-thirds of the Métis people moved out of the province of Manitoba, most between 1876 and 1884. This period of exodus coincided with the enactment of a series of statutes by the Manitoba provincial legislature (where the loss of population had eliminated the Métis majority position) facilitating the sale of the interests of Métis children in the 1.4-million-acre land grant and imposing provincial taxes on lands prior to the grant.

The Manitoba Act failed to resolve the grievances underlying the Red River Rebellion because Canada for the most part and from the outset had never been prepared to accept a Métis-majority province. In the words of Sprague, "The real opposition to Red River was that the colony was predominantly Métis. A collection of 'semi-savages' had taken it upon themselves to pretend that they could form a government and write their own terms for entry to Confederation—into behaving like Nova Scotians, Prince Edward Islanders or others, demanding better terms as their condition for admission to the federation."[17] Nonetheless, the Manitoba Act established the Métis as one of Canada's founding peoples or nations, and it is this status, together with the aspirations associated with it, in particular the right to a land base and political autonomy, that remains the driving force behind Métis nationalism to the present day—and would set the new nation on a collision course with Canada in the valley of the Saskatchewan.

THE NORTH-WEST REBELLION, 1885

Some Red River Métis moved farther north, some moved south into the United States, but most moved west to the South Saskatchewan River valley and to the settlements near Fort Edmonton, where they joined or founded Métis communities. There they resumed their demands for a land base in unison with those Métis resident in the North-West before 1870. As early as 1872, the Saskatchewan Métis had petitioned for an inalienable tract of 1.8 million acres (720,000 hectares) of land. Ottawa refused to recognize their claims as half-breeds and said they would have to make claims as ordinary settlers. The Métis were expected to apply for land as homesteaders, but they believed their contributions and rights were paramount to the new land regulations. They also claimed exemption from the township system of survey, which threatened to disrupt their pattern of river lots borrowed from Quebec.

As the federal government negotiated treaties with Indians and granted vast tracts

Gabriel Dumont, 1837–1906.
(Library and Archives Canada, PA-178147)

of land to the Hudson's Bay Company, the railways, and land-speculation companies, it ignored continuous Métis petitions for land title. When its indifference threatened to throw the North-West into disorder, the federal government, recognizing that the Métis could influence the Indians not to sign treaties, chose to settle their claims on the basis of extinguishing Indian title. The Dominion Lands Act, 1879, provided for the granting of land to half-breeds of the North-West toward extinguishment of Indian title, yet it was not until 28 January 1885, that the Macdonald government established a commission to review and settle Métis claims in the North-West. By then, the Métis were already on an inexorable course of rebellion against Ottawa.

In May 1884, the Métis of the South Saskatchewan River valley met in Batoche to adopt resolutions setting out their grievances and seeking the return of Louis Riel. A delegation then left for Montana to persuade exiled Riel, a teacher in a Jesuit mission school, to return to the North-West. On 19 March 1885, under the leadership of Riel, the Métis formed the Provisional Government of Saskatchewan. As in 1869–70, they demanded responsible government, parliamentary representation, and local control of public lands, as well as confirmation of land titles according to the river lot system of survey.

On 26 March 1885, fighting broke out at Duck Lake, where Gabriel Dumont and the Métis clashed with the North-West Mounted Police, prompting the federal government to dispatch a military expedition under the command of Major General Frederick Middleton. On 24 April, Dumont ambushed Middleton's column at Fish Creek. Between 9 and 12 May, Middleton's army defeated the Métis in the Battle of Batoche. A few days later, Riel surrendered and was transported to Regina for trial. On 1 August, he was found guilty of treason, and on 16 November he was hanged.

The trial and execution of Riel created Canada's first national unity crisis: Ontario, still seething over the execution of Thomas Scott, demanding a similar fate for Riel; Quebec, in support of the defender of the French language and Catholic faith in the West, demanding clemency. Macdonald's refusal to commute the death sentence—"He shall hang though every dog in Quebec bark in his favour"—and the execution itself led to massive street protests in Montreal (and would contribute to the victory of Quebec nationalists in the provincial election in 1886 and the decline of the Conservative Party in that province). As for the people whose actions in defence of their rights had led to the crisis in the first place, Macdonald offered

Métis Council prisoners in the courtyard of the Regina Court House, August 1885. L-R: Ignace Poitras, Pierre Parenteau, Baptiste Parenteau, Pierre Gariepy, Ignace Poitras Jr., Albert Monkman, Pierre Vandal, Baptiste Vandal, Joseph Arcand, Maxime Dubois, James Short, Pierre Henry, Baptiste Tourond, Emmanuel Champagne, Kit-a-wa-how (Alex Cagen, ex-chief of the Muskeg Lake Indians). (Library and Archives Canada, PA-118760)

a retrospective and blunt assessment of their status in an address to the House of Commons following the suppression of the rebellion:

> In 1870, in order to secure peace and order—in fact, to obtain possession of the country—it was necessary to enter into an arrangement by which that Province [of Manitoba] might be acquired, that turbulent feelings might be put down and Canada might secure peace and quiet in that country. In order to accomplish that result the Government of the day entered into negotiations with certain delegates from the Province of Manitoba, which culminated in the Act of 1870, creating Manitoba a Province. In that Act it is provided that in order to secure the extinguishment of the Indian title 1,400,000 acres of land should be settled upon the families of the half-breeds living within the limits of the then Province. Whether they had any right to those lands or not was not so much the question as it was a question of policy to make an arrangement with the inhabitants of the Province, in order, in fact, to make a Province at all. ... That phrase was an incorrect one, for the half-breeds did not allow themselves to be Indians. If they are Indians, they go with the tribe; if they are half-breeds they are white, and they stand in exactly the same relation to the Hudson's Bay Company and Canada as if they were altogether white. That was the principle under which the arrangement was made and the Province of Manitoba was established.[18]

For Macdonald, the recognition of Métis rights in Manitoba had been no more than an expedient for Canada to gain possession of the West. In the wake of Batoche and with the "redoubtable Riel" out of the way, it could be dismissed as a mistake. There would be no political accommodation of the Métis as a distinct people; their rights would be no different from those of white settlers.

Notwithstanding Macdonald's views on Métis rights (or the lack thereof), during the period of armed conflict in the spring of 1885, his government adopted orders-in-council authorizing the Street Commission to distribute half-breed grants. Given the nature of Métis grievances, which had led to two uprisings, and their perceived influence over the Indians, this policy was the most expedient means of concluding treaties and opening the public lands of the North-West to large-scale settlement. Moreover, since the half-breed land grants would come out of lands opened for homesteading purposes, the federal government was in reality conferring on the Métis benefits similar to those available to white settlers under homesteading legislation. Subsequent half-breed commissions would extend grants to Métis throughout the North-West.

Starting with the signing of Treaty Eight in 1899, half-breed commissions hearing Métis claims would sit simultaneously with Indian treaty commissions.

Grants under the Dominion Lands Act took the form of scrip, a coupon denominated in a fixed amount of acres or dollars that could be applied to the purchase of surveyed dominion lands opened for homesteading. Land scrip was non-transferable, but the process for redeeming it for land proved to be complicated and lengthy. Métis claimants had to travel to distant dominion lands offices to locate the land scrip on a dominion lands entry and then wait for the patent to be issued by Ottawa. Métis from large areas of the North-West that had not yet been surveyed could not use land scrip to obtain title to their traditional lands.

The most common form of grant issued by the half-breed commissions was transferable money scrip, which could be applied to the purchase of dominion lands or sold and assigned to land speculators, often lawyers and bankers, who were equipped to go through the onerous redemption process. Most Métis opted for money scrip and then sold it for a fraction of its value to scrip speculators. Ottawa's collusion with these speculators extended to every step of the scrip distribution and redemption process.

Scrip speculators travelled with and, in effect, became an integral part of the half-breed commissions. Dominion lands officials posted large cards in their offices with the names of speculators from whom scrip could be procured by the public and then applied to the purchase of dominion lands. Speculators opened scrip accounts with the Department of the Interior that would transfer scrip credits to dominion lands offices where speculators were doing business. When Edmonton

Money scrip with a face value of $160 issued by the North-West Half-breed Commission on 10 July 1908. (Library and Archives Canada, RG 15, vol. 1399) (Photo by Métis Archival Project, 2004)

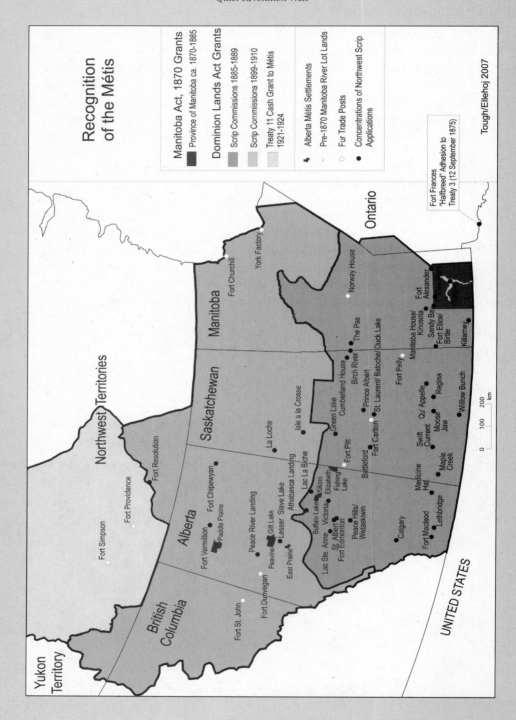

Recognition of the Métis

Manitoba Act, 1870 Grants
- Province of Manitoba ca. 1870–1885

Dominion Lands Act Grants
- Scrip Commissions 1885–1889
- Scrip Commissions 1899–1910
- Treaty 11 Cash Grant to Métis 1921–1924

- Alberta Métis Settlements
- Pre-1870 Manitoba River Lot Lands
- Fur Trade Posts
- Concentrations of Northwest Scrip Applications

Tough/Ellehoj 2007

Fort Frances.
"Halfbreed" Adhesion to
Treaty 3 (12 September 1875)

Yukon
Territory

Northwest Territories

British Columbia

Alberta

Saskatchewan

Manitoba

Ontario

UNITED STATES

Fort Simpson
Fort Providence
Fort Resolution
Fort St. John
Fort Dunvegan
Fort Chipewyan
Fort Vermillion
Paddle Prairie
Peace River Landing
Peavine
Gift Lake
Lesser Slave Lake
East Prairie
Athabasca Landing
Lac La Biche
Buffalo Lake
Kikino
Victoria
Elizabeth
Fishing Lake
St. Albert
Lac Ste. Anne
Fort Edmonton
Peace Hills/
Wetaskiwin
Calgary
Fort Macleod
Lethbridge
Medicine Hat
Maple Creek
Swift Current
Moose Jaw
Willow Bunch
Regina
Qu'Appelle
La Loche
Isle a la Crosse
Green Lake
Cumberland House
Fort Pitt
Battleford
Fort Carlton
Prince Albert
St. Laurent/ Batoche/ Duck Lake
Birch River
The Pas
Fort Pelly
Fort Ellice/
Birtle
Killarney
Sandy Bay
Manitoba House/
Kinosota
Norway House
York Factory
Fort Churchill
Fort Alexander

0 100 200
km

Recognition of the Métis

This map indicates some of the basic geographical expressions of the political/legal recognition of the Métis by the Crown. The *Manitoba Act, 1870*, made provision for a land grant to Métis children. Later, scrip coupons were issued to Manitoba Métis adults. These provisions applied to the "postage stamp" province of Manitoba, a territory depicted on this map and much smaller than present-day Manitoba.

Although the federal government treated with First Nations of the Northwest beginning in 1871, the claims of the Métis outside of the postage-stamp Manitoba were not considered until 1885, when the federal government initiated a non-negotiable claim process that was largely limited to the issuing of land or money scrip to Métis individuals. This map indicates the territory and timing of scrip commissions and it depicts locales in which a discernable concentration of scrip applications were taken.

It should be noted that scrip was not issued in Ontario, but recognition of the Métis took a peculiar form when the federal government took an adhesion from a Métis community to Treaty Three at Fort Francis on 12 September 1875. Similarly, scrip claims were largely outside of the experience of the Métis of British Columbia, however, scrip applications were taken at Fort St. John. Nonetheless, scrip applications asked claimants for information on places of birth and residence and this information indicates the presence of Métis in Ontario and British Columbia.

This map also depicts the present-day Alberta Métis Settlements, which were established by the province's *Metis Betterment Act, 1938*.

—Frank J. Tough

NOTE: The provincial and territorial boundaries in this map depict the situation in 1912.

millionaire Richard Secord was charged in 1921 with obtaining Métis scrip through fraud, Parliament amended the Criminal Code to impose a time limitation of three years on the prosecution of scrip offences, thereby nullifying the charges.

Without title to their land and facing a rapid decline of the fur trade economy, the Métis of the North-West were swept away by a tide of immigration in the decades following the North-West Rebellion. Some moved to the northern forests of the Prairies, where they joined established Métis communities or formed new ones. There they were able to continue their traditional pursuits of freighting, trapping, hunting, and fishing. In the southern part of the Prairies, some Métis managed to cling to their lands and earned a livelihood as farmers and farm labourers. Many others were forced into slums on the fringes of Indian reserves and white communities or on road allowances, strips of public land on either side of public roads. They eked out a subsistence gathering buffalo bones for shipment to fertilizer factories; picking stones on farms; doing other menial jobs; or hunting and fishing. Some got by on relief.

Métis emigrants from Manitoba who had been displaced by the earlier failed land grant distribution fared even worse than their brethren in the North-West. They were denied scrip in the North-West on the ground that their claims should have been settled in Manitoba. Likewise, they were denied homestead lands under the provisions of the Dominion Lands Act on the ground that their claims should have been settled by scrip.[19]

The records of the North-West Mounted Police provide a snapshot of Métis conditions.

20 April 1888—"Halfbreeds of Bresaylor area destitute."

16 May 1888—"Métis in North Battleford area starving."

7 May 1889—"Relief provisions provided to halfbreeds at St. Laurent."

8 October 1889—"N.W.M.P. are ordered by Sir John A. Macdonald to cease giving relief to destitute Métis."

31 November 1889—"Métis of St. Laurent area destitute."

24 December 1889—"Halfbreeds in North Battleford area destitute."

4 January 1891—"Halfbreeds at Fort-a-la-Corne destitute."

24 March 1891—"Relief supplies given to halfbreeds at Pincher Creek."

29 June 1892—"Destitute halfbreeds from Cumberland House arrive in Prince Albert."

July 1892—"Halfbreeds at Lac-la-Biche are destitute."

April 1894—"Halfbreeds at Willowbunch are destitute."

27 November 1900—"Halfbreeds in Athabasca region of Alberta are destitute."[20]

In 1930, the Natural Resources Transfer Agreements (NRTA) transferred control of the public lands and natural resources of the Prairies from Ottawa to the Provinces of Manitoba, Saskatchewan, and Alberta. The agreements made some provisions for Indian reserves and hunting rights but made no reference to the Métis. They marked an end to the sixty-year period of Ottawa's administration of the public lands of the Prairies to which the fate of the Métis Nation had been inextricably tied.

Starting with the turmoil behind negotiations of the Manitoba Act, 1870, and ending with the silence of the NRTA on the Métis, this period had seen two attempts by Métis provisional governments to establish political autonomy for the protection of the interests of the Métis Nation within the Canadian federation. On both occasions, Ottawa had contained the upsurge of Métis nationalism with military force and a policy of Indian title extinguishment, one that conveniently allowed Ottawa to terminate rights at the same time they were recognized. With the NRTA, the Department of the Interior closed the books on Métis land grants under the Manitoba Act and scrip allocations under the Dominion Lands Act. Métis claims, according to the Department of Justice (to this day), had been extinguished by law.

The expedience governing the distribution of Métis land grants and scrip allocations, together with the divergence in Ottawa's treatment of the land title rights of Indians and Métis in western Canada, calls into question whether these grants constituted a valid means of extinguishing the Métis share of Indian title. Notwithstanding the shortcomings in the treaty process, the federal government did extend the practice of British colonial authorities to adhere to basic principles and procedures set out in the Royal Proclamation of 1763 in its dealings with the Indian tribes. Hence, Indian treaty commissioners negotiated the terms of treaties with the leaders of the Indian tribes. The compensation offered in exchange for the extinguishment of Indian title was to have lasting benefits in the form of inalienable land reserves, annuities, hunting rights, and other benefits.

In dealing with Métis claims, on the other hand, Ottawa (and later the Province of Manitoba) generally proceeded through unilateral legislation and regulation. While the 1.4-million-acre land grant in Manitoba did result from negotiations involving the delegates of Riel's provisional government, its implementation was undermined by unilateral legislation and administrative action. In the North-West, Ottawa proceeded without even the appearance of negotiation to extinguish Métis claims by legislation and Orders-in-Council. Having rejected efforts by the Métis in Manitoba and Saskatchewan to secure control over the allocation of Métis lands by local governments, the federal government pursued a method of compensation—transferable money scrip—that fed a lucrative speculation industry and almost by design facilitated the alienation of Métis land grants. Whether the distribution of public lands opened for homesteading—and hence available to any settler in the West, albeit under different programs—constituted a valid means of compensating Métis for their share of Indian title remains another outstanding issue.

With its transfer of public lands and natural resources to the Prairies in 1930, the federal government absolved itself of any further responsibility for the Métis. Any future interventions on their behalf would have to come from the provinces. This denial of federal responsibility extended far beyond the question of formal jurisdiction. Métis history and culture were kept out of national museums and galleries and ignored in cultural policies. In 1941, the Métis were removed as a distinct people in Canada's census.

To avoid the stigma of "road allowance people," many Métis chose to assimilate. They became French or Scottish Canadians and achieved mobility in prairie society at the expense of their historical identity. Some managed to integrate into the dominant English and French groups while retaining a consciousness of their heritage and historical contributions. For those Métis stuck in limbo between white and Indian societies, identity shifting became a means of meeting the needs of the situation. Rick Hardy, the former president of the Métis Association of the Northwest Territories, would tell the Berger Inquiry (1974–77),

> I don't think that anyone, without having gone through the fire, can understand the feeling of being Métis. Belonging to both, but in reality to neither. Growing up in Fort Norman in the 1950s, I went through the fire. White and Indian accepting you on the surface, but rejecting you from the heart and soul. Imagine the feeling of a person being called a "Goddamned Halfbreed." So for a while we did what we thought was a smart thing; when with the Whites, we were White; when the Indian came, we became Indian, but this could only go on for so long without splitting ourselves apart trying to be two people.[21]

This marginalization of the Métis impinged on the integrity of their historical national identity. Like the English, Germans, or other nations, the Métis had originated as the mixed offspring of different peoples. Once they had evolved into a new entity, however, it did not matter how much ancestry they possessed from either side. In the words of Riel, "Why should we concern ourselves about what degree of mixture we possess of European or Indian blood? If we have ever so little of either gratitude or filial love should we not be proud to say, 'We are Métis'?"[22]

Riel's vision of a reborn Métis Nation would blur but never die. Predominantly Métis communities, Métis historical and cultural societies, and Métis political associations throughout the dark period of the Métis diaspora would preserve the history, culture, traditions, and political objectives of the new nation. They would offer a flicker of hope to the thousands wandering along the physical and psychological fringes of two societies, neither one their own.

Chapter 2

IN SEARCH
OF REPRESENTATION

For many Canadians, the Métis and the rebellions represented an interesting interlude in a somewhat dull Canadian high-school history course, significant for the firestorm generated in Quebec by the execution of Louis Riel and the crisis this created in confederation. A footnote to the historic conflict between English and French, the Métis people themselves, with the death of their leader, seemed to disappear. In fact, they and their societies persisted, albeit largely unseen and unheard, until conditions were created that would transform the ideals and objectives behind the rebellions into political action.

EARLY MÉTIS POLITICAL ORGANIZATION

In 1887, Métis at Batoche, Saskatchewan, organized a society named after their patron saint, Joseph, with objectives similar to those of Quebec's St. Jean Baptiste Society.[1] The society became a focal point for petitions to Ottawa regarding claims for property damage during the Métis resistance of 1885. Around this time, Métis people began annual observances of the resistance at Batoche that continue to this day.

Also in 1887, a group of Métis nationalists met in St. Vital, Manitoba, to found a historical and cultural society. Incorporated on 1 March 1888, l'Union Nationale Métis Saint Joseph du Manitoba was, and to this day remains, committed to fostering an awareness of the historical contributions of Manitoba's Métis. In 1891, it erected a monument on Riel's tomb in the St. Boniface Cathedral cemetery.

In 1910, l'Union Nationale Métis decided to correct what it believed to be the deliberate distortion of the history of the Métis Nation. This undertaking required decades of research and interviews with the Métis of Red River and Batoche. In 1936, the work culminated in the publication of *Histoire de la Nation Métisse dans l'Ouest Canadien* by A. H. de Trémaudan.[2]

During the Depression of the 1930s, dire conditions on the Prairies provoked a political mobilization of the Métis. With the transfer of control of public lands and

Founders of Métis Association of Alberta, March 1935. Rear, L-R: P. Tomkins, F. Callihoo. Front, L-R: M. Norris, J. Dion, J. Brady. (Glenbow Archives, PA-2218-109)

resources under the NRTA and Ottawa's entrenched opposition to dealing with them, new Métis political associations turned to the provincial governments for redress of their conditions and rights. The reaction of the provinces was to avoid the outstanding issue of Métis land rights, focus on existing social and economic conditions, and seek remedies through relief measures.

Founded in 1932, l'Association des Métis de l'Alberta (to be known as the Métis Association of Alberta [MAA]) pressured the United Farmers of Alberta government into appointing a royal commission to inquire into the conditions of the Métis in 1934. The chairman of the Alberta half-breed commission barred historical evidence regarding the past treatment of Métis land rights, arguing that "… scrip was issued in extinguishment of any supposed right which the halfbreed had to special consideration but the Government of this Province is now faced, not with a legal or contractual right, but with an actual condition of privation, penury and suffering."[3] In 1936, the commission recommended the establishment of a Métis farm colony system as a relief program,[4] prompting Métis to protest that they should receive land with full title as a matter of right.

Following the recommendations of the Alberta half-breed commission report,[5] the province enacted the Métis Population Betterment Act in 1938 to provide for the establishment of Métis settlement associations that would receive land from the province. Twelve settlement areas were set aside in the 1940s, but the province later terminated four unilaterally (Marlboro, Touchwood, Cold Lake, and Wolf Lake) and relocated their populations. Today there are eight Métis settlements—Fishing Lake, Elizabeth, Kikino, Buffalo Lake, East Prairie, Gift Lake, Peavine, and Paddle Prairie— comprising a land mass of 1.28 million acres (512,000 hectares).

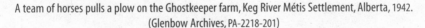

A team of horses pulls a plow on the Ghostkeeper farm, Keg River Métis Settlement, Alberta, 1942.
(Glenbow Archives, PA-2218-201)

Founded in 1937, the Saskatchewan Métis Society sought provincial assistance in directing its "constitutional claims" against the Government of Canada, which it held responsible for the historical dispossession of the Métis. Its objective was to procure federal compensation for extinguishment of the Métis share of Aboriginal title to the country in the form of assistance for the Métis to establish themselves in agriculture and industry. By the 1940s, twelve townships of public lands had been set aside for the Green Lake Settlement under a number of projects by the province (and prior to that by the federal Department of the Interior), providing Métis families with ninety-nine-year leases to land. Again the allocation of land was pursued as a relief measure; a report on Métis claims funded by the Saskatchewan government in 1943 concluded that "… in making any submissions to either the Dominion or Provincial Governments, stress should be laid on present conditions and needs rather than on compensation for past rights or alleged injustices."[6]

In Manitoba at this time, Métis associations were also working to press claims against Ottawa based on unextinguished Aboriginal title, but there was little if any federal or provincial response. A Northern Halfbreed Association formed in the 1930s was active in the Métis settlements near The Pas, Moose Lake, and Cedar Lake.

FIRST PROVINCIAL BOARD OF OFFICERS OF SASKATCHEWAN METIS SOCIETY ELECTED nov. 17, 1937

BILL LaROCQUE
BOB LaROCQUE
J. Z. LaROCQUE
JERRY LaROCQUE
MARTIN KNUDSTON

ED KLYNE
JOE McKENZIE
JACK BLONDEAU
JOE ROSS

Founders of Saskatchewan Métis Society, 17 November 1937.
(Collection of Clément Chartier)

Rose, Charlotte, and Helen Garneau, St. Paul, Alberta, August 1938. (Glenbow Archives, PA-2218-176)

Malcolm F. Norris and family, 1941. (Glenbow Archives, PA-2218-183)

It lobbied for the survey of crown land in the region in order for its members to gain title to their land and homes.

During this period, the constitutional case for federal intervention was given some impetus, albeit indirectly, by a judicial ruling. Section 91(24) of the Constitution Act, 1867, had given the federal government jurisdiction over "Indians and Lands reserved for the Indians." Ottawa had exercised this legislative authority for status Indians through the Indian Act, 1876, which excluded Eskimos and Métis. In 1939, the Supreme Court of Canada ruled that, despite the Indian Act, Eskimos were "Indians" for the purposes of section 91(24) of the Constitution Act, 1867, and therefore a federal responsibility. For Métis leaders seeking a direct relationship between the central government and a Métis Nation that transcended provincial boundaries, the ruling regarding Eskimos raised the possibility that they, too, would fit within the broad definition of "Indians" for constitutional purposes and hence fall within federal jurisdiction.

The outbreak of the Second World War derailed efforts to resolve the historical and constitutional issues of critical importance to the Métis. The years during and after the

Len and Marlene Belcourt playing a game outdoors, 1948.
(Glenbow Archives, PA-2218-296)

war proved to be difficult ones for Métis associations; hampered by the diversion of their leadership into the war effort and by a constant shortage of funds, they sometimes lapsed into periods of dormancy. With the formation of Métis settlements in the 1940s, the Government of Alberta bypassed the leadership of the Métis Association of Alberta—including leftist activists Malcolm Norris and Jim Brady—and dealt directly with government-controlled settlement councils.[7] Successive governments in Saskatchewan dealt with associations they considered too militant by funding rival groups.

During the 1960s, a new set of circumstances caused a revival of Métis political consciousness and organization. With the liberalization of North American society, minorities began to assert their identities. Among them were the Métis. According to Antoine Lussier and Bruce Sealey,

> The 1960s marked a sharp increase in the number of Métis students graduating from high schools in Manitoba. However, not until this time did they graduate as Métis. What led to their willingness to admit their heritage was a sudden surge of Métis nationalism, fostered in students by the media and liberal-minded teachers. They were encouraged to identify with a romantic past. As people recalled the days of sugar beet topping and cucumber picking with nostalgia, students increasingly developed a new sense of pride in the fact that their fathers were trappers, loggers, or construction workers; they were no longer so ready to deny their past.[8]

The upsurge of nationalism in Quebec during this period undoubtedly played a role in Métis political revival. Quebec's demands on the federal state and Ottawa's response to them—the Royal Commission on Bilingualism and Biculturalism (1963–69), with its mandate to find ways to develop the Confederation on the basis of an "equal partnership between the two founding races"—had a telling effect on many Métis who believed that, as a founding people, their nation had as much right to special status as Quebec. (During the next decade, the election of a separatist government in Quebec, the referendum on sovereignty association, and the Trudeau government's move to patriate the Constitution with entrenched official language rights would stimulate the Métis and other Aboriginal peoples to pursue their own forms of political autonomy and constitutional protection of their group rights.)

The success of independence movements in Europe's African and Asian colonies also contributed to a new outlook among the Métis intelligentsia in Canada. The themes of colonial exploitation and national liberation were paramount in the writings of Métis activist and revolutionary Howard Adams. Born and

Jean Cuthand, Malcolm F. Norris, and James Brady at a demonstration in Regina, Saskatchewan, 1 April 1961. (Glenbow Archives, PA-2218-943)

raised in the Métis community of St. Louis, a few kilometres from the battlefields of the North-West Rebellion, Adams had been radicalized while pursuing his PhD studies at the University of California at Berkeley in the mid-1960s. There he learned the tactics of the free speech movement—sit-ins, strikes, and demonstrations—which he would later apply in Saskatchewan. His written works offered a searing account of the psychological effects of colonialism on the Métis and other Aboriginal peoples.[9]

The 1960s witnessed the reorganization of older Métis associations and the formation of new ones. The MAA reorganized around the issue of natural resources. Despite the regulations of the Métis Population Betterment Act directing revenues from the sale of settlement natural resources into a Métis Trust Fund, the province denied any requirement to add to the fund the royalties and fees it was collecting on the oil and gas from Métis settlements. In 1961, MAA president Adrian Hope—veteran political organizer, rodeo rider, farmer, poet, and philosopher—collected one dollar from each association member to reactivate the organization and hire legal counsel. By the end of the decade, the MAA, under the leadership of Stan Daniels, was locked in a lawsuit against the province.

In 1965, the Métis of northwestern Ontario formed the Lake Nipigon Métis Association. Its members lived along the old fur trade route, where Métis communities had pressed Ottawa for a land base during the period of the Métis land grant scheme in neighbouring Manitoba. Led by Métis patriarch Paddy McGuire Sr., the association concentrated on enhancing economic opportunities for its members, particularly Métis fishermen.

The southern-based Saskatchewan Métis Society also reorganized and in 1967 amalgamated with the new northern-based Métis Association of Saskatchewan to form the Métis Society of Saskatchewan (MSS). In 1969, the MSS elected Howard Adams as president.[10] During the next decade, the MSS would remain the most militant of the Métis associations under the leadership of Adams and his protégé, Jim Sinclair.

In Manitoba, the Métis people saw the need for a political voice extending beyond the limited social base of l'Union Nationale Métis (comprising francophone Métis, by now a small proportion of the total Métis population) and its historical and cultural activities. The Manitoba Métis Federation (MMF) was founded in 1967 to unite the Métis throughout Manitoba and to work toward reconstruction of the Métis Nation. As custodian of the historical Métis nationalism that had created the Province of Manitoba, the MMF would offer ideological direction to the national Métis movement in the decades to come.

THE MÉTIS AND NON-STATUS
INDIAN ALLIANCE

After close to a century of adhering to its policy of non-recognition, the Government of Canada, under the leadership of Pierre Elliott Trudeau, began to respond to a revitalized Métis movement. Its approach was cautious, however, for Ottawa did not wish to raise expectations. Prime Minister Trudeau's attacks on *deux nations* in the 1968 election and his government's white paper of 1969 proposing a repeal of the Indian Act demonstrated his philosophical opposition to special status for any group in Canada. Instead, Trudeau offered Canadians the vision of a bilingual, multicultural country where all individuals had access to equality of opportunity. In line with these principles, his government's social policy departments were prepared to deal with the Métis as a disadvantaged minority group. In the process, they brought the Métis together with another Aboriginal group—non-status Indians—that had long been denied legal recognition by Ottawa.

The Indian Act of 1876 used a patrilineal rule—proof of Indian descent through the male line—to define who was entitled to live on lands reserved for Indians. Accordingly, subsection 3(3) of the act defined the term "Indian" as "any male person of Indian blood reputed to belong to a particular band; any child of such person; and any woman who is or was lawfully married to such person." Since 1876, successive Indian Acts had steadily shrunk the definition of "Indian" and forced a loss of status or exclusion of many Indians from band lists, reserves, and benefits. Section 12(1)(b) of the Indian Act, 1951, removed Indian status from Indian women who married non-Indians. In keeping with the patrilineal rule, Indian men who married non-Indians kept their status, and their wives and children automatically became eligible for registration under the Indian Act.

In western Canada, many Indians had lost status as a result of other measures. In the nineteenth century, the federal government had offered scrip as an incentive for treaty half-breeds to discharge from treaty, thereby reducing the Indian population. These "mixed-blood" Indians did not share the history, culture, or sense of nationhood of the Métis and saw themselves as members of the tribes with whom they had been raised. After the federal government amended the Indian Act in 1879 and 1884, many "full-blood" Indians were also induced by speculators to discharge from treaty to take scrip. (During the early 1930s, the MAA asked the province to take action on behalf of the descendants of 1,292 treaty Indians who had left treaty to accept scrip in 1885–86 and were swelling the growing Métis population in need).

Despite their fundamental differences in history, culture, and political aspirations, the Métis and non-status Indians found themselves in much the same relationship with the federal government. Both had suffered a loss of identity and land rights as a result of federal legislation and policy. Both had been considered "citizens like any other" and a provincial responsibility, unlike status Indians and Eskimos, for whom the federal government had exercised its constitutional responsibility. Now, under the Trudeau regime, both were recognized as Aboriginal minorities with special problems rather than special rights.[11]

In 1970, the federal Liberal government agreed to fund Aboriginal organizations. Three national associations were recognized, along with their affiliated associations. Status Indians formed the National Indian Brotherhood (NIB), while the Inuit formed the Inuit Tapirisat of Canada (ITC). Ottawa also offered funds to the existing Métis associations on the Prairies, which joined with the non-status Indians and Métis of British Columbia to form the Native Council of Canada (NCC). During the next five years, the NCC expanded to include new, predominantly non-status Indian associations from the other provinces and territories.

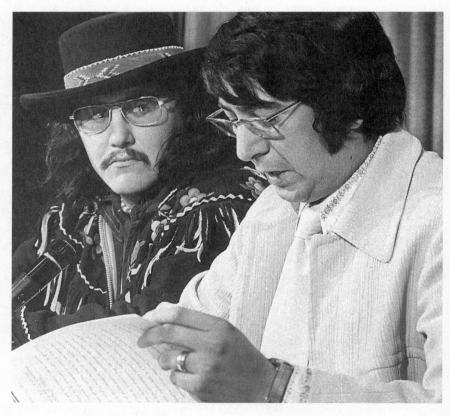

Tony Belcourt (right), first president of Native Council of Canada
with Harry Daniels, Ottawa, Ontario, 17 December 1971.
(CP Photo Archive)

In its "core funding" policy, the federal government encouraged the alliance of Métis and non-status Indians as it facilitated the delivery of special programs to both "disadvantaged" groups through a single association in each province or territory and at the national level. An alliance also made sense to Métis and non-status Indian leaders in order to alleviate common social and economic problems and to add to their political clout. In 1970, the Lake Nipigon Métis Association joined with non-status Indians to form the province-wide Ontario Métis and Non-Status Indian Association. In 1975, the MSS changed its name to the Association of Métis and Non-Status Indians of Saskatchewan (AMNSIS). While not changing their names, the Manitoba and Alberta organizations also admitted non-status Indians but, like Saskatchewan, placed emphasis on the aspirations of their Métis majorities.

During the 1970s, Métis and non-status Indian associations worked alongside the federal government (and on the Prairies with the provincial governments) to deliver housing, employment, and training programs to their members. Increasingly, they found themselves in an ambivalent position. On the one hand, they were confronting the government with claims for political autonomy. On the other, they were cooperating with the government, acting as arms of its bureaucracy in the provision of services and programs and as a buffer between government and association members.

The energy crises of the 1970s[12] accelerated penetration of the hinterland by resource corporations and forced a politicization of the Métis relationship with the federal and provincial governments. Many of the resource projects—uranium mining in northern Saskatchewan, hydroelectric development in northern Manitoba, and oil and gas extraction in Alberta—were located in areas with significant Métis populations who feared yet another wave of dislocation. Métis land claims would raise the consciousness necessary for the consolidation of a nationalist ideology.

MÉTIS LAND CLAIMS CAMPAIGNS

In 1973, the Supreme Court of Canada rendered an inconclusive judgment on a declaration sought by the Nisga'a Indians of British Columbia that their Aboriginal land rights had never been extinguished.[13] Three judges upheld the Nisga'a claim, three rejected it, and the case was decided against the Nisga'a on a procedural technicality. Nevertheless, six of the seven judges recognized the existence of land rights based on Aboriginal title, and the decision forced a reversal in federal policy.

While Ottawa had previously refused to recognize these rights, now it was prepared to negotiate land claims agreements in certain parts of the country where Aboriginal title claims based on traditional use and occupancy of the land had not been extinguished by treaty or other lawful means. These "comprehensive claims" included the Yukon, Northwest Territories, northern Quebec, and most of British Columbia. The only Métis organization to be included in a "comprehensive claims" negotiation process was the Métis Association of the Northwest Territories. Prairie Métis had been instrumental in opening transport on the Mackenzie River waterway system toward the end of the nineteenth century; in 1966, Richard Slobodin commented that "among Métis of the southern Mackenzie District, old traditions of Métis nationality and of the insurrections retain a vitality surprising to this observer."[14] Now, however, they were included in negotiations on the basis of claims they shared with the Dene of the Mackenzie Valley, not the prairie Métis. This placed the Métis in an ambivalent position, contributing to the on-again, off-again Dene-Métis talks with Ottawa during the next decade and politically isolating the Métis of the North from their prairie brethren.

In other parts of the country, the federal government asserted that Aboriginal title claims had been extinguished by treaties or other lawful means but recognized that it had not always honoured its legal obligations as set out in those agreements. These "specific claims" generally related to the lands or assets of Indian bands and involved issues such as shortfalls of promised reserve land, illegal sale of reserve land, or breach of obligation arising out of government administration of Indian funds. The long-standing opinion of the federal Department of Justice that Métis land rights based on Aboriginal title had been extinguished by law (the Manitoba Act, 1870, and the Dominion Lands Act, 1879) remained the position of the Trudeau government, reaffirmed in 1969 in a letter from Minister of Indian Affairs Jean Chrétien to the president of the MMF. At the same time, the government was willing to provide funding under its "specific claims" policy for Métis land claims research to determine if any of Ottawa's obligations remained outstanding.

Federal funding for Métis and non-status Indian land claims research first became available in 1976. Prior to this, research into Métis land claims had been undertaken by a group of Métis academics associated with the Manitoba Métis Federation Press, founded in 1972 to promote awareness of Métis history.[15] With the establishment of federally funded research teams on the Prairies, the history of the Red River Métis served as a starting point not only for the MMF but also for the Métis associations in Saskatchewan and Alberta, many of whose members traced their origins to Manitoba before the first dispersion. Then the research work expanded into the history of the administration of Ottawa's scrip issues in the North-West.

The research programs brought to the forefront of the Métis movement a Métis intelligentsia that had generally not figured prominently in leadership roles earlier in the decade, when "bread and butter" issues were pre-eminent. In undertaking research and workshops on Métis rights, these intellectuals rapidly gained the confidence of members and assumed leadership roles in their associations. Métis land claims research campaigns raised the political consciousness of the

Métis and made them aware of their historical nationhood. At annual assemblies and local and regional meetings, the attention of members began to shift from social and economic problems to Métis rights. Political issues began to dominate Métis news media. In making Métis from the different provinces and regions of the Prairies aware of their common history, identity, and aspirations, land claims research revealed significant differences between the two constituencies of the Native Council of Canada.

Métis claims, based on the historical and legal recognition of the Métis as a distinct Aboriginal people with land rights, were concentrated on the Prairies, in adjacent parts of British Columbia and the Northwest Territories where Métis had settled after the North-West Rebellion, and along the historical fur trade route in northwestern Ontario. Elsewhere, NCC constituents—even those of mixed ancestry—generally did not share the history and culture of the Métis. Their identity and rights were tied to Indian reserve communities and bands from which this population had been separated mainly as a result of discriminatory provisions of the Indian Act. While the Métis were seeking their own self-governing land base as a distinct Aboriginal people, non-status Indians sought the right to rejoin Indian bands and live on reserve lands.

This fundamental difference in objectives created considerable friction within the NCC. While its Métis affiliates on the Prairies stressed nationalism, its non-status Indian affiliates, particularly those in the Maritimes (consisting overwhelmingly of women who had lost Indian status through intermarriage), pushed for an emphasis on the discriminatory membership rules of the Indian Act. This friction was exacerbated by the structure of the NCC, where political representation and power in no way reflected population distribution.

The NCC was a federation of the provincial and territorial associations of Métis and non-status Indians, each with one vote on the NCC board of directors and an equal number of votes at the NCC's annual assembly, which elected national executive officers. This "equality of affiliates" caused dissatisfaction among the prairie Métis associations, which, with their large populations, had less strength within the NCC than the more numerous but generally less populous non-status Indian associations. Consequently, although the total population of Maritime non-status Indians (who tended to vote as a bloc at NCC assemblies) was less than that of the Métis in a single prairie city, such as Winnipeg, their three associations[16] had as many votes in the NCC as the three prairie Métis associations.

Métis alienation was a recurring theme throughout the history of the NCC, the opinion being that a "Native" alliance obscured the distinct identity and aspirations of the Métis. NCC assemblies tried to offset this discontent by electing prairie Métis as presidents for the greater part of the decade: Tony Belcourt from Alberta (1971–74) and Harry Daniels from Saskatchewan (1976–81). Nevertheless, by the end of 1977, both AMNSIS and the MMF had pulled out of the national organization.

The first attempt to bring about a political realignment of the Métis people was made in Cranberry Portage, a Manitoba village near the Saskatchewan border, at the end of January 1978. Organized by land claims research teams, the meeting brought together delegates from AMNSIS and the MMF to discuss the political direction of the Métis movement. MMF president John Morrisseau and predecessor Ferdinand Guiboche exhorted the assembly to think in terms of Métis nationhood and a Métis homeland spanning provincial boundaries.

According to researchers who addressed the gathering, the first Métis provisional government was formed in the absence of any constituted government and was therefore in accordance with the doctrines of international law (John A. Macdonald had considered this situation at the time, as outlined in a letter presented at the meeting). Delegates adopted a resolution to restore the provisional government that had fallen with Riel in order to negotiate a settlement of Métis rights with the Government of Canada. This new provisional government would remain the legitimate representative of the Métis until they reached a satisfactory agreement governing the terms of their union with Canada. A harbinger of things to come, a further resolution was passed to the effect that such an agreement had to be entrenched as part of the Constitution of a restructured and revitalized Canada.

The time for realignment, however, was not yet right. The MAA maintained its membership within the NCC, its indomitable president, Second World War veteran Stan Daniels, reluctant to walk away from an organization that he had helped found. Moreover, after years of building up an association at local, regional, and provincial levels and developing relationships with governments and the media, the AMNSIS leadership was reluctant to surrender its autonomy to a new, untested national body. Despite the enthusiasm at Cranberry Portage, the new "provisional government" died on the floor on which it was proposed.

Nevertheless, toward the end of the 1970s, the Métis on the Prairies were reaching a turning point in their political evolution. The land claims campaigns had evoked strong sentiments and an ideology capable of transforming these sentiments into strategy. It would take a new issue to catalyze the development of this strategy, one in which the Métis search for renewed nationhood would become caught up in Canada's search for a new Constitution.

Chapter 3

HARRY DANIELS AND THE QUEST FOR THE CONSTITUTION

*P*rime Minister Trudeau had made modernization and patriation of the Canadian Constitution a priority since coming to office in 1968, but he had been stymied by the failure of first ministers to reach an accord on constitutional reform at the Victoria Conference in 1971.[1] The election of a Parti Québécois government in Quebec in 1976 sparked renewed activity on the national unity and constitutional reform files, leading to public consultations, parliamentary committees, and intergovernmental conferences. The stage was being set for the expression of Métis aspirations by a new kind of leader, charismatic and telegenic.

CHALLENGING THE
"TWO FOUNDING NATIONS" MYTH

Born in Regina Beach, Saskatchewan, on 16 September 1940, Harry Daniels entered the Métis polticial movement in the radicalized environment of the 1960s. He was influenced by the revolutionary ideas of Howard Adams and by the strategies and organization of the Black Panther Party and American Indian Movement. There was another important side to Daniels that would play to his advantage on the political scene, that of the showman.

Daniels was a gifted dancer, writer, and actor. He studied with theatrical groups such as the Manitoba Theatre Centre Studio and Dora Mavor Moore's New Play Society in Toronto, and he acted in several award-winning plays on the stage, television, and radio, as well as in a number of television series. On the national political stage, starting with his election to the NCC presidency in 1976, he became renowned for his passionate oratory, sartorial splendour, and irrepressible humour. In his presentations on constitutional issues, he began to capture nationwide media attention for the Métis, his charismatic leadership allowing the NCC to assert its legitimacy as the national representative of the Métis people, despite the rumblings of discord on the Prairies.

For Daniels, Canada's historical suppression of the Métis as a founding nation and its perennial national unity crisis were inextricably bound together. He attacked the "two founding nations" theory by which the English and French were held to be the founders, or "charter groups," of Canada. Before the Task Force on Canadian Unity on 2 March 1978, he declared that the Métis, by virtue of the actions of the provisional government in Red River, were "the only charter group in Canada with a history of national political independence before joining Confederation."[2] In an address to the Special Joint Committee of the Senate and House of Commons on the Constitution on 23 August of that year, Daniels identified the Manitoba Act as the Métis cornerstone of Confederation and confirmation of their role as a founding nation but one that "proved to be an empty guarantee."[3]

Daniels was influenced in his thinking by an ongoing relationship with an unusual soulmate, President José Lopez Portillo of Mexico. A renowned historian, Portillo was intrigued by the Métis people and their affinity with his country's mestizo majority. Both had fused indigenous and European cultures and traditions into distinct New World identities but with very different outcomes: one embraced as the national identity of Mexico, the other suppressed and denied by Canada. In an article in *Le Devoir*, Daniels alluded to these divergent outcomes and their impacts on national identity when challenging English Canada and Premier René Lévesque to a "Founding Nations Conference" that would include the Métis, before further discussions of constitutional reform took place:

The Métis fact, not the Francophone or Anglophone, represents the true basis of Canadian culture. As historians know, the Red River Métis community was the embryo of a burgeoning Canadian identity but this identity was suppressed and denied by the federal government in Ottawa which looked to England and France for its notions of culture and thus blatantly violated the terms of the agreement by which Louis Riel's Métis Provisional Government negotiated Manitoba's entry into Confederation. Since then it has been the British and French notion of culture and not a distinctly Canadian one, which has dominated Canada. Mexico did not go this route and ... developed a vibrant culture and a strong national community. It is no wonder that Canadian unity and national identity are in a crisis.[4]

Daniels took this message to the country's ethnic and immigrant communities. On 27 October 1978, at the Third Canadian Conference on Multiculturalism in Ottawa, he portrayed Louis Riel as the father of multiculturalism, who sought possession of only one-seventh of the West for the Métis, with the remainder to be distributed to all the oppressed people of the world. He struck a responsive chord when he quipped that the Liberal government's multiculturalism policy "continues to feed us the 'two founding nations' myth while tossing in some Ukrainian Easter eggs, Italian grapes, or Métis bannock for some extra flavor."[5]

Daniels was alarmed by the prime minister's draft legislation for constitutional reform (Bill C-60, or the Constitutional Amendment Bill), released before the first ministers conference at the end of October. The accompanying policy paper, "A Time for Action: Toward the Renewal of the Canadian Federation," referred to "full respect for Native rights" but within the context of equality of opportunity and multiculturalism, in effect rights enjoyed by all Canadians. More alarming for the Métis, the document referred to Indian and Inuit peoples only.

In his brief to the First Ministers Conference on the Constitution (to which the NCC had been invited as an observer) on 30 October 1978, Daniels asserted, "We are not just another cultural group, but an historical national minority, that is, a people with a right to stay in Confederation or get out of it. Ethnic groups do not have this right. They are not historical national minorities and do require measures to guarantee access to equality of opportunity. We need more than this."[6] Historical nationhood, he argued, conferred collective rights on the Métis beyond the individual rights proposed for the new Constitution. Consequently, Daniels pressed for entrenchment of a Charter of Rights for the Aboriginal Peoples separate from the proposed Charter of Rights and Freedoms that would apply to all Canadians. As well, he insisted on full and equal participation for Aboriginal people in the process of constitutional patriation.

Although effective in setting out the case for Métis self-determination, Daniels was vague about how it would be exercised. He had called for a constitutional guarantee of Métis representation in Parliament and provincial legislatures, but he had not yet addressed the thornier issue of self-government on a Métis land base that, with a few exceptions, did not exist. This next giant step in the development of a Métis nationalist strategy would be taken in stride with Canada's venture into nation building.

The Constitutional Catalyst

With the defeat of the Liberal government in 1979, momentum on constitutional reform slowed. Although the national Aboriginal organizations had been limited to observer status at the first ministers conferences in October 1978 and February 1979 (the latter dealing with the economy), the agenda for the patriation process had been expanded to include the item "Canada's Native People and the Constitution." The new Conservative government, however, did not share Trudeau's zeal for constitutional amendments—especially if they meant conflict with the provinces. The future of the process was in doubt.

The return to power of the Liberals on 18 February 1980, and, more significantly, the defeat of the *oui* forces in the Quebec referendum on sovereignty association on 20 May, thrust the country back into the constitutional debate. Trudeau had promised the Québécois a new Constitution if they voted "no," and a new Constitution they would have—even if they didn't particularly like what the prime minister had to offer. He had also spoken of Aboriginal involvement in constitutional reform, which would follow a successful outcome of the referendum.[7] For Aboriginal peoples, the Constitution had become, like land claims, a vehicle for the articulation of their special status in the federation.

Daniels entered the new round of constitutional discussions fixated on the status of NCC participation in the patriation process, a preoccupation governed by two concerns: that, regardless of the progress in constitutional discussions between Aboriginal peoples and governments, the Métis might be left out again;[8] and that, without a formalized partnership for Aboriginal peoples in the patriation process, the entire Aboriginal rights issue could be dropped. Indeed, the prime minister's statement on 10 June, "Priorities for a New Canadian Constitution," had not included Aboriginal issues in its twelve-point agenda for the constitutional conference the following September. It had indicated in an adjunct that first ministers would also receive Aboriginal representations.

Frustrated by the exclusion of Aboriginal peoples from the intergovernmental work on the Constitution during the summer, Daniels resorted to a more militant stance. On 2 July, the annual meeting of the Joint Cabinet–NCC Committee in the

House of Commons deteriorated into a sit-in protest by Daniels and his board members. The protest was sparked by cabinet's refusal to state a definitive position on the meeting's two top agenda items: the status of Aboriginal participation in the patriation process, and the NCC's *Statement of Claim Based on Aboriginal Title of Métis and Non-Status Indians,* a product of three years of land claims research by the NCC and affiliates. According to Daniels, the eight-hour occupation of the parliamentary committee room wasn't a sit-in at all; it was an extension of the meeting with cabinet that had not been adjourned before the committee chairman, Minister of Justice Jean Chrétien, and his associates left at 2 PM for Question Period in the House of Commons. Daniels told reporters that the NCC would no longer accept observer status at first ministers conferences or the "take it or leave it" attitude of the government.

On 3 July, Daniels flew his board of directors in a chartered plane to Winnipeg, where the Liberal Party was holding its policy convention. At the convention centre, the NCC lobbied delegates to support full and equal Aboriginal participation in the constitutional review process. Referring to the site of the convention as an attempt by the government to counter western alienation, Daniels told the press, "We represent a whole nation of people who have been alienated. We have been trying for more than a century to get into Confederation, unlike those who are trying to separate."

In a surprise move on 4 July, the Liberal Party approved a resolution that Aboriginal peoples be included at all levels of constitutional reform discussions. Minister of Indian Affairs John Munro conceded that the party was endorsing a broader involvement for Aboriginal peoples in the talks than had been favoured until then by the government. Like other party resolutions, however, it was not binding on the government.

Nevertheless, the issue of Aboriginal participation in constitutional discussions was taking on national as well as international dimensions. When federal and provincial constitutional ministers gathered in Montreal on 7 July to study the agenda for September's first ministers conference, their hotel was surrounded by hundreds of protesters organized by the NCC's Quebec affiliate, the Laurentian Alliance.

More alarming for the federal government were threats emanating from the other side of the ocean. Bruce George, a British Labour member of Parliament (MP) with a keen interest in indigenous peoples, had become a spokesman for a group of MPs vowing to make patriation difficult if Aboriginal peoples were excluded from the process. To this threat, Trudeau retorted at the Liberal convention in Winnipeg, "Well, all I can say is they better not try."

In a letter to Daniels on 11 August 1980, Trudeau stated that constitutional discussions of Aboriginal issues would have to wait until late 1980 or early 1981.

The most he could promise before the first ministers conference in September was a meeting with a subcommittee of the Continuing Committee of Ministers on the Constitution,[9] set up to canvass Aboriginal views on the twelve agenda items. At this meeting on 26 August, Daniels vented the frustrations of Aboriginal Canada before the first ministers conference, referring to "fruitless meetings we have been subjected to over the years, where we were asked for our views, gave them, only to receive the response, 'Don't call us, we'll call you.'"

30 JANUARY 1981

It was during this period of uncertainty that Daniels launched his own innovative scheme to involve his constituents in the patriation debate. During the summer of 1980, the NCC had established a Métis and Non-Status Indian Constitutional Review Commission to canvass the views of Métis and non-status Indians on the subject of a new Constitution. The commission, comprising Daniels as commissioner and a number of Aboriginal deputy commissioners, would tour the country, using public hearings and conferences as forums for the expression of Aboriginal views on the Constitution. As well, non-Aboriginal Canadians, in particular political leaders and prominent academics, would be invited to appear before the commission. It was an interesting reversal of roles, with government representatives such as Premier Richard Hatfield of New Brunswick putting their views to an Aboriginal commission.

The First Ministers Conference on the Constitution in September of 1980 ended in failure and the decision of the Trudeau government to embark on unilateral patriation. At its first series of hearings on 14 and 15 October in Ottawa, the Métis and Non-Status Indian Constitutional Review Commission cast new light on the constitutional deadlock. Under the glittering chandeliers of the Skyline Hotel, British MP Bruce George reiterated earlier warnings to hold up patriation in the British House of Commons unless Aboriginal peoples were properly represented in the process. On the second day of the hearings, Premier Hatfield of New Brunswick startled the commission by stating that Métis and non-status Indians had largely been assimilated and therefore "should be treated as far as the decision-making process is concerned in constitutional reform ... no differently than any other people in Canada."[10]

Unilateral patriation loomed as a double-edged sword for Aboriginal peoples. On the one hand, it threatened to bring home a Constitution that only indirectly addressed Aboriginal rights. The sole reference to Aboriginal peoples in the patriation resolution introduced in the House of Commons in October stated that the Charter of Rights and Freedoms "shall not be construed as denying the existence of any other rights or freedoms ... that pertain to the native peoples of Canada."[11]

Without actually stating that Aboriginal rights did exist, the resolution left Aboriginal peoples in limbo. On the other hand, unilateral patriation offered Aboriginal peoples a chance to bypass the provincial governments in obtaining recognition of their rights. The provinces, which held jurisdiction in key areas (including land and resources, education, and health care) where Aboriginal peoples were seeking control, had at least as much to lose from the entrenchment of Aboriginal rights as the federal government and were expected to offer stiffer opposition. The leaked "Kirby memorandum"[12] had stated that entrenching Aboriginal rights would be very difficult after patriation since a majority of the provinces would have to agree to changes that might benefit Aboriginal peoples at the expense of provincial power. For the Métis and non-status Indians, who were treated as ordinary citizens within provincial jurisdiction, unilateral federal action offered particular potential. Harry Daniels had written to the prime minister on 17 September, stating that the NCC did not oppose unilateral patriation in principle as long as it could be assured of some movement on Aboriginal rights.

On 24 October, the Liberals applied closure on the constitutional debate and sent the patriation resolution to the Special Joint Committee of the Senate and House of Commons on the Constitution of Canada. In a televised appearance before the committee on 2 December, Daniels exhaustively reviewed the lack of Aboriginal participation in the patriation process. In an impassioned finale, he declared, "There is no such thing as selective justice. If our rights are not protected in this resolution, then neither are yours."

Weary from his incessant and seemingly futile battle to secure a place for his people at the bargaining table, Daniels had nevertheless emerged as an integral part of the opposition mounting against Trudeau's constitutional resolution as it stood. By the end of 1980, only two provinces—Ontario and New Brunswick—had voiced support for the federal initiative; the dissenting provinces had decided to challenge the resolution in the courts. In Quebec, Premier Lévesque had launched a crusade against the federal action. A Gallup poll in December showed that 58 per cent of Canadians opposed patriation without considerable provincial support.

The NCC found itself caught between the confrontational approach of the Indians and the cooperative approach of the Inuit. From its lobbying office in London, England, the National Indian Brotherhood (NIB) launched an anti-patriation campaign that would culminate in the British courts more than a year later.[13] In November, the Union of British Columbia Indian Chiefs brought hundreds of protesting Indians to Ottawa on a chartered train, "The Constitution Express." The Inuit, on the other hand, tried to work within the system to effect change. Upon the advice of their lawyers and MP Peter Ittinuar, they attended meetings of the special joint committee as observers, viewing the committee as a vehicle for amending the patriation resolution.

In spearheading NCC strategy, Daniels was wary of both approaches, fearing a backlash at home if the British lobby was pursued too vigorously but also harbouring a personal dislike for committee watching. He decided that if he couldn't bring his people into the process, he would bring the process to his people. As chairman of the Métis and Non-Status Indian Constitutional Review Commission, Daniels hosted a series of hearings, first in Sault Ste. Marie and then in Moncton, generating regional media interest in the hundreds of Aboriginal people showing up to express views on constitutional patriation and entrenchment of rights.

In January 1981, Minister of Justice Chrétien moved to strengthen the Charter of Rights and Freedoms to generate broader public appeal. Regarding the rights of Aboriginal peoples, however, the government remained firm: it wouldn't recognize rights that had not been defined. Within the month, this argument would crumble under political pressure.

On 29 January, a British parliamentary select committee headed by Sir Anthony Kershaw recommended that Westminster not patriate because of provincial opposition. At home, the federal New Democratic Party (NDP), an ally of the Liberals on the patriation issue, made its continued support conditional upon recognition of Aboriginal rights in the resolution. To reverse the momentum mounting against patriation, appease its parliamentary ally, and legitimize its patriation package as an expression of national will, the Trudeau government acceded to an Aboriginal rights amendment. It stated simply that "The Aboriginal and treaty rights of the Aboriginal peoples of Canada are hereby recognized and affirmed."

Worked out in NDP leader Ed Broadbent's office by Aboriginal leaders and legal advisers, the amendment was to be put before the special joint committee at 4 PM on 30 January by Chrétien. As TV camera operators prepared for the historic moment amid the elegance of Room 200 in Parliament's West Block, committee members and Indian and Inuit leaders awaited the leader of Canada's third Aboriginal group, conspicuous by his absence during the day. Minutes before 4 PM, Harry Daniels entered the committee room. Greeting Daniels at the door, Chrétien confirmed that a deal had been reached. Daniels asked if there was a specific reference to Métis in the amendment. Chrétien said no but assured Daniels that the term "Aboriginal peoples" would be interpreted broadly. Daniels told Chrétien in not-so-polite terms that the deal was off unless Métis were specifically recognized.

A frenzied chain of events ensued, with Daniels accosting committee members in the room and in corridors and a perplexed minister of justice feeling a much-needed deal slipping through his fingers. Finally, Chrétien approached a Daniels aide[14] and asked him to "call Harry off." As Chrétien would soon tell reporters, the day's events had generated a momentum that couldn't be stopped.

With television cameras rolling and Aboriginal leaders seated behind him, Chrétien then introduced his Aboriginal rights amendment, calling on Inuit MP

Peter Ittinuar to read it in English and former Minister of Indian Affairs Warren Allmand to read it in French. What the public did not know was that the amendment had undergone further change only minutes before. Now, in addition to the recognition of Aboriginal and treaty rights, a new subsection stated that the Aboriginal peoples of Canada included Indian, Inuit, and Métis peoples.

What may have appeared to be a simple statement of fact represented a monumental triumph for the Métis people. After a century of being denied their territorial and cultural integrity, they had been recognized in the Constitution of Canada. The subsection also represented a personal triumph for Harry Daniels. He had seized the magic of the moment and opened up a new era for the Métis.

Chapter 4

The Pitfalls

of Patriation

The breakthrough achieved by Harry Daniels and other national Aboriginal leaders was but part of a national bargaining process that was far from over. In fact, given the extent of provincial opposition and the pending decision of the courts on the legality of patriation, there was no guarantee that it would even happen. For the Métis, who stood to gain the most from the resolution of all the Aboriginal peoples, 30 January 1981 had opened the door to great opportunity but exposed them, on a number of fronts, to considerable risk.

THE CHRÉTIEN LETTER

During the deliberations leading up to 30 January 1981, Aboriginal leaders had insisted that Aboriginal consent be required for constitutional amendments affecting Aboriginal rights. Governments had countered that only sovereign powers (meaning themselves) could figure in an amending formula and that an Aboriginal consent clause would impose limitations on the legislative authority of federal and provincial governments (which is precisely what Aboriginal leaders wished to do). On 30 January, Jean Chrétien had assured Aboriginal leaders that, with the inclusion of their rights in the patriation package, their interests would be taken into account when the government dealt with changes to the Constitution's amending formula. His remarks had been construed by some as support for an Aboriginal consent clause or veto over amendments affecting Aboriginal rights.

This hopeful speculation was shattered the following Monday when Chrétien introduced a further amendment allowing Ottawa and any province to bilaterally amend the Aboriginal rights provisions as they would apply in that province. Foremost in Harry Daniels' mind was the possibility of the federal government and the Conservative government of Sterling Lyon in Manitoba doing away with the Métis land grant provisions of the Manitoba Act, which Daniels knew were about

Harry Daniels and Peter Ittinuar confront Justice Minister Chrétien over omission of Aboriginal "consent"
in patriation resolution, Ottawa, Ontario, 2 February 1981.
(CP Photo Archive)

to become the subject of a major litigation by the MMF. Together with Indian and Inuit leaders, Daniels cornered Chrétien in the cloakroom outside the special joint committee hall and persuaded him to drop the amendment. Chrétien, however, refused to build an Aboriginal consent clause into the resolution, promising at most to make Aboriginal rights subject to the general amending formula, which at that time required the support of the federal Parliament, as well as any province having or once having had 25 per cent of the total Canadian population (Quebec and Ontario), and at least two of the four provinces in Atlantic Canada and two of the four provinces in western Canada representing at least 50 per cent of the population of each region.

The aborted Chrétien amendment did much to sour the atmosphere of goodwill of the previous Friday. To Aboriginal leaders, it seemed to be an attempt to allay the fears of the provinces that recognition of Aboriginal rights would diminish their jurisdiction over public lands and natural resources. For Daniels—who on 30 January had told the press he was prepared to bring the Constitution home by himself if necessary—the amending formula controversy forced a reconsideration of his newfound enthusiasm for unilateral patriation. Events during the next two months would reinforce these doubts.

Daniels would receive legal advice that the patriation resolution, as it applied to Aboriginal peoples, was deficient in areas other than the amending formula. To be entrenched in the Constitution, rights had to be enforceable through the courts and applicable to both the federal Parliament and provincial legislatures (in order to have priority over federal and provincial statutes). Daniels was advised that, because Part II of the resolution (The Rights of the Aboriginal Peoples of Canada) lacked the enforceability and applicability provisions contained in Part I (The Canadian Charter of Rights and Freedoms), Métis rights had not been entrenched.

Together with Indian and Inuit leaders, Daniels met with Chrétien and Minister of Indian Affairs John Munro a number of times to discuss further amendments, but the federal government would go no further. Compounding Daniels' concern over lack of entrenchment was a letter sent by Premier Richard Hatfield to the Métis and Non-Status Indian Constitutional Review Commission on 2 March 1981, in which the premier stated that "provincial legislatures must be able to make laws regarding the Aboriginal and treaty rights of Aboriginal people who are not under federal jurisdiction."[1] New Brunswick, and perhaps other provinces, did not believe that the rights of Métis and non-status Indians were binding on their legislatures.

Whatever misgivings Daniels had were reinforced when his Métis and Non-Status Indian Constitutional Review Commission held hearings on the Prairies. The Saskatchewan Métis association, not a member of the NCC, was so angry at his public support for patriation that Daniels wouldn't hold a hearing in his home province.

At a hearing in Winnipeg on 4 March 1981, MMF President John Morrisseau explained to the commission, "We can't draw up the rights of a new constitution when our rights entrenched in the Manitoba Act of 1870 are still outstanding. We're only putting ourselves back and giving them another way out. First of all, let's settle the issue that's there, that's the issue of land claims."[2] Moreover, the absence within the patriation resolution of a requirement for Métis consent to constitutional amendments affecting them raised the real possibility of the government removing the Métis land rights sections of the Manitoba Act that the MMF intended to make the subject of major litigation. According to Morrisseau, "If the Government of Canada was to repeal Sections 31 and 32 of the Manitoba Act through an amending process, we would consider such a maneuver to be the greatest breach of faith in Canadian history."[3]

This was a message to which a disillusioned Daniels was now—somewhat belatedly—receptive. On 15 April, the NCC joined the MMF in a major land claims suit against the federal government and the Government of Manitoba, seeking a court declaration that sixteen federal and provincial statutes altering the Métis land rights sections of the Manitoba Act were unconstitutional. Then, at a press conference in Ottawa on 20 April, Daniels made the NCC's continued support for patriation conditional upon the inclusion of consent and entrenchment clauses in the resolution.[4] Pressed by reporters, he called Canada a racist state. The next day newspaper headlines across the country announced that the Métis had jumped off Trudeau's bandwagon.

On 24 April, in a terse letter from the minister of justice to the NCC, the Government of Canada formally rejected Métis and non-status Indian land claims. In ruling out land as federal compensation, Chrétien reaffirmed his government's commitment to improve social and economic conditions for Métis and non-status Indians. At one level, the Chrétien letter was the natural response of a defendant in a lawsuit, but coming as it did only a few months after 30 January, it appeared to some Métis leaders to trivialize the Aboriginal rights provision to the point of meaninglessness. Despite the agreement of 30 January, the Métis were still considered a special problem, not a special rights, group.

The Chrétien letter represented a personal defeat for Daniels and signalled an end to his regime in Ottawa. To his critics, concentrated on the Prairies, the government's rejection of Métis land claims proved that Daniels had become detached from the grassroots issues of the people. While he had been preoccupied with the often abstruse details of constitutional patriation, the historic and still burning issue of a Métis land base remained unresolved. Nonetheless, Harry Daniels, in his own inimitable way, had given the Métis a foot in the door; the task of forcing the door open would fall to others.

THE LULL BEFORE THE STORM

During the spring of 1981, a Newfoundland court took the wind out of the sails in the prime minister's race toward unilateral patriation, ruling it illegal. Shortly afterward, the Liberals agreed to postpone the final vote on the constitutional resolution until the Supreme Court ruled on its legality. With the constitutional debate on hold, the NCC's constituents turned inward to the political void left by the impending departure of their national leader.

Harry Daniels' decision to step down as NCC president before the tenth annual assembly in Ottawa in July 1981 threatened to upset a delicate balance in the national office. Despite the absence of the Manitoba and Saskatchewan Métis from the NCC during his term, Daniels had projected a Métis image for the organization while accommodating eastern-Canadian non-status Indians to whom he was beholden for votes. Now his departure cast into doubt the ability of the NCC to manage the competing interests of Métis and non-status Indians.

The tenth annual assembly of the NCC in Carleton University's main hall marked the return of the Manitoba and Saskatchewan Métis associations to the NCC fold, a return prompted by the federal government's insistence on dealing with national Aboriginal organizations only on constitutional issues. The first test of this new found unity would be the presidential election to replace Daniels. Frontrunners were Jim Sinclair, the fiery leader of the Saskatchewan Métis, and Louis (Smokey) Bruyère, an affable, mild-mannered Ojibway from Ontario, the favourite of the non-status Indians east of the Prairies. In addressing the assembly, each candidate, in his own way, captured the hopes and fears of his people during this lull before the constitutional storm.

Amid a display of historic Métis flags, the powerful, resolute Sinclair, hands on hips, referring to himself as spokesman for the Métis Nation, radiated the growing confidence of the prairie Métis. The constitutional process, he warned, represented the last opportunity in a lifetime for the Métis to negotiate their entry into Confederation. The defeat of the Parti Québécois in the Quebec referendum precluded a sovereignty approach for the Métis; what was needed was a partnership in the new federation.

While evoking a strong response from Métis delegates, Sinclair's emphasis on Métis nationhood did little to allay the concerns of non-status Indian delegates. The patriation resolution's recognition of Indians, Inuit, and Métis, without a specific reference to non-status Indians, had aroused fears that constitutional rights would apply only to those Indians registered under the Indian Act. They listened carefully to Bruyère's low-key speech, which emphasized his ability to reconcile different interests. To many in the hall, what Bruyère said was less important than what he was. As New Brunswick non-status Indian leader Gary Gould reminded the delegates in his nomination address, "Smokey is a leader—an Indian leader."

After five years of Daniels' leadership, culminating in the constitutional recognition of the Métis, the non-status Indians believed their turn had come. Capitalizing on the non-status bloc vote from eastern Canada, Bruyère was elected president of the NCC. At the same time, delegates elected Audreen Hourie, a Métis nationalist from Manitoba, to the office of vice-president. As well, the NCC board of directors would later name Jim Sinclair to head its all-important constitutional committee. For a while, at least, this balancing act would keep a fragile coalition together.

THE NOVEMBER CRISIS

On 28 September 1981, the Supreme Court of Canada rendered its long-awaited decision on unilateral patriation. In an ambiguous ruling claimed by both sides as a victory, the court ruled that it was legal for the federal government to make constitutional amendments affecting federal-provincial relations without the consent of the provinces but unconstitutional in that a convention had been established that these amendments did require provincial consent. The decision would bring first ministers back to the bargaining table at a constitutional conference on 5 November in Ottawa. With the turnaround in position of both Indians and Métis since 30 January and their anti-patriation lobbying in Britain, the Trudeau government did not feel bound to protect Aboriginal rights in the final round of talks with the dissident provinces. Only the Inuit had remained steadfast in support of the constitutional resolution, and they were too few to hold Ottawa to its bargain.

In a secret bargaining session, resource-rich provinces tied their support for the Charter of Rights and Freedoms to an elimination of the Aboriginal rights provision, which was dropped. Later, congratulating each other on their accord before a television audience of millions, first ministers (with the exception of René Lévesque, also dealt out of the "national deal") maintained a solidarity of silence on the fate of Aboriginal rights. It was as if the provision had never existed.

Within days, however, their covert compact sparked nationwide protests. A coalition of Aboriginal organizations was thrown together to lobby for the restoration of Aboriginal rights. Prime Minister Trudeau stated that the federal government had acceded to the deletion because the Aboriginal peoples themselves opposed patriation, prompting criticism that Ottawa had used the Aboriginal demand for more as an excuse to give them nothing. Under fire, Trudeau agreed to include Aboriginal rights once again if the provinces agreed.

The campaign to restore Aboriginal rights in the patriation package targeted Alberta, whose premier had become identified as a key player in dropping the Aboriginal rights provision. Peter Lougheed continued to assert that Alberta could not support undefined rights that had been included without provincial involvement. At the same time, faced with an outpouring of Aboriginal anger in massive demonstrations on the streets of Edmonton, Lougheed agreed to explore the possibility of a compromise, preferably on his terms. With Alberta's treaty Indians insisting on an exclusive relationship with Ottawa and opposed to any provincial involvement in the constitutional process affecting treaty rights, Lougheed turned to the Métis Association of Alberta.

The MAA had reorganized in the 1960s to litigate against the province for oil and gas rights on the Métis settlements but had lost control of its action when the eight settlements formed their own association in 1975. After that, much of the political energy of Alberta's Métis had been channelled through the Federation of Métis Settlements (FMS). Nonetheless, given its status as the Alberta affiliate of the NCC that was likely to add credibility to any agreement reached, it would be the province-wide MAA—the weak link in the chain of Métis associations across the Prairies—that was suddenly blown onto the political stage by the storm surrounding Lougheed.

On 16 November, Premier Lougheed met with the MAA leadership, intent on reaching a deal and offering positive statements on an expanded Métis land base to sweeten the pot. The meeting was adjourned until 19 November, with an agreement that the government and MAA lawyers would each work on wording for a revised Aboriginal rights section. On 19 November, with 5,000 Aboriginal people protesting on the doorstep of his legislature, Lougheed and the MAA reached an agreement on wording. The following day, the Alberta-MAA accord was made formal in a letter from Premier Lougheed to the president of the MAA, Second World War veteran and retired civil servant Sam Sinclair.

The accord stated that affirmation of Aboriginal and treaty rights would be restricted to those rights existing prior to the coming into force of the new Constitution. It identified Aboriginal peoples as Indians, Inuit, and Métis. It also required the prime minister to convene a constitutional conference of first ministers and Aboriginal leaders to define the rights of Aboriginal peoples to be included in the Constitution. The Alberta-MAA accord provided the basis for a modified section 35(1) of the Constitution Act—"The existing Aboriginal and treaty rights of the Aboriginal peoples of Canada are hereby recognized and affirmed"—that was reinserted in the constitutional resolution and adopted by Parliament in December 1981.

Although the province intended to use the new wording to restrict the courts' interpretation of Aboriginal and treaty rights, the MAA emerged from the November Crisis with some satisfaction. Confronted by a sudden and formidable challenge, the association had managed to negotiate a settlement on behalf of all Aboriginal peoples in Canada. Most important, the MAA—the only prairie Métis association to have maintained its membership within the NCC during the previous decade—had begun to realize that, in a crisis threatening to take away their recognition as Métis, the Métis would have to go it alone.

Chapter 5

ELMER GHOSTKEEPER

AND "MÉTISISM"

*B*efore releasing the terms of the Alberta-MAA accord on 20 November 1981, Premier Lougheed met with the leader of the organization representing Alberta's eight Métis settlements. Elmer Ghostkeeper hadn't yet figured in the constitutional wrangling in Ottawa—the province-wide MAA represented Alberta in the NCC—but he had a deep-seated interest in the constitutional question, an interest that would send shock waves through the entire Aboriginal political establishment.

A DATE WITH DESTINY

Born and raised on Paddle Prairie Métis Settlement in northern Alberta, Ghostkeeper, a University of Alberta graduate, assumed the presidency of the Federation of Métis Settlements in 1980 during a period of political ferment on the settlements. In 1979, the province had staged a controversial raid on settlement offices to seize files helpful to its case in the natural resource litigation with the settlements.[1] Under Ghostkeeper's leadership, the FMS would continue to pursue the litigation despite exhausting procedural delays by the province. At the same time, Ghostkeeper pressed settlement leaders to exercise as much authority as possible under the Métis Population Betterment Act, 1938. Settlement councils began to negotiate their own surface rights agreements with oil and gas companies even though the fees generated amounted to small change compared to the millions of dollars in subsurface revenue bypassing the Métis Trust Fund en route to provincial coffers.

Ghostkeeper had viewed the breakthrough on Aboriginal constitutional rights and Métis constitutional recognition on 30 January 1981 as a golden opportunity for the Métis settlements to gain control over their lands and resources and to expand their self-government powers. For this reason, and despite the lack of FMS representation in the NCC, he had accepted Harry Daniels' invitation to serve as a deputy commissioner of the Métis and Non-Status Indian Constitutional Review Commission at a hearing on Kikino Métis Settlement on 18 February 1981. The commission heard that the settlements were seeking constitutional protection from the kind of unilateral action by the province that had resulted in the termination of four settlement areas without compensation, the withholding of subsurface resource revenues, and the reduction of local self-government powers.

Alberta Métis Settlements leader Elmer Ghostkeeper burns ceremonial sweetgrass outside Alberta legislature to protest the deletion of Aboriginal rights from the constitution, Edmonton, Alberta, 16 November 1981.
(CP Photo Archive)

The testimony of settlement members plus the environment surrounding the hearing in Kikino proved to be an eye-opener for the NCC leaders on the commission. While they had been pressing governments for the recognition of special status and the resolution of land claims, they had not yet converted the aspirations of their membership into specific proposals for a self-governing land base. Now they were hearing from people who considered themselves the vanguard of the Métis nationalist movement and, in fact, equated the establishment of the Métis settlements with the rebirth of the Métis Nation.

By the time Ghostkeeper met with Premier Lougheed on 20 November, events had thrust him into the national spotlight. In a personal act of protest against the first ministers' deal of 5 November, he had captured media attention by burning sweetgrass on the grounds of the Alberta legislative building in Edmonton five days in a row. On 19 November, he had addressed a crowd of 5,000 Aboriginal people in the provincial capital. In his meeting with the Alberta premier, Ghostkeeper pressed for reinclusion of the original Aboriginal rights section in

Elmer Ghostkeeper following a meeting with Premier Lougheed, Edmonton, Alberta, 20 November 1981.
(CP Photo Archive)

the patriation resolution but finally acceded to the Alberta-MAA draft accord. While insertion of the word *existing* in the Aboriginal rights clause was seen as a setback, Ghostkeeper was already focused on another clause of the accord—what was to become section 37 of the new Canadian Constitution—requiring the prime minister to hold a constitutional conference of first ministers and representatives of Aboriginal peoples within one year of patriation. This conference would address the identification and definition of the rights of Aboriginal peoples to be included in the Constitution. For Ghostkeeper, leader of a unique community charged with a historic mission, this was a date with destiny.

Toward a "Made-in-Alberta Agreement"

On 17 April 1982, Queen Elizabeth II proclaimed Canada's new Constitution. Among the guests at the patriation ceremonies in Ottawa was a thirty-five-year-old rising Métis political star from Alberta's Peace River country who had been nominated by his Member of Parliament to represent the region as a "young achiever." Elmer Ghostkeeper's unequivocal decision to attend had defied a feeling at the time that Indian and Métis "young achievers" should join their national associations in a boycott of the patriation ceremonies. Ghostkeeper, however, was betting on Canada in the hope that in gaining the ability to alter its own makeup, the country would be ready for a new relationship with its Aboriginal peoples.

Ghostkeeper was also betting on Alberta in the belief that the events in November had ushered in a new era in Alberta-Métis relations. Sensing a willingness by the premier to move toward broader local self-government for the settlements, Ghostkeeper reached an agreement with the province in early 1982 to establish a joint Government of Alberta–FMS committee to review and propose revisions to the Métis Population Betterment Act. A committee member and the author of its terms of reference, Ghostkeeper would bring the committee, headed by Alberta patriarch and former Lieutenant-Governor Grant McEwan, onto the settlements for a first-hand look at Métis lifestyles, issues, and aspirations.

Ghostkeeper adopted a similar approach to the constitutional conference on Aboriginal rights to be held within one year of patriation. He believed that the resolution of the November Crisis in Alberta had set an important precedent. In resolving the crisis, Premier Lougheed had struck an accord with Métis representatives and then proceeded to sell this consensus to the other provinces and Ottawa. Perhaps a "made-in-Alberta agreement" approach could form the basis of a national consensus at the section 37 conference. At a series of meetings with provincial cabinet ministers during the spring of 1982, Ghostkeeper and MAA president Sam Sinclair suggested a joint Government of Alberta–Métis constitutional committee to shape consensus on Métis rights that could be taken to the section 37 constitutional conference.[2]

Ghostkeeper was aware that his approach set the FMS apart from other Aboriginal organizations. For Indians, provincial involvement in the identification of their rights was anathema; a special and exclusive relationship with the federal government was the cornerstone of their special status. In fact, one year earlier, the Assembly of First Nations, or AFN, (formerly the NIB) had withdrawn its support for the patriation resolution because of provincial involvement in the amending formula as it affected Aboriginal rights and in the section 37 constitutional conference. The FMS approach also diverged from that of Métis associations in Manitoba and Saskatchewan since the 1930s; considered ordinary citizens within provincial jurisdiction, these Métis had no choice but to work with the provinces, but at the same time they asserted (as did their provinces) that the historical and constitutional responsibility to deal with Métis lay with the federal government.

For Ghostkeeper, demands for an exclusive relationship between Ottawa and Aboriginal peoples did not seem practical. The Constitution Act, 1982, made the rights of Aboriginal peoples subject to the general amending formula that required the support of Parliament and at least seven of the provinces representing at least 50 per cent of Canada's population. Moreover, the experience of the Métis settlements in Alberta had proven that the foundations, however fragile, of a self-governing Métis land base could be laid within the confines of provincial legislative authority. Alberta had accepted primary responsibility for its Métis population and addressed the land issue through establishment of the Métis settlements in the 1940s, Métis land cooperatives in the 1970s, and an individual land tenure program in the 1980s. In fact, the Alberta experience highlighted the paradox of a failed federal policy: beginning with recognition of Métis Aboriginal title, Ottawa's policy had been implemented through unilateral legislative action, alienable land grants, and termination of any form of special status; in Alberta, on the other hand, a policy premised on Métis needs rather than rights had been implemented through negotiated agreements with Métis representatives, inalienable land allocations, and continuing special status for Alberta Métis through provincial legislation.

On 30 June 1982, the FMS released its constitutional position paper, a slick report entitled *Métisism*, largely a reflection of Ghostkeeper's philosophy and testimony to his desire to work with the province. *Métisism* asserted the belief of settlement residents that they were the owners of their land and resources. It sought constitutional protection for their control of the land and natural resource base so that federal and provincial laws would not apply in these areas. In other areas, though, it did not seek exclusive jurisdiction and generally was amenable to delegated powers from the provincial government, in marked contrast to First Nations proposals for a third order of government without any provincial involvement. In deviating from the generally accepted Métis position outside Alberta that the Métis should fall within federal jurisdiction, *Métisism* underscored the historical struggle to fit into the new western provinces as a distinct entity: "Perhaps the most compelling reason for us opting out of an exclusive relationship with the federal government is that, while it might enhance our political status, it does not fit with the Métis way of doing things. More than any other Canadians, we recognize the importance of western provincial rights: our ancestors formed two provisional governments to defend them. We are proud to be western Canadians and proud to be Albertans."[3]

History and demographics had long precluded the option of provincehood to meet Métis aspirations as a nation within Canadian federalism; in seeking an alternative approach to achieving Métis political autonomy within the existing division of powers, *Métisism* sought not only to strengthen the foundations of a self-governing Métis territory but also to guarantee its participation in provincial (and federal) institutions. It proposed guaranteed representation of the settlements in the provincial legislature as a single electoral constituency and on the Northland School Division Board. It also sought protection and promotion of the Métis (Michif) language through the minority language education framework of the Alberta School Act.

In the report's cover letter, Ghostkeeper reminded Premier Lougheed that the preamble to the Métis Population Betterment Act stated the Alberta government's intention to implement the recommendations of the Alberta half-breed commission by means of conferences and negotiations between the government and representatives of the Métis people of Alberta. In the same spirit, *Métisism* sought the support of the province in joining Métis representatives to forge a consensus. On 28 July 1982, Premier Lougheed agreed to the establishment of a Joint Constitutional Committee of Alberta Ministers[4] and Presidents of the FMS and MAA to see if such a consensus could be reached. A working group of officials from the province and Métis associations began a series of discussions on Métis agenda items in August. The first steps had been taken toward realization of a "made-in-Alberta agreement."

A CASE FOR DIVORCE

While Elmer Ghostkeeper's maverick style of dealing with a province was certain to arouse suspicion among a variety of Aboriginal groups, nothing could compare with the intensity of feeling generated by his next foray into national Aboriginal politics. Ghostkeeper was convinced that, in order for the Métis people to negotiate a new future through the constitutional process, they needed a coherent ideology to express their long-standing political aspirations as a "new nation." In an analysis of the NCC undertaken as a university student, Ghostkeeper had concluded that the NCC could not satisfy the political needs of Métis people for a number of reasons. First, it depended on federal funding, which ensured that its priorities would be those of government, not those of the Métis people. Also, its organizational structure copied that of Canadian federalism, thereby ignoring natural constituencies such as the Métis settlements that didn't fit the national or provincial model of Aboriginal organization favoured by the federal funding agency. Most significant, it comprised two basic constituencies with inherently divergent objectives; thus the lack of a coherent ideology.

The summer of 1982 marked the turning point in Ghostkeeper's stance toward the NCC, from critical skepticism to open defiance. As a guest of the MAA, he attended a number of NCC meetings, which reinforced his earlier conclusion that the national organization had failed as a vehicle for Métis nationalism. At the NCC's

annual assembly in Ottawa, Audreen Hourie, the Métis vice-president of the organization, was defeated in her re-election bid by Bill Wilson, a lawyer from British
Columbia. Wilson, a status Indian, would assume his executive post alongside the
non-status Indian president of the NCC, Louis Bruyère. Ghostkeeper assumed that,
since the Constitution identified three Aboriginal peoples—Indians, Inuit, and
Métis—and made no reference to non-status Indians, the NCC seats were there for
the Métis. Now, in an ironic twist, the NCC would head into the constitutional conference with an all-Indian executive.

By this time, it had become readily apparent that the "non-status" issue was not
a constitutional one since the primary objective of non-status Indians—reinstatement to full Indian status—required revisions to the Indian Act, not the
Constitution. Indeed, with the entrenchment of sexual equality in the Constitution
Act, 1982, the federal government had until 17 April 1985, to do away with the discriminatory membership rules of the Indian Act, such as section 12(1)(b), which
had removed Indian status from thousands of Indian women who had married
non-status men. Nonetheless, Indians comprised a majority on the NCC board of
directors—the three national executive members plus the presidents of affiliated
provincial associations in the Atlantic provinces, Quebec, Ontario, British
Columbia, and the Yukon—and had no intention of relinquishing the NCC seats to
the prairie Métis.

The non-status Indian women on the board insisted on participation in the
constitutional process not so much to define Aboriginal and treaty rights as to
ensure that, when defined, these rights would apply equally to male and female persons. Their male counterparts, including status Indians from British Columbia and
the Yukon who had become disenchanted with the AFN, had been on the political
scene for a long time and didn't want to miss the high-profile action on the constitutional front. They intended to present their own version of Indian rights at the
constitutional conference. Thus, there was the possibility that the NCC seats at the
constitutional conference—what Ghostkeeper termed the "Métis seats"—would be
occupied by Indians pursuing positions in conflict with those of the AFN, with the
Métis caught in the crossfire.

Ghostkeeper was not the only Métis leader alarmed by the prospect of the
Métis being denied their day at the negotiating table. The spark that would ignite
the powder keg of Métis discontent was a summit conference of the prairie Métis
associations held in Jasper, Alberta, on 19 and 20 September 1982. Ghostkeeper
openly questioned the legitimacy of an organization that no longer represented
Métis interests. His remarks elicited instant support from the president of the MMF,
Don McIvor, who had also been chafing over the issue of constitutional representation. On 23 September, Ghostkeeper brought the issue to a head in a controversial
letter to the NCC and affiliates. A summary of the grievances and concerns of the

Métis, it concluded that "The NCC was established in 1970 as a marriage of convenience between Métis and non-status Indians. With the inclusion of Métis in the Constitution Act and the need to prepare a definition of Métis rights for the Section 37 Conference, it is time for a divorce." Ghostkeeper called on the Métis associations within the historical Métis homeland in western Canada to create a new national body to represent the Métis at the constitutional conference. He also stated no objection to the participation of the NCC at the conference but only as the representative of non-status Indians. Whether it was accorded its own seating or shared that already reserved for Indians was a matter to be resolved by the NCC, the AFN, and the Government of Canada.

On 7 October 1982, at a formal signing ceremony in Winnipeg, Ghostkeeper and McIvor, on behalf of the FMS and the MMF, declared their independence from the NCC on constitutional issues in the form of a Métis proclamation. They formed the Métis Constitutional Alliance to present the Métis consensus on inalienable Métis rights to be included in the Constitution of Canada. They declared their moral obligation, as custodians of Métis rights, to represent Métis people at the Section 37 Constitutional Conference.

The first test of the Métis Constitutional Alliance (MCA) would come at an NCC board meeting in Winnipeg on 13 and 14 October, scheduled to coincide with the first meeting of officials from the federal government, the provincial governments, and the three national Aboriginal organizations (AFN, NCC, and Inuit Committee on National Issues, or ICNI) to develop an agenda for the First Ministers Conference on Aboriginal Constitutional Matters. Ghostkeeper had been invited to attend the board meeting alongside McIvor to deal with the fallout from his letter. During two days of heated and acrimonious debate, NCC board members excoriated the new alliance for threatening what, in their eyes, was an inviolable union of Métis and non-status Indians. By the end of the second day, the groups reached an impasse, with Ghostkeeper and McIvor still unswerving in their commitment to the MCA and a Métis nationalist position.

In the late hours of the evening, with NCC board members packing for their flights the next day, a solitary but resolute Ghostkeeper walked in the dark to a cemetery in St. Boniface. There, alongside the grave of Louis Riel, he pondered the fate of the Métis Nation. But Ghostkeeper was not as isolated as he thought. Waiting for him in the lobby of his hotel was a Métis leader who had kept his own counsel during the two-day slugfest but had listened carefully to Ghostkeeper's forceful arguments. Waiting for a conversation that would alter the landscape of Métis politics for decades to come.

Chapter 6

IN THE BEAR PIT
WITH JIM SINCLAIR

*I*f the fledgling Métis Constitutional Alliance was to take flight, it would need the support of the other Métis associations within the historical Métis homeland, the MAA and AMNSIS. Both groups had been conspicuous by their absence at the founding of the MCA and by their quiescence during the stormy NCC board meeting in Winnipeg. Their reluctance to respond to the Ghostkeeper initiative resulted in part from a genuine concern of their boards that a split from the NCC—which had already been given two seats at the constitutional conference—would leave the Métis out in the cold. Other reasons lurked below the surface—more partisan, more personal, and ultimately, more important.

PRAIRIE POPULISM (MÉTIS STYLE)

The weak leadership of the MAA had not responded to Ghostkeeper's letter because it resented Ghostkeeper's high-profile role in the MCA, which it perceived as undermining the legitimacy of the MAA as the province-wide representative of the Alberta Métis. The uncharacteristic wavering of the Saskatchewan Métis, and in particular of its leader, was a more complex matter. With his experience in Aboriginal politics stretching back longer than that of any of his peers, AMNSIS president Jim Sinclair had a profound understanding of the implications of the Ghostkeeper challenge: that the constitutional recognition of Métis was forcing a realignment of interests along historical and cultural lines among the disparate groups under the umbrella of the NCC; that some leaders, like many of their constituents, would continue to sit on the fence between Aboriginal identities or continue to shift identities to meet the needs of the situation; and that, while the Ghostkeeper letter marked the point of no return for Métis nationalists, the "marriage of convenience" would not end without a bitter contest. Together this added up to a formidable personal dilemma for Sinclair, the most complex personality of the Métis movement and its supreme paradox. Sinclair was a non-status Indian.

How he captured the presidency of the Métis Society of Saskatchewan in 1971 and held onto it for the next seventeen years attested to Jim Sinclair's relationship with the Métis people and their struggles. Sinclair was born on 3 June 1933, in a shack on the edge of Punnichy, a town in southern Saskatchewan. His parents, Cree Indians, had lost Indian status before his birth and were prohibited from living on his mother's nearby reserve. Sinclair grew up among "road allowance people," destitute Métis living in slum dwellings on the sides of public roads. At night, he heard tales of the 1885 resistance told in hushed tones by people still fearful of reprisals. "Road allowance people" were regularly harassed by local authorities wishing to avoid making relief payments. Sinclair's family was evicted from their shack and forced to live in a tent farther from Punnichy. From there, Sinclair attended the mostly white school, where he was subjected to incessant racism and brutality.

In 1950, his family moved to Regina and the half-breed tent city alongside its "nuisance grounds," or garbage dump. Welfare and occasional manual labour were his only means of support. At night, local whites drove cars through the camps, hurling insults and sometimes trampling tents. As Regina grew and the "nuisance grounds" moved farther out, the tents moved with them. Succumbing to the hopelessness of poverty, Sinclair turned to alcohol. For the next ten years, he drifted from half-breed slums to skid row sections of towns, his life a continuous drunken stupor. For two years, he lived out of a derelict car. On more than one occasion, he woke up on a floor after a party near someone who'd been stabbed to death.

His sole source of inspiration during this period was Napoleon Lafontaine, a Métis Society local leader whose followers fought for their dignity with their fists. Under Lafontaine's influence, Sinclair began to realize that his condition and those of many other "road allowance people" could be overcome through self-help and organizing. Sensing a purpose to his life, Sinclair fought off alcoholism. Then he plunged into work, banding poor, alcohol-plagued Métis into self-help groups so they could gain control over their lives. In the process, he tangled with welfare authorities, the police, and the church, which branded him a dangerous radical.

The self-help movement became an integral part of the reorganization of the Métis Society of Saskatchewan (MSS) later in the l960s. Under the influence of radical activist Howard Adams, Sinclair became aware of the political roots of Métis problems. The MSS used community organizing and confrontational politics to politicize Métis people. This heavy emphasis on political action and control at the local level would influence Sinclair's distrust of distant and top-heavy national organizations.

In contrast to the ideological approach of the MSS during Adams' presidency in the late 1960s (cut short due to illness), Sinclair practised pragmatism from the day he succeeded Adams. He believed that Métis people could not grasp the political objectives of nationalism as long as they were locked in poverty and dependency. Only by first assuming responsibility for themselves as individuals could the Métis achieve self-determination as a people. While Adams had distrusted government-funded programs as attempts to depoliticize and bureaucratize Aboriginal associations, Sinclair encouraged their creation as a means for his followers to gain control over their lives and as a focal point for political awareness.

Scores of marches, sit-ins, and camp-ins to improve living conditions helped to release more government funds for social and economic programs. When given a miserly $5,000 for a housing program, Sinclair ordered it converted into nickels that were then carted in wheelbarrows to the Central Mortgage and Housing Corporation office in Regina. As the floor flooded with coins, he told reporters that the Métis were fed up with "nickel and dime" programs.

Sinclair made sure to channel the energy that went into these programs through the MSS. Unlike in other provinces, where governments often funded independent Aboriginal agencies and societies to provide services to Aboriginal people, in Saskatchewan all these functions, including housing, communications, and job training, were kept under Sinclair's central control. The crowning achievement of Sinclair's drive for Métis self-reliance was the founding in 1978 of the Gabriel Dumont Institute, the educational arm of AMNSIS.

Later to become affiliated with the University of Regina and expanded into a network of centres throughout Saskatchewan, the Gabriel Dumont Institute developed the educational components of AMNSIS programs in areas such as economic development, employment, job training, and culture. It also involved Métis in the public education system, training teachers, developing curricula, and launching adult/community education programs. Sinclair viewed the Dumont Institute as a training ground for the development of professional management of Métis affairs and institutions that would accompany any successful exercise of political autonomy.

A prairie populist, Sinclair believed that Aboriginal leaders had to be directly elected by and responsible to people at the grassroots level. In the late 1970s, his association had pioneered the province-wide "one person, one vote" ballot box electoral system; thus, Sinclair could claim that the thousands of people going to the polls on Métis election days made him as legitimate a leader as an MP or MLA. Whether giving speeches, debating opponents in his favourite "bear pit session," or "rapping" with reporters, Sinclair personified the populist politician: he was a large, powerful man, at least a decade older than he looked, who exhorted his audience in a style reminiscent of the Bible Belt preachers he'd heard so often on skid row. Once, fed up with public stereotyping of "half-breeds" as welfare cases, he declined an invitation to meet the queen, telling reporters she was the "biggest welfare bum in the world."

By the end of the 1970s, Sinclair had become the closest thing to a household name and AMNSIS the closest thing to a well-greased political machine among Métis people anywhere in Canada, with Sinclair lieutenants Jimmy "D" Durocher and Wayne "Millions" Mackenzie dispensing largesse to the faithful, who didn't have to be reminded of the source of the start-up money for a gas bar, the new roof on the house, or a seat in a training centre. From his headquarters in Regina, Sinclair commanded the support of more than 120 locals, regional offices, salaried board members, full-time legal counsel, and hundreds of employees throughout Saskatchewan. The annual "Back to Batoche" celebrations were expanded into massive expositions of Métis culture, drawing as many as 20,000 people to the site of the 1885 resistance.

The same combination of pragmatism and populism that had made Sinclair such a formidable figure in Saskatchewan also made him an implacable foe of the NCC. He opposed what he considered the NCC's undemocratic structure and in particular a national executive indirectly elected by a handful of delegates from each of its member associations at an assembly. He opposed a national organization competing with its affiliates for the minimal amount of influence possessed by Aboriginal people. In short, Sinclair saw the NCC as a barrier rather than a bridge to Ottawa and for that reason had pulled the Saskatchewan Métis out of the NCC shortly after its inception.

With the inclusion of Aboriginal rights in the patriation package in 1981, Sinclair and MMF president John Morrisseau had no choice but to reaffiliate their organizations with the NCC in order to participate in constitutional issues at the national level. In his run for the NCC presidency during the summer of that year, Sinclair committed to restructuring the NCC as a lobby office for its provincial affiliates with decision-making by provincial presidents rather than a national executive; in a pledge guaranteed to cost him the election, Sinclair declared that, if elected NCC president, he would stay home and lead the Saskatchewan Métis. Shortly after his defeat, the NCC board of directors, in a move to offset Métis alienation, named Sinclair chairman of the NCC Constitutional Committee, a position he coveted more than the presidency itself. This was the position he occupied a year later on 7 October 1982, when Elmer Ghostkeeper swept like prairie fire into Winnipeg for the founding of the Métis Constitutional Alliance. Ironically, now that the NCC's legitimacy as Métis representative was under assault, Sinclair—its harshest critic for more than a decade—was in charge of its constitutional policy.

Ghostkeeper's call for an end to the "marriage of convenience" between Métis and non-status Indians caused problems for Sinclair at the provincial level. A small splinter group of Métis dissidents was now attacking Sinclair for being a non-status Indian leader of a Métis movement. Sinclair was determined to crush what he considered to be the racism of opportunists who couldn't beat him at the polls. He suspected a link between this splinter group and the MCA.

After listening carefully to Ghostkeeper's defiant defence of his position for two days at the NCC board meeting in Winnipeg, Sinclair was willing to set aside his doubts. Ghostkeeper had impressed him with his clearly articulated ideas and tenacity in pursuit of *Métisism*. He sensed in the younger man, a leader of the only Métis land base in Canada, a valuable ally in strengthening the Métis position in the constitutional process. In the hours following the breakup of the meeting, Ghostkeeper returned to his hotel from a graveyard in St. Boniface to find Sinclair waiting patiently in the lobby, ready to "rap."

In the early hours of the morning, Sinclair and Ghostkeeper reached a deal. As chairman of the NCC Constitutional Committee, Sinclair was prepared to recommend that the MCA (including AMNSIS and MAA) should occupy the two existing NCC seats at the constitutional conference in order for the Métis to have their own representation and present their own distinct constitutional position. In return, he wanted Ghostkeeper to give him time to sell the plan to the NCC and avoid dealing with the Métis dissidents in Saskatchewan. The likelihood of having to relinquish his newly established power base within the NCC by moving to the Métis Constitutional Alliance did not daunt Sinclair. A survivor and master of Métis politics since the 1960s, he had felt the winds of change blowing off the prairie and had decided to travel with them.

SECTION 35 VERSUS SECTION 37

In the weeks following his commitment to Ghostkeeper, Sinclair worked to arm-twist a slim majority of the NCC board into supporting a compromise measure to avert a breakup of the organization. In a letter on 3 November 1982, his Constitutional Committee formally requested four seats at the constitutional conference so that each part of the NCC's dual constituency could participate on a basis equal to that of other Aboriginal groups. A week later the Federal-Provincial Relations Office in Ottawa rejected the request and suggested a split of the two existing seats between Métis and non-status Indians.

Upon receiving the news in his office in Edmonton, Elmer Ghostkeeper telephoned Jim Sinclair and Don McIvor. The snub from Ottawa had not surprised him since he had received reports that the NCC executive had been covertly lobbying the federal government against Sinclair's compromise. He pressed Sinclair and McIvor to commit to a withdrawal from the NCC and the founding of a Métis national organization to force Ottawa's hand on constitutional representation.

Sinclair urged caution. He said a collapse of the NCC could derail the constitutional conference—in his words, a once-in-a-lifetime opportunity for the Métis to negotiate a new deal in Confederation—and, to make matters worse, there were reports that the AFN was also experiencing intense internal friction in its preparation for the constitutional conference. He asked Ghostkeeper and McIvor for more time to pressure both the federal government and the NCC into accepting full and equal Métis representation. In the interim, he encouraged them to set out the Métis position both to the non-Métis majority on the NCC board and to the participants in the preparatory constitutional discussions.

Ghostkeeper had little choice but to heed Sinclair's advice. His FMS, despite its representation of the only Métis land base in Canada, had no standing within the NCC. Fearing precipitous moves that could cost them their day at the constitutional table, the other Métis associations were maintaining their tenuous affiliation with the NCC. If a Métis realignment was to materialize before the constitutional conference, Ghostkeeper would have to accept Sinclair's invitation to expose the NCC's inherent and irreconcilable contradictions.

Before the next round of constitutional preparatory talks in Ottawa on 17 and 18 November 1982, the NCC board and advisory staff assembled in the organization's downtown Ottawa office to develop a comprehensive position paper. By this time, it had become apparent that all Aboriginal organizations wanted to restructure Part II of the Constitution Act, 1982 (Rights of the Aboriginal Peoples of Canada), as a "Charter of Rights for the Aboriginal Peoples." Like the Canadian Charter of Rights and Freedoms in Part I of the Constitution Act, an Aboriginal charter would contain a list of specific rights as well as enforcement mechanisms. The immediate task at hand for the NCC was to decide on an approach to identifying the rights in the Aboriginal charter. The issue would become whether to focus on "existing Aboriginal and treaty rights" in section 35(1) of the Constitution Act, 1982—that is, to elaborate on rights already existing in law—or to focus on the purpose of the section 37 constitutional conference—that is, to identify and define the rights of Aboriginal peoples to be included in the constitution.

With Jim Sinclair, chairman of the NCC Constitutional Committee, moderating the debate, Indian representatives on the board made it clear that the NCC had to build upon the "existing Aboriginal and treaty rights" clause in order to construct an Aboriginal charter. Gary Gould, president of the NCC's New Brunswick affiliate and occupant of the Aboriginal rights portfolio on the NCC board, stated his intention to argue that Aboriginal and treaty rights existed in law and would present a broad and modern interpretation of what was contained in historical treaties (pre-Confederation in the Maritimes) and covenants. The status Indians on the NCC board also sought to build upon section 35, but rather than citing and elaborating on legal agreements, they intended, like their counterparts in the AFN, to present their conception of "existing" rights, the foremost being Aboriginal title encompassing underlying title to all of Canada and a basis for sovereignty.

Ghostkeeper had come to the NCC meeting at the invitation of Sinclair to explain how Métis constitutional rights could be accommodated within an Aboriginal Charter of Rights. Ghostkeeper viewed the section 37 constitutional conference as an opportunity to negotiate the rights of Métis outside the narrow legalistic context of "existing Aboriginal and treaty rights" and in the tradition of Riel's provisional governments in Red River and the North-West that had rejected the paternalism and wardship of the treaties in favour of pursuing political equality as a distinct people and nation with English Canada and French Quebec. He told board members that the Métis would not foreclose on the possibility of pursuing Métis Aboriginal rights but would reserve these arguments for the courts in the event that they could not achieve their goals through negotiations. With insertion of the term "existing," he observed, section 35 had become a "closed box" that the government did not intend to open. He stated his intention to use the constitutional conference to define Métis rights as a nation—the rights to a land base and self-government—over and above Aboriginal rights.

During a break in discussions, Ghostkeeper confronted Sinclair with the agenda for the constitutional conference that was being developed by government and Aboriginal officials, including those of the NCC, simultaneous to the NCC board meeting.[1] He told Sinclair that it would be exceedingly difficult for the Métis to enter into meaningful discussions of a land base and self-government with an agenda focused on "existing rights," including Aboriginal title.[2] He reminded Sinclair of the entrenched opinion of the Department of Justice that the Manitoba Act and the Dominion Lands

Act had extinguished Métis Aboriginal title. He insisted that Métis land base and self-government be added to the constitutional agenda as distinct items.

By this time, Sinclair needed no more convincing; the debate had had a telling impact on its moderator. For him, the prospect of Aboriginal politicians heading into a bargaining session with arguments that ultimately had to be determined by the courts represented a complete abrogation of responsibility and filled him with disdain. He was appalled when he learned of the legal precedents that Gary Gould intended to cite as a case for self-government within an Aboriginal charter. (One of these, a 1677 treaty between the governor of Virginia and the queen of Pamunkey, prompted an associate to quip to the speechless Sinclair, "Well, you'll be a Pamunkey's uncle.")

The critical issue would become the separate Métis agenda items demanded by Ghostkeeper, the venue, the NCC board meeting in Montreal on 8 and 9 December 1982. This meeting would coincide with the last preparatory meeting of officials before federal and provincial constitutional ministers and Aboriginal leaders were to meet to finalize the agenda for the constitutional conference. With board members deadlocked on the agenda in a salon of the Queen Elizabeth Hotel in Montreal, Sinclair abandoned his stance as moderator, heaping scorn on those who wanted to "dust off old treaties" to establish their rights. After a century of waiting for a chance to reach a new deal in Confederation, he warned, the Saskatchewan Métis were going to the table to talk politics, not law. Ghostkeeper and McIvor, now joined by MAA president Sam Sinclair, demanded the seating of an MCA candidate at the officials' table the next day to present the Métis agenda. Indian board members initially resisted what they saw as a thinly veiled bid by the alliance to take the NCC seats at the first ministers conference but relented when the Métis started to walk out.

The next morning Jim Sinclair confirmed their worst fears when he appeared at the intergovernmental meeting and took the NCC seat. He informed the federal chairman that the Métis did not seek to pursue narrow legal rights such as Aboriginal title when they were at the table for a political settlement. Like any other nation, the Métis needed a land base and self-government to survive. A stony silence gripped the conference room, Indian and Inuit representatives reacting to what appeared to them to be the Métis abandoning Aboriginal title in order to anchor their rights in the murky waters of nationalism. As the meeting adjourned for lunch, a shouting match broke out in the hallways outside between Sinclair and a livid Gary Gould, who warned that he wouldn't sit back if the NCC ignored the "existing" rights of its Indian constituents.

The next morning Gould took his threat a step further. With Sinclair and the MCA on the conference floor pressing for inclusion of a Métis land base and self-government in the agenda for the constitutional conference, the rest of the NCC board met upstairs. Their strategy for putting an end to what they saw as the carnage below was simple: exercise their board majority in the future to unseat the alliance and protect their Aboriginal and treaty rights.

A DIVORCE AT LAST

With the players in Canada's newest constitutional game breaking for Christmas, leaders of the now-expanded Métis Constitutional Alliance assembled in a cold, windswept Regina on 20 December 1982. The foremost question for the Métis, Jim Sinclair assured the conclave, was not whether to bolt from the NCC but, given its hold on the Métis seats at the constitutional conference and Ottawa's refusal to create more, when and how to do so. At Sinclair's suggestion, the alliance sent a telex to NCC president Louis Bruyère, calling on the NCC to facilitate the presentation of a strong Métis constitutional position and to pursue non-status Indian objectives by increasing its involvement in parliamentary committee hearings on revisions to the Indian Act. It also called for an urgent meeting of the NCC board in early January.

On 21 December, the NCC president, acknowledging that the NCC had not yet adopted a unified constitutional position, mailed a new draft position to NCC affiliates with an emphasis on "existing" rights. At a meeting in Don McIvor's office in downtown Winnipeg on 6 January 1983, the MCA dismissed the NCC document out of hand, informing Bruyère by telex that his document was meaningless since it didn't reflect the Métis position. On 10 January, the alliance telexed Gérard Veilleux, the new secretary to cabinet for federal-provincial relations, and pressed for the separation of a Métis land base and self-government from Aboriginal title on the constitutional agenda.

On 13 and 14 January, the NCC board of directors gathered in downtown Vancouver, where NCC vice-president Bill Wilson was based. In contrast to Gary Gould's non-status Indians from eastern Canada, who wanted to advance novel legal arguments to define Aboriginal rights, Wilson advanced a politicized interpretation of Aboriginal title as the basis of Indian sovereignty. He also advocated the need to replace elected chiefs under the Indian Act with hereditary chiefs. For the Métis leaders, the emergence of the various Indian positions within the NCC highlighted the irrelevance of an organization that had once purported to represent Métis interests and the alien and somewhat bizarre situation in which they now found themselves.

On the second morning of talks, after an inconclusive first day, Gould attacked the premise that the two NCC seats at the constitutional conference were there for the Métis. He made a motion to split the two seats between Métis and Indians. As hands went up in support of the motion, the Métis associations from the three prairie provinces sat alone in opposition. An infuriated Sinclair declared that the NCC had become a "melting pot of left-over Indians" into which the Métis were expected to assimilate. Both seats were Métis seats, and the Métis were not going to back down. Then he resigned as chairman of the NCC Constitutional Committee.

In a final gesture of defiance, Jim Sinclair, Ghostkeeper, McIvor, and Sam Sinclair stormed out of the room.

On 18 January, members of the Métis Constitutional Alliance telexed Prime Minister Trudeau to announce their withdrawal from the NCC and to seek decertification of the latter as Métis representative at the constitutional conference. They stated their intention to form a new national body in Edmonton on 22 January to occupy the two Métis seats. The marriage of convenience between Métis and non-status Indians had ended in divorce.

Chapter 7

MÉTIS POLITICAL
REALIGNMENT

*O*n 22 January 1983, more than one hundred elected Métis representatives gathered in the conference hall of a suburban hotel in Edmonton. Delegates from northwestern Ontario, Manitoba, Saskatchewan, Alberta, the Métis settlements, and northeastern British Columbia[1] sat in an expansive circle to capture the continuity of the Métis Nation. With the realization that Métis people throughout their historical homeland were finally achieving the elusive goal of political unity, a palpable sense of accomplishment filled the air. Their objective was to establish a new national organization to represent the Métis at the constitutional conference, their keynote speakers the leaders of the Métis political realignment, Elmer Ghostkeeper the ideologue and Jim Sinclair the tactician.

THE MÉTIS CONSTITUTIONAL COUNCIL

Elmer Ghostkeeper set the tone of the gathering in his opening address, invoking Riel's prophecy that the Métis Nation would rise again within a century of his death. He chronicled the struggle of the Métis for a land base and self-government and challenged delegates to establish a new provisional government and a new List of Rights that would become as much a part of the new Constitution as Riel's List of Rights had become a part of the Manitoba Act. Sinclair roused the delegates with an emotionally charged speech in which he identified with those Indians who had broken treaty in order to fight alongside the Métis in their war of national resistance in 1885:

> Treaty Indians today don't even recognize or talk about the Indians who were hanged along with Riel. Those poor martyrs have not even been recognized by their own people. At least you people have had the decency to honour your own people who died for you in those battles. You've got something to go there [the constitutional conference] with, a sense of history, and a sense of pride. Don't throw it away now and if once you think I'm throwing it away, kick me out of this room and I'll go.

The Métis had not opted for full sovereignty in the nineteenth century, noted Sinclair, nor did they seek it in the constitutional process. What they did want was political autonomy as well as participation in the larger political system. The contemporary situation of Métis required self-government on Métis lands, a more limited form of autonomy off Métis lands, as well as guaranteed Métis representation in Parliament and provincial legislatures.[2]

The assembly also heard from Clément Chartier, the vice-president of the Saskatchewan Métis association but an outsider to Sinclair's political machine. Born and raised in Buffalo Narrows, a predominantly Métis community in northern Saskatchewan, Chartier had graduated from Athol Murray's Notre Dame College and later the University of Saskatchewan Law School. The soft-spoken, erudite lawyer had played a significant but behind-the-scenes role in many of the events leading to the Métis political realignment, including the MMF–AMNSIS summit in Cranberry Portage in 1978, when he was a third-year law student, and the November crisis in Alberta when he had advised the MAA on the revised Aboriginal rights clause. Chartier was grounded in international legal issues affecting Aboriginal populations and in 1982 had represented the World Council of Indigenous Peoples (an international federation of Aboriginal organizations from four continents) at the first session of the United Nations Working Group on Indigenous Populations in Geneva. His work in extending the principle of self-determination in international covenants from UN member states to Aboriginal and national minorities within those states had helped to shape his outlook on the issue of Métis constitutional rights.

Chartier appealed to the delegates to look beyond the "closed box" of section 35 to their inalienable right to self-determination as a people and a nation. He referred to Aboriginal rights and title as a "legal fiction." The Métis had always known of their right to their land, but, as for Aboriginal title, they didn't know they had it until the government extinguished it. Governments could give and take away Aboriginal and treaty rights but could never diminish the right of Métis to an autonomous homeland.

Chartier explained to the delegates how the unique aspirations of the Métis could be accommodated in the Constitution alongside those of other Aboriginal peoples who were trying to build their case on Aboriginal rights. While a general principle such as the right of Aboriginal peoples to self-government could be recognized in the Constitution, separate processes would have to be established for the negotiation of the specific forms of self-government favoured by Indians, Inuit, and Métis. In the case of the Métis, this meant a tripartite process involving Ottawa, the western provinces, and the Métis Constitutional Alliance. The specific rights and powers emerging out of these separate processes would then be set out in separate schedules of the Constitution Act.

Despite the unanimity of delegates on the need for a new national body for Métis political representation, significant differences emerged over the structure of that organization. A "nationalist" wing of delegates called for the establishment of a third Métis provisional government with a mandate transcending provincial boundaries and, in effect, replacing provincial Métis associations. The concept was sweeping: a directly elected national legislature or Métis Parliament located in Batoche (close to Saskatoon), Saskatchewan; an executive branch initially responsible for intergovernmental negotiations leading to a land base and self-government and then applying the legislation of the Métis Parliament; an administration to absorb the service-delivery apparatus of the provincial bodies and Métis institutions such as the Dumont Institute; and a judicial branch to adjudicate disputes over matters within the jurisdiction of the Métis government. Thus, the third Métis provisional government would articulate the political will of the Métis to be self-governing and would legislate and administer broadly based policies, programs, and institutions in those areas of Métis government jurisdiction to be derived from agreements with Ottawa and the provinces. Its foremost proponents were Elmer Ghostkeeper, who believed that the Métis settlements would constitute a natural electoral district for representation in this national legislature, Clément Chartier, and the Manitoba Métis.

A "confederalist" wing of delegates opposed the proclamation of Métis government on the ground that it was premature for established provincial associations to give way to an untested national structure. Their opposition rested on the same argument used to block the creation of provisional governments and governments-

in-exile throughout history: in the general absence of a Métis self-governing territory, what was the point in empowering a body, no matter how representative of or
accountable to its constituents, that lacked the land base, legal authority, and financial resources to act on its decisions? Worse still, one that could usurp the limited
power and resources of the provincial associations. Drawn mainly from the AMN-
SIS and MAA boards, the "confederalists" argued that a new national body had to be
limited in mandate and accountable to the boards and presidents of affiliated
provincial associations. In fact, Jim Sinclair, the leader of the wing, surpassed the
"confederalists" in his desire for a decentralized national body, insisting on a loose
alliance of existing associations on constitutional issues with, perhaps, a lobby
office in Ottawa to act on behalf and upon the instruction of provincial presidents.
In effect, it would be a structure that was literally the sum of its parts.

With the debate over structure proving to be far too complex and potentially divisive to resolve on the floor, delegates agreed to put off a decision to another day and
focus on the task at hand. For the purpose of constitutional representation, they agreed
to formalize their alliance as a Métis Constitutional Council (MCC) consisting of the
prairie provincial associations and the FMS, with provision made for future participation of Métis from British Columbia and northwestern Ontario. They also ratified the
list of Métis rights, now reconstituted as a Métis Charter of Rights, for presentation at
the constitutional conference.

On 24 January 1983, the MCC informed Prime Minister Trudeau of its Edmonton
mandate. It stated its intention to attend the meeting of constitutional ministers and
Aboriginal leaders scheduled for the end of the month. Furthermore, it advised the
prime minister that Jim Sinclair would be going to Ottawa to secure the two Métis seats
held by the NCC.

In Ottawa, Sinclair learned that the Government of Canada was adamant in its
refusal to rearrange the table at the constitutional conference now set for 15 and 16
March 1983, and that the NCC intended to hold both seats to the exclusion of the prairie
Métis. Federal officials assured Sinclair they were concerned by the recent events. They
promised that steps would be taken to ensure distinct Métis representation at the conference—but only under the NCC umbrella. Toward that end, federal-provincial relations chief Gérard Veilleux sent senior officials Reeves Haggan and Pierre Gravelle to
pressure NCC president Louis Bruyère into yielding a seat to the Métis.

On 27 January, Sinclair met with the NCC board to explore the possibility of peaceful coexistence. He laid out three unconditional terms for sharing the NCC seats at the
conference: NCC members would not be part of the Métis Constitutional Council; they
would not interfere in the strategies or decisions of the council; and they would not participate in the selection of a spokesperson for the Métis seat. With neither side particularly happy, the NCC agreed, later telexing the compromise to the prime minister.

The first test of this new arrangement would be the meeting of federal and provincial constitutional ministers and Aboriginal leaders in the capital's Intergovernmental Conference Centre on 31 January and 1 February 1983, the first opportunity for Aboriginal organizations to engage political ministers rather than tight-lipped bureaucrats. Heading into these talks with the objective of securing their priorities for the constitutional agenda, the leaders of the MCC had become the pariahs of the process: despised by the organization that had been invited to represent them; distrusted by other Aboriginal peoples for their pursuit of a nationalism that appeared to conflict with the infallible doctrine of Aboriginal rights; and trapped in a conflict over the division of powers between federal and provincial governments equally intent on doing as little as possible for them.

WRANGLING OVER JURISDICTION

As Jim Sinclair took his seat at the table in the Intergovernmental Conference Centre on 31 January, he sensed how Ottawa's denial of jurisdiction had placed the Métis at an acute disadvantage in the process relative to other Aboriginal peoples. Sinclair had been in power for as long as Pierre Elliott Trudeau and had witnessed the evolution of federal policy from one oriented toward the repeal of the Indian Act to one recognizing and enhancing the special status of those Aboriginal peoples for whom it had accepted and exercised constitutional responsibility. Accordingly, status Indians and Inuit had established processes outside the constitutional talks through which they could pursue self-government and land claims with Ottawa in the event that the constitutional conference failed. Even non-status Indians would have a process to be reinstated to Indian status. Without a special relationship with Ottawa, the Métis had been forced to put all their eggs into the constitutional basket.

Sinclair had also dealt with Liberal, NDP, and Conservative governments in Saskatchewan. He knew that his province (and, for that matter, Manitoba and British Columbia) would support the historical Métis position on federal jurisdiction for Métis people, but its willingness was shaped by a desire to be reimbursed for the cost of services provided to the Métis population and stopped short of transferring public lands to the Métis. Therefore, determining whether the federal or the provincial government had jurisdiction with respect to the Métis question (outside Alberta) begged the issue of a Métis land base.

In his opening remarks, Sinclair insisted that a Métis land base remain a distinct priority item on the agenda for the constitutional conference. The Métis were prepared to be flexible at the bargaining table, but accepting anything less than a land base would be agreeing to the articles of surrender disguised as a charter of rights. The meeting chairman, Minister of Justice Mark MacGuigan, stated that the Government of Canada was prepared to include a Métis land base on the agenda but did not have any legal obligation to provide Métis with land. He alluded to the Métis settlements of Alberta as an example of what the provinces could do. Sinclair responded that the Métis had rebelled against Ottawa, not the provinces, and had been subjected to Ottawa's land grant and scrip schemes.

Manitoba's attorney general, Roland Penner, reminded MacGuigan that the Manitoba Act, a federal statute and part of the Constitution, provided for a Métis land base that still needed redress. The inevitable impasse over jurisdiction took on ethical dimensions in a clash between the justice minister and Saskatchewan's attorney general, Gary Lane:

> MacGuigan: "I said we didn't regard ourselves as having a legal obligation to a [Métis] land base. Do we have a moral obligation? Well, we can talk about that but we are not acknowledging a legal obligation."

> Gary Lane: "Morality is not jurisdictionally divided."

> MacGuigan: "Can I ask you the same question, Mr. Lane?"[3]

According to some constitutional ministers, the complexity of a Métis land base and self-government required these issues to be handled in an ongoing process rather than at the first ministers conference itself. An irate Sinclair responded, "... I thought I came to a political meeting this morning but I see many of the Attorneys General around the table hiding behind their law degrees and they are not talking politics. They are talking to us like lawyers and I want to remind you people that you are politicians first and lawyers second. You were elected by people to deal with issues such as these and if these issues are too complex, maybe you should leave the room and bring in somebody who can."[4]

After the second day of the meeting, as Sinclair and other members of the Métis Constitutional Council prepared for return flights to the Prairies, the NCC Constitutional Committee held a debriefing in its Ottawa office. Committee members were disturbed by Sinclair's emphasis on Métis nationalism and opposed keeping a Métis land base on the agenda as a distinct item (along with self-government). They denounced the federal government's "strong-arm tactics" that had led to Sinclair's seating. They referred to the Métis as "dissidents."

As for the seat of the Métis Constitutional Council (which the NCC called the Métis Constitutional Committee), one member said, "All of us have the right to sit on that Committee and we can exercise that right anytime we want. The Committee is open for joiners. When the crunch comes, we can all say, 'yes, we are members' and then take a vote and elect our Committee Chairman and spokespersons."[5] The NCC was about to commit the greatest blunder ever made by an Aboriginal organization in Canada.

EXPULSION

The second test of the new seating arrangement would be the final meeting of federal, provincial, and Aboriginal officials in Ottawa on 15 February. The MCC selected Elmer Ghostkeeper as its spokesperson, a decision likely to exacerbate NCC hostility since Ghostkeeper was viewed as an outsider who had led the move to break up the national organization. To make matters worse, Ghostkeeper had every intention of renewing the Métis offensive at the meeting.

In his opening remarks, Ghostkeeper raised the issue of full and equal Métis participation at the constitutional conference. Chairman Gérard Veilleux stated that the NCC had worked out a compromise and that he did not wish to interfere in its internal matters. Ghostkeeper retorted that Métis representation was not an internal matter but a national issue. He further stated that the Métis were participating to express their nationalism and their rights tied to their nationality. Accordingly, Aboriginal title and treaty rights were not issues of concern to the Métis and should properly be addressed to the AFN.

Tensions continued to mount leading up to the final meeting of constitutional ministers and Aboriginal leaders at the end of the month. On 17 February, the MCC telexed NCC president Bruyère to seek separate opening statements and a separate delegation to back up its spokesperson at the first ministers conference. On 24 February, Jim Sinclair attended an NCC board meeting to explain the Métis position and strategy. He was attacked by vice-president Bill Wilson, who accused the Métis of selling out their Aboriginal rights.

On a quiet Sunday afternoon, 27 February 1983, the Métis Constitutional Council gathered in Ottawa's Holiday Inn to prepare its strategy for the final ministers' meeting the next day. Unknown to the Métis, elsewhere in downtown Ottawa representatives of the NCC, the AFN, and ICNI were also meeting to draft a joint agenda for the conference. Later that night the Métis learned that their seat had been taken away by a resolution of the NCC. A decision had been made to put vice-president Wilson in what had been the Métis seat next to a representative of the eastern Canadian non-status Indians. The NCC's eastern and western Indian constituencies had found room for their different conceptions of "existing" rights by carving up the NCC seats among themselves.

On 28 February, shortly into the morning session at the Intergovernmental Conference Centre, conference chairman Mark MacGuigan challenged the credentials of the NCC, refusing to allow it to speak until the issue of Métis representation was resolved. Then he adjourned the meeting so that efforts could be made to resolve the problem. When the meeting reconvened, MacGuigan informed participants that, as a result of interventions by the AFN and ICNI,[6] the Government of Canada would recognize the NCC as the representative of the Métis for the purpose of the meeting. AFN and

Jim Sinclair listening to reporters' questions after the Métis are denied representation in constitutional talks, Ottawa, Ontario, 1 March 1983.
(CP Photo Archive)

ICNI leaders then defended their action by citing the principle of non-interference by the government in the internal affairs of an Aboriginal organization.

The constitutional ministers of Manitoba, Saskatchewan, and Alberta immediately protested the chairman's decision. Alberta's intergovernmental affairs minister, Jim Horsman, introduced Ghostkeeper to put forward the Métis case through the Alberta delegation. Ghostkeeper, noting that Louis Riel had been denied his seat in the House of Commons, charged the chair with repeating history. He suggested that the constitutional meetings themselves had become illegal without Métis representation.

Horsman and his prairie counterparts objected to the constitutional agenda being set in the absence of the Métis; indeed, the joint agenda tabled by the AFN, ICNI, and the NCC highlighted Aboriginal title and treaty rights but lacked any reference to a Métis land base. When Manitoba's attorney general, Roland Penner, pressed for inclusion of this item on the agenda, Wilson suggested its deletion had resulted from an "oversight"[7]; he added that with the concurrence of the AFN and ICNI, there was a possibility it could be attached to Aboriginal title. Wilson tried to press the case that Métis exclusion was really an internal matter, drawing an analogy between the Métis and the opposition parties in Parliament and provincial legislatures. Penner responded that, when 90 per cent of Canada's Métis lived in the four western provinces, the NCC could not call their representatives an opposition. He warned Wilson not to read him lectures about the principles of democracy without first looking in his own backyard.

By this time, Ghostkeeper, Chartier, McIvor,[8] and the Sinclairs had walked out of the meeting and retreated into the recesses of the conference centre. They had lost their only seat and their agenda priorities had been dropped. Virtually on the eve of the constitutional conference, the Métis had been expelled from the constitutional talks. Regrouping in a coffee room upstairs, they quickly drew two conclusions: first, the Métis needed more than a loose constitutional alliance to protect their interests; second, the constitutional conference had to be stopped.

Chapter 8

THE MÉTIS NATION VERSUS PIERRE ELLIOTT TRUDEAU

*M*étis leaders had never relied on the courts for justice, but Jim Sinclair sensed a no-lose situation in a legal battle with Ottawa over representation at the constitutional conference. If the Métis sued and won, they would have their seats. If they sued and lost, they would go home to mobilize outraged communities, and the conference—with "false pretenders" in the Métis seats—would be a sham. Thus began the most important legal confrontation with Canada by the Métis since Louis Riel addressed a Regina court from the prisoners' box in 1885.

A NO-LOSE SITUATION

During the noon recess of the ministers' meeting on 28 February, Jim Sinclair met privately with Senator Jack Austin, the minister of state for social development. Austin voiced deep concern over the lack of Métis representation and proposed a further meeting with Sinclair along with the other Métis leaders and Minister of Justice Mark MacGuigan. That evening the Métis Constitutional Council met with Austin and MacGuigan in the venerable justice building on Parliament Hill. The justice minister reiterated Austin's concern and indicated that the federal government had to consider options to ensure a Métis presence at the constitutional table.

On the morning of 1 March, the Métis leaders informed Prime Minister Trudeau by letter of their intention to form a permanent national representative body for the Métis people. They set 4 March as a deadline for two seats at the constitutional conference as well as reinclusion of a Métis land base in its agenda. At a major press conference that afternoon, Ghostkeeper, McIvor, and the Sinclairs blasted the Government of Canada for the expulsion of the Métis from the talks. For the first time, they referred to the possibility of legal action to regain seating at the table. Prior to leaving Ottawa that night, the members of the MCC mandated Jim Sinclair—whose Métis association was the only one with full-time legal counsel—to begin work on an injunction against the prime minister.

On 2 March, Sinclair made it clear in a telex to MacGuigan that, if the new national Métis representative body was not invited to the first ministers conference, the prime minister would fail to meet his obligation under section 37 of the Constitution Act. He also emphasized that the Métis did not wish to deprive Indians or Inuit of their representatives; they only wanted the representation to which they were entitled. With obvious reference to the NCC, he stated, "It is difficult enough for us to reach a consensus amongst ourselves without having to compromise positions with diverse groups of status and non-status Indians." On 3 March, he and his legal counsel met with a Regina law firm to commence proceedings against the Government of Canada.

In Regina on 4 March, addressing the Special Parliamentary Committee on Indian Self-Government on behalf of his non-status Indian constituents, Sinclair stated that the rights of Métis had to be resolved at the constitutional conference and those of non-status Indians through revisions to the Indian Act. Later, at a press conference, he launched a blistering attack on Ottawa's denial of Métis representation at the table and warned that papers to commence legal action would be filed on 8 March. The case, he insisted, would be against the Government of Canada, not the NCC.

By now, Manitoba's attorney general, Roland Penner, had telexed MacGuigan to press for Métis representation at the constitutional conference. Even the federal

Indian affairs minister, John Munro, had told the press that the NCC did not represent the Métis; moreover, he questioned its continued participation in the constitutional talks since it now appeared to represent non-status Indians only.[1] Nevertheless, the deadline for Trudeau to invite the Métis, Friday, 4 March, had passed, and the Métis were out in the cold.

During the weekend, the documents for the court case were prepared by a Regina law firm working under the direction of AMNSIS lawyer Rob Milen. A University of Saskatchewan activist from the 1960s, Milen had never stopped fighting the establishment, having publicly fired himself as the provincial government's negotiator of Indian land entitlement in 1980 in protest against the slowness of the talks.[2] A Saskatchewan cabinet minister had once likened him to "a thoroughbred who gets lathered up when you pull the reins back on him."[3] Milen had always advised the Saskatchewan Métis to avoid the courts if possible—advice that complemented the philosophy and style of his boss and friend, Jim Sinclair—but both men now recognized that, under the circumstances, the courts would serve as the most effective platform for launching what was essentially a political campaign.

In Edmonton on 6 March, representatives of the MMF, AMNSIS, and MAA reached an accord on charter membership in a permanent Métis national representative body. The accord provided for the establishment of a Métis National Council by the prairie associations and, in anticipation of the eventual admission of Métis from regions contiguous to the Prairies, for representation by population in the national body. It also bound members to the principle of non-interference in the internal affairs of fellow members.

In Regina on Monday, 7 March 1983, with the boards of the council's chartered members meeting across the Prairies to ratify the Edmonton accord, Sinclair and Milen prepared to sue the Government of Canada for not having fulfilled its requirement under section 37 of the Constitution Act, 1982, to invite the Métis to the constitutional conference. Milen had earlier reached an agreement with the federal government to hold hearings in the Federal Court in Regina, but the court registrar suddenly refused any documents for filing. In a curious twist, the Federal Court couldn't rule on the matter because it had no jurisdiction over the Constitution Act, 1982, a British statute. Since section 37 required the prime minister of Canada to invite representatives of the Aboriginal peoples to the constitutional conference, Trudeau himself would have to be sued in the province of his residence and work. Hence a shift in legal action to the Supreme Court of Ontario, which would have to scramble for available court space given that the prime minister was being sued in a personal capacity to prevent the first post-patriation constitutional conference, just a week away.

BIRTH OF THE MÉTIS NATIONAL COUNCIL

On Tuesday, 8 March, the prairie Métis associations formally established the Métis National Council (MNC) in Regina. Hastily assembled delegates pledged themselves to the cause of Métis nationalism and vowed to fight the court case until the bitter end. In a letter to the prime minister, they demanded two seats for the Métis at the constitutional conference and warned that they were no longer prepared to compromise on this issue. To back up their demands, they gave Trudeau official notice that they were proceeding with an injunction to ensure the first ministers conference did not take place until Trudeau exercised his responsibility under section 37 of the Constitution Act and invited the Métis to the table.

The MNC's founding delegates also confirmed understandings inherent in the Edmonton accord that would cast long shadows of discord on the organization. Arriving in Regina on 8 March, Elmer Ghostkeeper learned that the MAA had made its participation in the court case conditional upon its sole representation of Alberta within the MNC. The MAA may have been the weak link in the chain of Métis associations on the Prairies, but it was still the only province-wide Métis association in Alberta and thus in a position to exploit the MNC in its most vulnerable hour. To maintain a united prairie Métis front in the battle with Ottawa, the MMF and AMNSIS had reluctantly conceded to the MAA demand. An appalled Ghostkeeper, the architect of the Métis realignment, had been sacrificed on the altar of *realpolitik*. Although the MNC would later try to accommodate Ghostkeeper and the FMS within its constitutional decision-making, Ghostkeeper considered the exclusion of the Métis settlements from charter membership in the MNC a great and personal betrayal.

Delegates also decided to establish the position of national representative to embody the political will of the entire Métis Nation at the first ministers conference and elected Clément Chartier to the post. This decision may have addressed the exigency of the moment—the need to establish the credibility of a new national body if it was to assume its place at the first ministers' table—but it masked fundamental and long-standing differences over ideology and strategy within the Métis movement. For the nationalists, the selection of Chartier as leader and Saskatoon as the seat of the new organization comprised an interim step toward the establishment of a directly elected Métis Parliament and government to be located in Batoche once the institutional framework and an electoral system were agreed upon by the existing Métis associations. Confederalists viewed the office of national representative in a somewhat different light. They saw it as an ad hoc measure to get the MNC into the conference and believed that it would later become a lobby office for the presidents of its charter members, or the sum of its provincial parts. With the clock ticking down to the conference, and in the absence of Jim Sinclair, who was en route to

Toronto, it was unlikely that this potentially divisive issue would be aired, much less resolved, in Regina. As it had been at the founding of the MCC in January, a decision on the internal constitution of the Métis Nation would simply be put off.

In the nation's capital on the morning of Wednesday, 9 March, a perplexed minister of justice and his associates met with Sinclair in a final bid to defuse a legal powder keg about to blow up in their faces. MacGuigan, who had earlier told the press that the Métis should take the NCC to court for their seats, now encouraged Sinclair to sign an out-of-court settlement offering one NCC seat to Sinclair in a personal capacity. Sinclair rejected the offer; the Métis people, not an individual, were taking on the state, he declared, and the NCC was irrelevant to their action.

Deputy Minister of Justice Roger Tassé advised Sinclair that the prime minister didn't have a constitutional obligation to invite the MNC to the conference. Sinclair replied that, when the AFN was invited, the Indians were invited; when ICNI was invited, the Inuit were invited. "Who did you invite when you invited the NCC—Indians or Métis?" he asked accusingly. Tassé's expression conveyed to Sinclair the impression that the feds had not only bungled the case politically but perhaps legally as well.[4] It appeared that the Department of Justice had assumed that the Métis were claiming the seats due to their withdrawal from the NCC. In fact, Sinclair intended to dispute the prime minister's original invitation to the NCC on the grounds that it had not been made to the Métis, only to an organization of which the Métis had been a part. As a consequence, no invitation had ever been extended to the Métis people to participate in the constitutional conference as required by the Constitution Act.

On Wednesday afternoon, Sinclair appeared in a prestigious law office in downtown Ottawa to be cross-examined under oath on his affidavit in support of the Métis position. The affidavit was a blow-by-blow chronology of the political realignment. It concluded that the Métis people would suffer irreparable harm to their future political, economic, and cultural rights as a result of their exclusion from the constitutional conference. A nervous Ottawa-based legal counsel retained by the MNC asked Rob Milen how the veteran politician would do under cross-examination. Milen replied, "He'll circle but he won't land. The feds won't make a mark on him."

Assistant Deputy Minister of Justice Ian Binnie tried to establish that Métis were a diverse population represented by the NCC from coast to coast. Sinclair retorted that Sir John A. Macdonald hadn't sent troops to crush any Métis in the Maritimes but to Manitoba and Saskatchewan. When a frustrated Binnie reminded Sinclair that this was a legal case, Sinclair shot back that it was a political case.

Following Sinclair's cross-examination, a surprise witness suddenly appeared in the law firm office. Louis "Smokey" Bruyère had come to give his own affidavit evidence. In a move totally unexpected by the Métis, the NCC had intervened in the case in support of the Government of Canada. Under cross-examination by counsel for the Métis plaintiffs, Bruyère claimed that the NCC represented Métis,

Indians, and by virtue of its Native Women's Association affiliate, half of the Inuit population. He stated that a Métis was a half-breed, anyone of mixed blood, and that the distinction between Métis and non-status Indian was really only a legal one put forward by the federal government. He himself identified as both a non-status Indian and a Métis. Ottawa's ace of spades had turned out to be a joker.

By the end of the day, the die had been cast for a landmark court battle. Section 35(2) of the Constitution Act, 1982, had recognized but not defined "Métis." To determine whether the Métis had been invited to the constitutional conference, the courts would have to rule on who, exactly, were the Métis. Bruyère's testimony caused problems for the feds, for if the terms "Métis" and "Indian" were inter-changeable, as Bruyère had claimed, why were the Métis even included in the Constitution as a distinct Aboriginal people? As well, if the NCC represented all three Aboriginal peoples in the Constitution (including the Inuit), how could Ottawa claim to have invited the Métis?

On Thursday, 10 March, legal proceedings moved to the Supreme Court of Ontario in Toronto, the only available space for a court hearing. With the case generating widespread media coverage, the federal government was under considerable pressure to settle with the Métis. Premier Lougheed of Alberta had by now telexed the prime minister, calling for separate representation for the prairie Métis.[5] In the House of Commons, the Tories were attacking the Liberal government for not having "shouldered its responsibility" by guaranteeing two seats for the Métis.

A confident Jim Sinclair entered Osgoode Hall at 10:15 AM to appear on behalf of the prairie Métis plaintiffs against defendant Pierre Elliott Trudeau. The Métis were applying to a judge of the High Court of Justice for declarations that they were enti-tled to participate in the upcoming first ministers conference and that the prime min-ister had failed to invite them. They sought a writ of mandamus[6] compelling the prime minister to invite them and an injunction restraining the prime minister from convening the conference until such time as they were invited. In short, the case was a political hot potato the courts of Canada would not want to touch.

When proceedings began at 10:30 AM, Associate Chief Justice William Parker encouraged the litigants to reconcile their differences elsewhere and adjourned the court until the afternoon, when the case would be heard by three judges of the divi-sional court. This set the stage for further talks behind closed doors between Crown Counsel Binnie, Sinclair, and Milen. With Prime Minister Trudeau and his justice minister maintaining in the House of Commons that it was up to the Métis to sort out their differences with the NCC, Binnie's new offer was no different from MacGuigan's the day before.

Sinclair's response reflected the finality of the Métis decision. The fight was with Ottawa, not with the NCC, which as far as the Métis were concerned could have its own seats to represent non-status Indians. Furthermore, there would be no compromise on the Métis demand for separate representation under the name of the Métis National Council.

Minutes before the court reconvened in the afternoon, Rob Milen telephoned national representative Chartier, who had arrived in Ottawa to monitor negotiations with the Department of Justice as the lawsuit proceeded in Toronto. Moments before Milen's call, Chartier had received news from the Federal-Provincial Relations Office that the Government of Canada had acceded to the Métis demand for separate representation. Milen rushed back to inform Sinclair, who was facing three divisional court judges. Justice R. F. Reid announced an adjournment of the case for a day with the consent of both parties. Armed with Ottawa's agreement in principle, Sinclair left the courtroom with Milen to fly to Ottawa.

Awaiting them in Chartier's room in downtown Ottawa's Holiday Inn was a letter from Justice Minister MacGuigan stating that he had been authorized by the prime minister to invite the Métis National Council to the constitutional conference on the condition that it withdraw its court proceedings against him. As well, Chartier had been assured privately that the prime minister would agree to the reinclusion of a Métis land base in the first ministers' agenda if and when the MNC raised the matter at the conference. However, the feds would offer only one seat at the table to the MNC and fourteen additional delegate seats.

Chartier had already contacted the prairie associations, and they had concurred with the settlement. Sinclair also agreed, recognizing the discrepancy in seating as a face-saving gesture by the government that could easily be erased after the conference. Besides, he noted, the Métis could say as much from their one seat as the Inuit or status Indians or non-status Indians could say from their two seats, and having a sole representative at the table would only highlight the inequality to which the Métis had been subjected by Ottawa.

On the morning of Friday, 11 March, Chartier signed the documents for an out-of-court agreement. At the request of the federal government, the Métis had remained silent on the accord until Friday despite a curious and importunate media. This curiosity would be further aroused when lawyers for the Métis plaintiffs appeared in Osgoode Hall at two in the afternoon, withdrew court proceedings against the prime minister, and directed the media to a press conference in Ottawa for details of the settlement.

At 3 PM, Jim Sinclair and Clément Chartier appeared in the Parliamentary Press Theatre at the largest press conference ever held by the Métis. They emphasized that the Métis Nation had won what rightfully belonged to it and not at the expense of any other Aboriginal people. Meanwhile, the NCC was informing reporters that it would continue to speak for all Métis and non-status Indians regardless of the action taken by the MNC and attacked the "blasphemy" of Métis claims rooted in nationalism.[7]

THE 1983 FIRST MINISTERS CONFERENCE

At nine in the morning of 15 March 1983, the pounding of the chairman's gavel echoed through the cavernous depths of Ottawa's old railway station, now known as the Intergovernmental Conference Centre. Joining the prime minister and the premiers around the expanded oval table were the leaders of the Aboriginal peoples and territorial governments. Members of one Aboriginal delegation were conspicuous by their lone seat at the table and the crimson *Assumption*[8] sashes around their waists. National representative Clément Chartier occupied their seat. Immediately behind him sat Ferdinand Guiboche, a veteran Métis activist from Manitoba who had been chosen marshal of the delegation, and Jim Sinclair.

In his opening remarks, Prime Minister Trudeau addressed the controversy over Métis representation. He stated that, as a result of his requirement to invite Indian, Inuit, and Métis representatives to the conference, he had determined that the AFN, ICNI, and NCC should participate in constitutional discussions. In recent months, however, it had become evident that the Métis people "in great majority" did not feel properly represented by the NCC, and for that reason he had invited the Métis National Council to the table. In a thinly veiled warning to the NCC, he stated his hope to avoid multiplication of spokespersons for each of the Aboriginal peoples in the future.

The prime minister recognized that the diversity of Aboriginal peoples and aspirations made for varying models of Aboriginal self-government across the country. He limited the choices by what he considered the two unacceptable extremes of assimilation and absolute sovereignty. He supported Aboriginal self-government within the existing division of powers, with Aboriginal governments obtaining powers delegated from federal and/or provincial governments through legislation rather than exclusive powers entrenched in the Constitution.

In the MNC's opening address to the fully televised conference, Chartier chronicled the struggle of the Métis in the nineteenth century for a land base and self-government in western Canada, the indignities suffered after military defeat, and the vilification of Riel. He reminded Canadians that "The death and martyrdom of Riel has been a symbol to our people of the injustice they have suffered. Others who stood up for their rights in Canada such as Howe, Mackenzie and Papineau became heroes and influential leaders. Riel was instead branded a traitor."[9]

Chartier voiced concern that the Government of Canada, despite its constitutional recognition of Métis in 1981 and its promise of rights negotiations through section 37, had foreclosed on a settlement with the Métis before the conference. The Métis had "one more chance" to negotiate rights, and their priorities were still a land base and self-government, as they had been a century before. In conclusion, he asserted that the MNC was participating in the talks to fulfill the historical mission

Prime Minister Trudeau and MNC National Representative Clément Chartier
at FMC '83, Ottawa, Ontario, 15 March 1983. (Collection of Clément Chartier)

of the Métis Nation: to secure a place they could call their own.

Then Chartier vacated his chair to make way for Jim Sinclair, who declared that the continuous fight for basic rights to land and identity attested to the failure of Canadian democracy for the Métis people. Democracy had failed because it "looked after the majority" and "trampled" on the rights of minorities. If Métis rights were to be protected, he said, they had to be placed beyond the reach of "oppressive governments," regardless of their political stripe, and entrenched in the Constitution. Furthermore, if the new Charter of Rights and Freedoms for all Canadians was not "balanced" by a Charter of Rights for Aboriginal Peoples, then the Constitution itself would work against the Métis.

For Sinclair, the concept of partnership underlying the historical Métis position fit squarely between the two unacceptable extremes of sovereignty and assimilation set by the prime minister. In what would prove to be among the few promising exchanges during the conference, Sinclair informed the prime minister and Premier Lougheed that the Métis were prepared to start with a model such as Alberta's Métis settlements and build from there in cooperation with governments.

Unfortunately for the Métis, the AFN, ICNI, and NCC had set the agenda for the constitutional conference in the absence of the Métis. On day one, the conference bogged down on Aboriginal title, with governments refusing to move on the seemingly non-negotiable position of Indians from the AFN and NCC. A frustrated Sinclair used the impasse to raise the MNC proposal for separate schedules of constitutional rights for Métis, Indians, and Inuit and separate processes to define the rights in these schedules. On day two, the conference bogged down on sexual equality. As Sinclair had feared, non-status Indians would be pitted against status Indians on this issue. Premiers René Lévesque, Bill Davis, and Richard Hatfield as well as the NCC introduced non-status Indian women whose personal accounts of discrimination under the Indian Act were designed either to embarrass the federal government or undermine the demand for control over citizenship by the AFN, or do both.

With most provinces unwilling to budge on self-government, it became clear to the Métis that the most they could hope for was an agreement to keep talking. The constitutional conference concluded with a political accord being signed by the prime minister, all the premiers except Lévesque, and leaders of the four national Aboriginal organizations and territorial governments. The accord provided for a number of constitutional amendments, the foremost of which guaranteed two more constitutional conferences on Aboriginal issues in 1985 and 1987 (with a third conference guaranteed in 1984 by the political accord itself). A second amendment offered constitutional protection to land claims settlements. A third guaranteed "existing" Aboriginal and treaty rights equally to male and female persons. A fourth required the prime minister to hold further constitutional conferences with Aboriginal participation before any amendments were made to those sections of the Constitution directly affecting the rights of Aboriginal peoples.

As the prime minister brought proceedings to a close, the Métis delegation could draw some satisfaction from the conference. They had entered it as the least understood of all Aboriginal peoples and had conveyed to the hundreds of thousands of Canadians following it on television a clearer picture of who they were and what they wanted. Furthermore, in an exchange with the prime minister, Chartier had been able to reinstate "a Métis land base" on the constitutional agenda. An entrenched, ongoing process of constitutional negotiations offered the possibility of future breakthroughs.

The morning after the conference, a relaxed Jim Sinclair ate a hearty prairie breakfast of sausage and eggs in the coffee shop of Ottawa's Chateau Laurier. For the fifty-year-old political veteran, the conference marked the end of a long, hard road that had started twenty-three years earlier when Sinclair had overcome the scourge of alcoholism and set out to restore to the Métis the sense of self-worth he had won back for himself. In the process, he had championed the cause of Métis nationalism that would make him, an Indian leader of a Métis movement, particularly vulnerable.

On the other side of the restaurant, an attractive woman had taken notice of the solitary figure in the corner. In a sudden surge of emotion, she rushed over and embraced a pleasantly surprised Sinclair. She said she was a Vancouver model in town on business and had watched part of the conference on television. More than that, she was an Alberta Métis and had been inspired when he had spoken to Canadians about her people.

Later that morning, Sinclair window shopped his way down the Sparks Street Mall to the Holiday Inn, where the MNC had assembled to assess the conference and plan for the future. As Sinclair entered the dimly lit basement hall, he received a standing ovation from delegates, a rare event in the rough-and-tumble world of Métis politics. For Sinclair, it was a gratifying moment, one to be savoured as he headed back to the Prairies to an uncertain political future and into the pages of Métis history.

Chapter 9

IMPASSE

*T*he battle for full and equal Métis representation at the constitutional table came to an anticlimactic conclusion shortly after the 1983 first ministers conference. In mid-June in Ottawa, moments before the first preparatory meeting to set the priorities for ongoing constitutional talks, federal officials informed the MNC that it would have two seats, as did other conference participants, in all future meetings. With this issue out of the way, the question of who would occupy these seats imposed itself upon the MNC founders. An issue pushed to the sidelines in the rush to the constitutional table, the MNC's power structure would not lend itself to such speedy resolution.

NATIONALISTS VERSUS CONFEDERALISTS

As national representative of the Métis Nation, Clément Chartier had signed the 1983 Constitutional Accord on behalf of the MNC. Whether this position was to be ad hoc or permanent would be determined by the first annual MNC assembly in Winnipeg on 14 and 15 November 1983. The assembly became a showdown between the nationalist and confederalist forces within the MNC, a referendum not only on the direction of the movement at the national level but also on what was happening within the charter members as a result of the Métis political realignment.

Chartier, the leader of the nationalists, was an outsider to the Métis political establishment who had managed to get elected AMNSIS vice-president in 1982 independent of Jim Sinclair's political machine. He was an intellectual and a theoretician in a movement that had measured its progress in hard practical gains. His challenge was to convince the Métis masses that the nationalists and a political superstructure built on nationalism would pay greater dividends than the provincial associations they sought to supersede.

Leadership of the confederalist or status quo forces was clearly vested in the personality and political machinery of Jim Sinclair. His supporters feared that a centralized body would usurp the limited power and resources of the provincial associations some of them had spent a lifetime building. The provincial associations and their locals and the programs they provided were the only type of organization they understood; moreover, many depended on the functionary positions within the associations for their livelihood.

Adding fuel to the fire was the continued representation of non-status Indians by AMNSIS. With the formation of the MNC, the Indian minorities within the MMF and MAA had withdrawn and formed new provincial organizations to represent the interests of non-status and soon-to-be-reinstated Indians. Sinclair's association, on the other hand, decided to retain its dual membership but to pursue the constitutional objectives of its Métis electorate through the MNC.

The continuing alliance of Métis and non-status Indians in Saskatchewan reflected loyalty to Sinclair and the benefits such as jobs, housing, and small business assistance flowing from his political machine. Any split of the AMNSIS membership would inevitably entail a division of the assets, a nasty prospect for all concerned. But loyalty to Sinclair was not based on benefits alone; his credentials as a champion of the Métis cause had been enhanced by his lead role in the court case to seat the MNC at the 1983 first ministers conference.

Sinclair also proved to be highly adept at appealing to the sympathies of his Métis members, themselves classic underdogs, not to "kick people out" of the organization. Research by his legal team had revealed that Sinclair and approximately 3,000 of his non-status Indian members would not qualify for reinstatement to Indian status with the repeal of the discriminatory provisions of the Indian Act. Forming a separate non-status Indian organization affiliated with the NCC, such as had occurred in Manitoba and Alberta, was a non-starter for Sinclair; the NCC and its affiliates, by failing to adopt the ballot box method of election, had proven to be undemocratic, "top-down" organizations easily manipulated by Ottawa. Forming a separate non-status Indian organization without NCC affiliation was a possibility but, in view of the fight over programs and institutions that would inevitably occur, a painful last resort.

Chartier and his supporters within AMNSIS and its board of directors felt stifled by the failure of the association to split its membership. That failure, coupled with Sinclair's staunch opposition to the development of a national representative body of Métis people, had convinced them that his removal was imperative. The growing antagonism toward Sinclair was exacerbated by his manipulation of internal MNC politics to keep the nationalist wing at bay.

After the first ministers conference of 1983, the MNC had to deal with requests for admission from Métis associations from those regions of Ontario, British Columbia, and the Northwest Territories contiguous to the prairie provinces, taking in communities along the historical fur trade routes of the Métis homeland. The Louis Riel Métis Association of British Columbia was admitted to the MNC soon after the conference, followed by the Northwestern Ontario Métis Federation. In seeking assistance to build their fledgling organizations, the BC and Ontario associations—dubbed the "bookends"—turned to the individual MNC politician with the most respect and clout in Ottawa, Jim Sinclair. In return for pressing their case for federal government funding in his meetings with cabinet ministers, Sinclair could expect their unswerving support in his showdowns with the nationalists on the structure of the national organization.

These were the competing interests at play on the floor of the annual assembly in Winnipeg. Support for the nationalist and confederalist positions existed within each of the MNC's founding associations—a majority of AMNSIS delegates supported a confederalist structure (despite a significant Chartier nationalist minority), while a majority of MMF delegates supported Chartier and the move toward a nationalist governing body. The MAA, meanwhile, with indecisive Sam Sinclair at the helm, was divided but prevailed on the confederalist side largely to keep the FMS out of the formal structure.

The result was a decision of the assembly to eliminate the position of national representative occupied by Clément Chartier at the 1983 first ministers conference and to maintain a small MNC lobby office in Ottawa that would be accountable to the provincial presidents. At the same time, to avoid a rupture that would undermine their position at the first ministers' table, the nationalist and confederalist wings forged a compromise over constitutional representation. A constitutional committee under the chairmanship of Chartier and including Elmer Ghostkeeper of the FMS would steer the MNC's policy development and occupy one of the MNC seats at the 1984 first ministers conference alongside a seat to be occupied by the executive committee of provincial presidents. Notwithstanding this delicate balancing act, the MNC was the only national Aboriginal organization in the ongoing constitutional process without a national leader.

THE 1984 FIRST MINISTERS CONFERENCE

At the same time that it grappled with the leadership question, the MNC had to contend with the issues long used by governments to justify their inaction on Métis rights. First was Ottawa's denial of jurisdictional responsibility for dealing with the Métis. Second was the alleged difficulty in identifying who, how many, and where the Métis people were for the purpose of rights entitlement.

In advance of the first meeting of federal and provincial constitutional ministers and Aboriginal leaders prior to the 1984 conference, the MNC telexed Minister of Justice Mark MacGuigan on 27 September 1983 to press for a separate process involving the MNC, the federal government, and provincial governments in western Canada. If the Métis could be assured of a parallel process to break the federal-provincial impasse on jurisdiction and identification, then the MNC would be prepared to participate alongside the Indians and Inuit in negotiating a common statement of principles or rights for inclusion in the Constitution followed by separate schedules of rights for the different Aboriginal peoples.

The justice minister's response on 13 October did little to allay Métis concerns. MacGuigan stated that the agenda items in the 1983 Constitutional Accord contained fundamental matters of "crucial significance for all Aboriginal peoples and it would, in my opinion, be counterproductive, at this stage, to attempt their resolution in a fragmented manner." He added, ironically, that a separate process "could prejudice certain essential requisites of equity."

Therefore, the MNC had no choice but to work within the existing agenda and multilateral process flowing from the 1983 Constitutional Accord. At the meeting of constitutional ministers and Aboriginal leaders in Ottawa on 2 and 3 November 1983, the MNC focused on the agenda item "Land and Resources," under which it included the key Métis priority issues—a land base and resources, self-government, Métis self-identification, and the resolution of federal responsibility for Métis. During the multilateral meetings leading to the first ministers conference in 1984, the MNC would pursue its constitutional issues solely within the context of "Land and Resources," which came to be viewed as the "Métis" agenda item.[1]

Toward breaking the impasse on who, how many, and where the Métis people were, the MNC pressed for entrenchment of criteria for Métis self-identification in the Constitution. It identified the national Métis community as descendants of the Métis who had been entitled to land grants under the Manitoba Act and scrip under the Dominion Lands Act and others of Aboriginal ancestry who were absorbed by this historical community. Criteria for identifying the Métis would rest on self-declaration and community confirmation or proof of ancestry for those whose self-declaration could not be confirmed by Métis communities or locals.[2]

Work on Métis issues in the multilateral process would soon bog down on the issue of identification. The NCC decided to participate in working group sessions on Métis identification/enumeration. It insisted on a "pan-Canadian" concept of Métis to be included in any enumeration process. According to the NCC, the MNC self-identification criteria were elitist, and non-status Indians had the right to be considered Métis for the purposes of the Constitution and subsequent legislation.

For the MNC, the continued seating of the NCC at the table (at least on Métis issues) represented a thinly veiled ploy by the federal government to obfuscate Métis identity and justify its inaction on Métis rights. At a meeting with the MNC on 17 January 1984, the minister of justice stated that, as long as both the MNC and the NCC claimed to represent the Métis people, "it would not be desirable for the federal government to act unilaterally to exclude one or the other." At the meeting of constitutional ministers and Aboriginal leaders in Toronto on 13 and 14 February 1984, the minister cited the existence of another group of Métis as grounds for refusing an accord on Métis self-identification with the MNC. A few days later, a clearly frustrated Clément Chartier responded to MacGuigan:

> Regardless of what people outside the territorial and cultural boundaries of the Métis homeland might call themselves, they, indisputably, are not part of the historic Métis Nation. If your government feels strongly about their situation, it and the eastern Provinces are free to do whatever you wish. However, as representative of the Métis Nation, the Métis National Council expects the Government of Canada to initiate a tripartite process with the western provinces and the Métis National Council to address Métis rights. If the First Ministers' Conference is to prove successful, the Government of Canada must show political will to deal honestly with the Métis Nation.[3]

This lack of federal political will extended to the impasse over federal-provincial jurisdiction and the Métis. As Jim Sinclair's exchange with Premier Lougheed at the 1983 first ministers conference had demonstrated, the MNC was willing to work with the provinces in establishing models for a self-governing land base; in the absence of provincial will to move on Métis issues, however, the MNC believed the federal government had the constitutional and historical responsibility to resolve Métis rights. In private discussions with the MNC, MacGuigan reiterated that primary responsibility for the Métis lay with the provinces, but Ottawa had a role to play in bringing the provinces forward to deal with Métis concerns, particularly the provision of lands. His Office of Aboriginal Constitutional Affairs (OACA) was satisfied that progress was being made on the provincial front: Alberta had asserted its responsibility for Métis, and the Pawley government in Manitoba had stated its willingness to negotiate a settlement of Métis claims under the Manitoba Act. As for the Province of Saskatchewan, OACA's director had assured the MNC that "We're working on them."

The Trudeau government had assumed the role of cheerleader in what it believed should be a Métis-provincial process, ignoring MNC requests for the establishment of a federal interlocutor for Métis. The MMF had suspended its litigation against the governments of Canada and Manitoba in response to Manitoba's offer to settle Métis claims. Ottawa welcomed the provincial initiative and acted as if it wasn't a co-defendant in the litigation; in fact, it was the principal target of the Métis action. The federal government certainly didn't see itself as part of any out-of-court settlement.

In the by-now familiar venue of the Intergovernmental Conference Centre on 8 and 9 March 1984, the MNC pursued the impasse over Métis issues with first ministers. In its opening remarks, the MNC stated its intention to leave the conference the following evening with a firm agreement on Métis self-identification and the enumeration process by which Métis citizenship would be established. Toward this end, it tabled draft constitutional accords on Métis identification and enumeration.[4] On the issue of jurisdiction, it stressed the need for a practical solution:

> Being a practical people, the Métis recognize the necessity of working out an agreement on our rights with a full understanding of the existing division of powers, in particular, provincial jurisdiction over lands and resources. We know that the assumption of constitutional responsibility for Métis by the Government of Canada is not a panacea. We know that the only way a Métis land base and self-government can become a reality is if Canada and the provinces within the Métis homeland mount the political will needed to release the Métis from the jurisdictional straitjacket in which we have found ourselves for decades. We appeal to First Ministers at this table not to argue over who does or does not have responsibility to deal with us but instead to determine how Métis aspirations can be accommodated through joint federal-provincial action.

> If the provinces are willing to transfer lands to the Métis, surely
> the Government of Canada can assume primary fiscal responsi-
> bility. Political will on the part of both levels of government is
> also required for the transfer of entrenched or delegated powers
> to Métis government on the land base. In short, Mr. Chairman,
> when there is a will, there is a way.[5]

The conference ended in a deadlock, with the federal government able to
muster the support of only a few provinces for its proposed constitutional
amendment for a limited form of Aboriginal self-government with powers delegated by Ottawa and the provinces. By the end of the conference, however, the
MNC had at least impressed upon the first ministers the need to tackle the obstacles faced by the Métis. The prime minister elevated the MNC priority issues—
federal jurisdiction under section 91(24) of the Constitution Act, 1867, and iden-
tification/enumeration—to the top of the agenda for the 1985 conference.

Moreover, in the closing days of the Trudeau era, the prime minister had
started to come around on the critical issue of federal responsibility for dealing
with the Métis. In a letter to the MNC on 30 April 1984, the prime minister stated that, "With respect to the question of responsibility for the Métis people, the
federal government has held the view that matters in this field fall to the provincial governments. It may well develop that another arrangement would be considered preferable both by governments and by the Métis representatives. Any
such determination would, however, have to follow from a thorough examina-
tion of the legal, economic and social consequences. As I stated at the conference, the question of jurisdiction over lands would be among those to be thor-
oughly explored. These matters will doubtless be closely examined over the next
several months."[6]

In Alberta, meanwhile, Peter Lougheed was drawing his own conclusions
from the exchanges on jurisdiction at the 1984 conference. On 28 March 1984, he
had written to MAA president Sam Sinclair requesting a statement of the position of the MAA on the matter of jurisdiction and responsibility for Métis.
Sinclair replied on 24 April that the question of jurisdiction was not a "burning
issue" with the MAA. After Lougheed and a number of his ministers met with the
MAA leadership on 28 April, Lougheed reported to the Alberta legislature that he
had asked the MAA to clarify the MNC and by association the MAA position that
the federal government should have primary responsibility for programming for
the Métis people. The premier expressed a desire to continue working closely
with the MAA on the improvement of the province's Métis programs but said
that it would be difficult to do so if the Métis leadership wanted responsibility
transferred from the provinces to the federal government.

Alberta's minister of Native affairs, Milt Pahl, reaffirmed the premier's position in a letter to Sam Sinclair on 29 May 1984. Pahl stated that jurisdictional authority for Métis governments would not flow directly from the Constitution but would have to flow either from the federal or the provincial government. The Métis of Alberta would have to indicate which level of government they wished to relate to. He suggested that the Government of Alberta would have difficulty enhancing or even maintaining special programs and services to Métis people beyond fiscal year 1984–85 if the Métis people of Alberta did not wish to be under provincial jurisdiction.

Alberta's "hard-ball" approach underscored the vulnerability of the MNC position. With provinces generally treating the Métis as ordinary citizens, it had made sense for the Métis to press Ottawa to assume and exercise responsibility for them as an Aboriginal people, but this position threatened the Métis relationship with the only province that had done something for them. The MAA tried (and managed) to dodge the bullet, replying somewhat cryptically to Lougheed that "neither jurisdiction has even come close to fulfilling its responsibility whatever it may be."

The fallout over jurisdiction focused the province on moving forward with the one group of Métis people with whom it had worked closely within the confines of provincial legislation. That year the joint Alberta–FMS MacEwan Committee had reported to the province, recommending changes to the provincial legislation governing the Métis settlements with a focus on greater Métis self-determination. The province believed it could proceed with the implementation of recommendations under its powers for local government and property and civil rights.

Following the 1984 first ministers conference, Elmer Ghostkeeper retired from politics to start a business on Paddle Prairie Métis Settlement. As a member of the MNC's constitutional committee, Ghostkeeper had worked to ensure that the constitutional protection of the only existing Métis land base became an integral part of the MNC's agenda item, "Land and Resources."[7] His high profile in the Métis political realignment and in the initial stages of the multilateral process had placed the Métis settlements on the political map, but exclusion of the FMS from charter membership in the MNC had taken a personal toll on him and had soured the FMS on the multilateral process in general.

Ghostkeeper's successors would be more inward-looking and focused on working within the province to achieve their objectives. Given the unwieldy nature of the multilateral process, with minefields such as jurisdiction, the province was also looking inward for a constructive way out. Hence the increased attractiveness of Ghostkeeper's "made-in-Alberta agreement" as an approach and the FMS as a partner (since it was not a formal participant in the multilateral process).

With the retirement of Prime Minister Trudeau shortly after the 1984 conference and the calling of a federal election by his successor, John Turner, the

Aboriginal constitutional process was put on hold. In the September 1984 election, the Progressive Conservatives under Brian Mulroney swept to power. The MNC, meanwhile, was heading into its annual assembly of member association boards in October, and its earlier compromise on constitutional leadership was about to fall apart.

THE 1985 FIRST MINISTERS CONFERENCE

The trigger for renewed infighting within the MNC was the election of Yvon Dumont to the presidency of the MMF after the 1984 first ministers conference. Dumont came from the town of St. Laurent, near Winnipeg, where he and his brothers were partners in a construction firm. The Dumont family could trace its roots in St. Laurent back to the 1790s and was part of the French Michif-speaking community that had managed to persevere in southern Manitoba following the great dispersion of the 1870s. Dumont had sought the MMF presidency in order to renew the Métis court case against Ottawa and the province.

In his lawyer, former BC Supreme Court justice Thomas Berger, Dumont had found a renowned and respected champion of Aboriginal rights who was prepared to keep the MMF court case moving despite a lack of funds. The MMF's statement of claim, to be revised in 1985, was sweeping. It sought a court declaration that twenty-one federal and provincial laws and Orders-in-Council were unconstitutional alterations to the Métis land grant sections of the Manitoba Act, 1870, and had resulted in the Métis being denied the land promised under the act.

Dumont believed that the Métis people required national leadership on constitutional issues that could not be provided effectively by provincial presidents elected to deal with "bread and butter" issues. He envisaged a national assembly and leader directly elected by the Métis people at the same time as the leadership of the provincial associations—in effect, a federal system of governance for the Métis with two levels of representation, each with its exclusive areas of authority. Toward this objective, Dumont became a forceful advocate of effective national representation for the Métis and a Chartier supporter.

On the floor of the MNC annual assembly in Spruce Grove, Alberta, in October 1984, Dumont proved his mettle in a clash with the indomitable Jim Sinclair. He gained majority support for Chartier to reassume the post of national representative as an interim measure toward the development of a national assembly. Much to the surprise of delegates, Sinclair promptly announced his resignation as AMNSIS representative to the MNC, prompting a series of stinging denunciations by his followers of the narrow nationalism of the Métis (some calling it racism) that had forced Sinclair out.

Chartier suddenly found himself in an unusual situation. A few weeks before the MNC assembly, he had been elected president of the World Council of Indigenous Peoples (WCIP) at a meeting in Panama City. Chartier—the perennial outsider—was now AMNSIS vice-president, MNC national representative, and WCIP president at the same time.

The counterattack followed swiftly in the weeks to come. The pro-Sinclair majority on the AMNSIS board "ordered" Sinclair to reassume his leadership of the organization. Moreover, they declared, Sinclair—not a national representative—would speak for AMNSIS at the constitutional table. Sinclair, for his part, moved quickly to consolidate support among other provincial presidents, namely Fred House of British Columbia and Paddy McGuire of Ontario, who were relying on him for government funding. Thus, the Métis headed toward the third first ministers conference in a state of utter confusion over national representation.

In Ottawa, the Conservative government was developing a new approach to the final first ministers conferences on Aboriginal constitutional matters in 1985 and 1987. The two lead ministers in the process, Minister of Justice John Crosbie and Minister of Indian Affairs David Crombie, would inject a candour and wry sense of humour that helped to animate what was becoming a more and more complex and legalistic process. At the first meeting of these ministers and their provincial and Aboriginal counterparts in Ottawa on 17 and 18 December 1984, the new federal approach was unveiled.

To be known as the "contingent right" approach, it was premised on the assumption that governments would not agree to entrench enforceable rights they didn't understand, and there was insufficient time before the next first ministers conference to obtain an adequate understanding of how courts would interpret rights such as Aboriginal self-government or a land base. Therefore, the federal government was proposing a constitutional amendment to recognize the right of the Aboriginal peoples to self-government where those rights were set out in negotiated agreements, to commit the government of Canada and the provincial governments to participate in negotiations directed toward concluding those agreements, and to identify elements of self-government to be negotiated, such as institutions, powers, jurisdiction, and financial arrangements. These elements would then be negotiated at the community level, and the resulting self-government agreements would receive constitutional protection in much the same way that modern land claims settlements had gained constitutional protection through a section 35 amendment agreed to at the 1983 conference—by way of declarations in the agreements themselves and in the federal and provincial enabling legislation putting them into effect stating that they were self-government agreements for the purposes of the Constitution.

The proposed amendment fell short of the AFN's demand for a free-standing, justiciable right to self-government (capable of being decided by a court), but its constitutional commitment to negotiate and its mechanism for protecting self-government agreements would enable the AFN and other Aboriginal organizations to leave the conference hall in a stronger bargaining position. From the Métis perspective, the proposal also shifted the focus of the conference and the ongoing process from the long and cumbersome agenda inherited from 1983, replete with section 35 issues such as treaty rights and Aboriginal title, to the single, all-encompassing issue of self-government. Moreover, it shifted negotiations from the unwieldy multilateral level (seventeen players at the conference table) to the tripartite level, thereby allowing Métis communities backed by the MNC and its provincial associations to pursue self-government arrangements and a land base with Ottawa and those provinces within the Métis homeland.

Crosbie also surprised the MNC with an offer to address the jurisdiction issue. While reiterating the Department of Justice view "that Parliament cannot legislate for Métis as a people distinct from Indians, under section 91(24) of the Constitution Act 1867,"[8] he offered the MNC leaders a Supreme Court reference on whether or not the Métis fit within that section. The MNC did not take him up on the offer; rather than risk a setback in the Supreme Court, it would continue to seek through negotiation an amendment to section 91(24), which would make explicit the inclusion of all Aboriginal peoples within federal jurisdiction.

On the eve of the first ministers conference on 2 and 3 April 1985, the MNC's internal impasse over constitutional representation was broken when a majority of provincial presidents backed Jim Sinclair's position that only the provincial presidents would sit at the constitutional table. Having come to terms with Sinclair's grip over the "bookends" and a quiescent Sam Sinclair, Yvon Dumont, who had led the move in Spruce Grove to reinstate Clément Chartier as national representative, did not put up a fight. Sensing the futility of pressing for structural reform in the near term, he had resigned his MMF to coexisting with other provincial associations within the MNC solely to pursue common constitutional objectives. Thus, Chartier was deposed as national representative for the second time.

The success of the 1985 conference hinged on the prime minister's ability to swing the hard-line provinces, particularly British Columbia, Alberta, and Saskatchewan, into accepting the constitutional commitment to negotiate self-government agreements. After the first day of the conference, at the insistence of at least two provinces, the commitment to negotiate was removed from the federal government's proposed constitutional amendment and placed in a non-binding political accord. The final offer at the table, the "Saskatchewan Accord" (named after the province that had made the weakening of the commitment to negotiate a condition for its support for the package) had the support of Ottawa and seven provinces representing more than 50 per cent of the population of Canada— enough for a constitutional amendment under the general amending formula—but only two of the Aboriginal organizations, the MNC and the NCC.

With the weakening of the commitment to negotiate, the AFN rejected the federal proposal, as did the Inuit leaders, albeit on a conditional basis. Prime Minister Mulroney offered the Inuit a sixty-day period to reconsider, but at a follow-up meeting of ministers in Toronto on 5 and 6 June 1985, the Inuit reaffirmed their rejection of the proposal, thereby sealing the fate of the accord. It would be the closest the conference players would ever come to an agreement on self-government.

Harry Daniels conferring with Jim Sinclair at FMC '85, Ottawa, Ontario, 3 April 1985.
(CP Photo Archive)

Chapter 10

The Fiery Front

The World Council of Indigenous Peoples had been established in 1975 at a conference in Port Alberni, British Columbia, with the objective of promoting international solidarity among indigenous peoples that could lead to action on their behalf at the international level. The election of a Métis to head this body and a dangerous mission he would undertake to a remote region of the Americas would illustrate to the Métis people how their struggle for an autonomous homeland was shared by indigenous peoples around the world. Occurring in the midst of constitutional talks that appeared to be heading nowhere, these events opened up a new fiery front stretching from the mangrove coast of Nicaragua to the frozen banks of the Rideau.

CLÉMENT CHARTIER, MISURASATA, AND THE SELF-DETERMINATION QUESTION

With the 1985 first ministers conference and the MNC setbacks behind him, Clément Chartier plunged into his new work as president of the WCIP. [1] A central objective of that organization, and of Canada's Aboriginal peoples, who had taken the lead role in its founding, had been the establishment of standards and instruments in international law that would recognize and protect the rights of indigenous peoples and put pressure on states to recognize the land claims and political autonomy of their indigenous populations. At the core of the issue of indigenous peoples' rights in international law lay the principle of self-determination.

The principle of self-determination[2] was defined in article 1 of the United Nations International Covenant on Civil and Political Rights (which became international law in 1976): "All peoples have the right of self-determination. By virtue of that right they freely determine their political status and freely pursue their economic, social and cultural development." Although hailed as a universal right of peoples, in practice, self-determination had been applied to independent states or to externally colonized peoples on their way to becoming independent states. It had not been extended to minority nationalities and indigenous peoples (of which the Métis are both) within independent states. These minorities and indigenous peoples saw themselves as being subject to an internal form of colonialism, a denial of their collective right to develop as distinct national communities within these states.

Recognizing that the equality or "prohibition on discrimination" articles of its existing human rights instruments had proven inadequate when applied to the situation and aspirations of indigenous populations, the UN Commission on Human Rights had authorized its Sub-Commission on Prevention of Discrimination and Protection of Minorities to commence work on the rights of indigenous peoples early in the 1980s. The sub-commission had assigned this task to a Working Group on Indigenous Populations (WGIP), which met for the first time in Geneva, Switzerland, in 1982 (with Clément Chartier in attendance as part of the WCIP delegation). In 1985, the WGIP began work on the drafting of a Declaration on the Rights of Indigenous Peoples for eventual adoption and proclamation by the UN General Assembly.

Through its work on the declaration, the WGIP would introduce the world community to the political aspirations of indigenous peoples. Its work influenced another international body concerned with human rights protection, the Organization of American States (OAS). Headquartered in Washington, DC, and comprising the thirty-five independent states of the Western Hemisphere, the OAS was becoming increasingly concerned with the situation of the indigenous citizens of North, Central, and South America. The only reference to indigenous peoples in OAS human rights instruments had been in the individual equality and non-discrimination articles of the American Declaration of the Rights and Duties of Man of 1948 and the American Convention on Human Rights of 1969. The OAS Inter-American Commission on Human Rights believed that an inter-American instrument should be drafted on the collective rights of indigenous peoples similar to that being developed at the UN.

Chartier's assumption of leadership at the WCIP had come at a time of mounting concern in both the UN and the OAS over the persecution of the Mayan people in Guatemala by that country's repressive military government. Chartier decided to conduct an investigation of the conditions of indigenous peoples in Central America that would figure in a report to the United Nations, where the WCIP had consultative status. During the summer of 1985, Chartier visited Mayan villages in Guatemala. In the fall, he visited Mayan refugee camps in neighbouring Mexico. But it was another conflict in Central America that was to consume Chartier's energy, a lesser-known conflict that many supporters of indigenous peoples did not want to know about.

The Sandinista National Liberation Front (Frente Sandinista de Liberación Nacional) had come to power in Nicaragua in 1979 in a popular revolution against the corrupt and repressive regime of the military dictator Anastasio Somoza. Under the direction of the Marxist minister of the interior, Tomas Borge, the Sandinistas had launched an aggressive "modernization" program on the isolated, jungle-clad Atlantic seaboard of the country, which was inhabited largely by indigenous peoples. Thousands of Miskito, Sumo, and Rama had been forcibly removed from their traditional lands and relocated to labour camps. In 1981, under the leadership of the MISURASATA[3] movement, the indigenous peoples began to wage armed resistance against the Nicaraguan government; by 1985, close to half of their villages had been burned, bombed, or occupied by government forces.

During the Christmas period in 1985, Chartier as WCIP president visited Nicaragua at the invitation of the Sandinista government to investigate the treatment of the Miskito people and to help mediate the conflict. He was received cordially by President Daniel Ortega and Tomas Borge, but to his surprise he discovered that the "investigation" would not include a tour of the Miskito homeland. After returning to Costa Rica and trying unsuccessfully to gain official permission to visit their homeland, Chartier slipped into the region on a clandestine mission. During the first three weeks in the new year, he toured fourteen Miskito communities, all demanding Managua's recognition of their right to a land base and self-government.

WCIP President Clément Chartier and Daniel Ortega Saavedra, President of Nicaragua, Managua, December 1985. (Collection of Clément Chartier)

On 21 January 1986, a village that Chartier was visiting came under rocket attack from government planes. Chartier's group of eighteen, which by now included Miskito guerrilla commander Brooklyn Rivera, escaped in a large dugout canoe. A few hours later the planes returned, strafing the canoe on a lagoon, killing three and leaving five injured. Among the injured was David Rodriquez, a MISURASATA fighter who, the previous summer, had attended an international indigenous youth conference that Chartier had organized as part of the centenary of the North-West Rebellion at Batoche.

Somehow, amid the carnage in the lagoon, the dugout and motor had remained intact. For the next sixteen days, Chartier's party canoed through the jungle, pursued by Sandinista ground forces and helicopters, receiving assistance from Miskito villages along the way. Finally, Chartier's group arrived at a Miskito coastal community under Sandinista military occupation. Alerted to the arrival of the fugitives, the villagers erected their own sound barrier to conceal their presence. An instant and noisy church service was arranged while fishermen in their dugout canoes added their own clatter to the singing. Amid this activity, other villagers pulled the boat of Chartier's group through a shallow channel into the mouth of the river emptying into the Caribbean.

Entering the pounding surf of the ocean, the group started up the motor but soon encountered a government naval vessel, forcing them to head out into the open sea with a broken compass. Following a twenty-two-hour voyage and with fuel supplies virtually exhausted, the party sighted the island of San Andreas, controlled by Colombia. Upon beaching their craft, the group—by now reduced to rags and caked in salt—was promptly arrested by the Colombian authorities. The three wounded were taken to a hospital (where the wounded Rodriquez had his leg amputated), while Chartier and company were jailed. Shortly afterward, with their identities confirmed, the group was released from prison[4] and taken to a luxury hotel filled with a group of Canadian tourists.

En route back to Canada following an international press conference in Costa Rica, Chartier could not imagine that his nightmare was to continue. While reports of his disappearance had aroused widespread concern in the Aboriginal community in Canada and calls for Canadian diplomatic intervention on his behalf, the indigenous peoples' political establishment was drawing knives. Other members of the WCIP executive were accusing Chartier of making an unauthorized foray into the Miskito homeland within the sovereign territory of the state of Nicaragua and com-

Clément Chartier travelling to inland Miskito villages in Nicaragua, January 1986.
(Courtesy Clément Chartier)

promising the WCIP's role in the mediation process. They expressed fears that Chartier (and by association the WCIP) would be branded a "contra."[5]

In reality, the WCIP establishment feared the loss of financial and political support from foreign aid agencies and left-leaning non-governmental organizations that championed the Sandinista cause in addition to that of indigenous peoples. In a blunt assessment of the crisis brought on by his actions, a WCIP rival told Chartier that the government in Managua and the WCIP were "milking the same cow." The showdown between Chartier and his detractors would occur in March 1986, when Chartier reported to the UN Human Rights Commission in Geneva.

After addressing the UN body with a focus on the plight of the Miskito, Chartier discovered that the two WCIP vice-presidents had tried to strip him of his credentials. What they failed to achieve before Chartier's address they achieved afterward; at a meeting of the WCIP board of directors in Geneva, Chartier's responsibilities and duties as WCIP president were suspended. Of all the member associations present, only the MNC stood in support of the Métis leader of the world's indigenous peoples.[6]

THE "BOTTOM-UP" APPROACH

Back in Canada, Métis leaders were trying to manoeuvre through minefields of their own in the constitutional talks. The MNC had accepted the final federal proposal at the 1985 first ministers conference—despite its watered-down commitment to negotiate—largely on the basis of a commitment given near the end of the conference by Prime Minister Mulroney that he would use his influence with the provinces to set in motion a process to ensure that the Métis priorities of self-government and a land base would be pursued through tripartite negotiations on the Prairies. At the follow-up ministers' meeting in Toronto in June 1985, Minister of Justice John Crosbie reiterated the prime minister's intention to move ahead on tripartite negotiations with willing Aboriginal and provincial partners in what came to be known as the "bottom-up" approach to self-government.

The "bottom-up" approach was of no interest to the AFN and ICNI. Their constituencies already had parallel processes on self-government and land claims, and they didn't wish to repeat the exercise as a substitute for constitutional negotiations. The proposed tripartite talks would occur outside the constitutional process, and there was no guarantee that any agreements reached would eventually gain constitutional protection. Moreover, the talks would make it possible for governments to bypass the national Aboriginal organizations and deal with local Aboriginal groups, thereby creating the potential to undermine the national organizations at the constitutional table.

In the absence of any parallel process for its constituency, the MNC felt tripartite talks at the regional and local levels would provide the western provinces with a clearer understanding of Métis self-government and its impact on their jurisdiction. The talks could also address the priorities of the MNC's large constituency that would remain off a land base. The MNC explained its position at the ministers' meeting in Toronto: "We realize that we have taken a different approach than the Indian and Inuit people. This does not mean we are any less committed to entrenching self-government, only that we differ in the approach to achieving that common goal. Our decision should come as no surprise to the participants around this table, considering our unique legal position in Canada."[7]

Not surprisingly, the Province of Alberta responded to the decentralization of talks by identifying issues of concern to Alberta's Métis settlements as its top priority in the post-1985 conference period. On 3 June 1985, the Alberta legislature passed a resolution in support of the Lougheed government's commitment to grant fee simple title to Métis settlement lands to Métis settlement government and to amend the province's constitution to protect the land base. The land transfer would occur only after provincial legislation respecting the settlements was revised to include reasonable land allocation, membership criteria, and democratic forms of local government. As for the Métis off-settlements, the premier wrote to Sam Sinclair on 11 April 1985, inviting the MAA to submit a proposed agreement for self-government as an example of what was outlined in the federal government's proposed accord on self-government at the 1985 conference. The MAA response was a proposed framework agreement on self-government to be concluded solely by the MAA and the province.

In the long run, the same barriers that had stood in the way of Métis aspirations at the multilateral level would block meaningful advances in tripartite talks in Manitoba and Saskatchewan. Regardless of how detailed the Métis proposals were, the talks inevitably foundered on the questions of whether Ottawa or the province had jurisdiction on a particular matter, which one was responsible for financing self-government arrangements, and which one was responsible for providing land. Even when a government such as Howard Pawley's in Manitoba could embrace the concept of self-government, the support was qualified by his "have-not" province's insistence on primary federal responsibility for financing Aboriginal governments. Worse still, the federal and provincial officials participating in the talks had no authority to push the talks beyond the impasse. As unwieldy and unresponsive as the multilateral process was, the MNC had no choice but to seek the breakthrough at that level.

The seemingly endless series of preparatory meetings in the two-year period leading up to the 1987 conference would produce a myriad of documents and permutations on the same issues but little if any substantive progress on the critical issue of the right to self-government. The three westernmost provinces would not commit to the entrenchment of a concept that they claimed they did not fully comprehend and, they feared, could be interpreted by the courts in a manner encroaching on their jurisdictions. British Columbia and Alberta remained unconvinced of the need for any self-government amendment. With Quebec a non-participant, the support of at least one of these western and the six other provinces was required if the federal government was to draw the required support for a self-government amendment under the general amending formula.

The federal government had retained the MNC's support for its "contingent right" amendment since 1985 and had sweetened the pot in the weeks before the final conference. In a breakthrough on the issue of jurisdiction, Ottawa proposed mechanisms to ensure that Métis self-government negotiations and agreements would not be affected by jurisdictional disputes related to section 91(24) of the Constitution Act, 1867.[8] The MNC submitted proposals in the multilateral talks to bridge the gap between the AFN's insistence on a free-standing, justiciable right to self-government and the federal government's "contingent right." In the dying moments of the 1985 conference, Jim Sinclair had tried in vain to forge a compromise with a proposal for explicit recognition of a right to self-government accompanied by a "sunrise" clause delaying its justiciability for a period of five years.[9] Whether a proposal like this had any chance of succeeding this time depended on how hardened positions had become by the time first ministers and Aboriginal leaders gathered in Ottawa's Intergovernmental Conference Centre on 26 and 27 March 1987, for the final conference on Aboriginal constitutional matters.

THE "BLOWOUT" 1987 CONFERENCE

According to Jim Sinclair, the Métis, after their battle to gain entry into the constitutional talks, should be the last to leave the bargaining table. He was determined to keep all lines of communication open until the end. Sitting amid the MNC delegates was Saskatchewan's former minister of intergovernmental affairs (and future premier), Roy Romanow, who had been invited by Sinclair to direct the MNC's advisers. Romanow's group was expected to monitor the conference proceedings from the MNC caucus room and undertake the liaison work with other delegations toward the development of a consensus proposal.

The opening remarks by other conference participants quickly brought to bear the polarization on self-government that Sinclair had feared. Aboriginal positions congealed around the unconditional justiciable right to self-government—now termed the "inherent" right—as quickly as the three westernmost provinces reaffirmed their opposition to even a "contingent" right with a binding commitment to negotiate self-government agreements. Sufficient support for the federal proposal—basically a repeat of its 1985 draft accord—was not there.

The MNC's opening remarks were delivered by Yvon Dumont, who had come into his own as an MNC spokesman after playing a largely passive role at the 1985 conference. Like MMF leaders before him, Dumont was of the view that Métis constitutional claims ultimately would have to be resolved through the proper implementation of the Manitoba Act, which embodied the terms of union of the Métis as a founding nation within Confederation. Under his stewardship, the MMF had advanced in its litigation of claims under the Manitoba Act. On 18 February 1987, the Manitoba Court of Queen's Bench had dismissed a federal government application to strike out the MMF statement of claim,[10] finding there were real issues to be decided at trial, namely whether the Manitoba Act promised a Métis land base and whether the alleged actions were unconstitutional and undermined the descendants of the Métis.

The procedural motions of the Department of Justice had only convinced Dumont that Ottawa feared the case going to trial. While he, like Sinclair, was keen on keeping doors open at the conference, he was wary of making undue concessions that could undercut the land claim. In the MNC's opening remarks, Dumont cut straight to the heart of the issue for the Red River Métis:

> The legitimacy of the Manitoba Act of 1870 was shattered by Canada's refusal to adhere to its promise to guarantee land rights for the Métis and their descendants. That promise had always been understood by the Métis to be given for their acceptance of the Manitoba Act. And, since it was not lived up to, since those basic promises were not kept, we feel that the Manitoba Act and the Constitution of Canada are void.[11]

Premier Bill Vander Zalm of British Columbia, after praising Canadian Aboriginal soldiers who had participated in the liberation of his native Netherlands two years before his immigration to Canada in 1947, concluded his remarks by flatly stating, "My government recognizes that the Fathers of Confederation divided all powers to govern between the federal and provincial governments. My government cannot commit to self-government as proposed by the AFN or its entrenchment in the Constitution."[12]

Premier Grant Devine of Saskatchewan, citing heavy provincial expenditures on Aboriginal peoples, would go no further than his proposed 1985 Saskatchewan Accord (with its non-binding commitment to negotiate): "Through the contingent rights approach it seems to me our approach bridged the gap between our concern that we did not understand the meaning of self-government—and clearly Canadians do not today—and our desire to recognize the rights and aspirations of native people. ... We do not believe it to be in the interest of Canadians to have those questions just holus bolus answered by the courts without having some involvement in the process."[13]

Premier Don Getty of Alberta prefaced his position on the proposed self-government amendment by reviewing the progress that his government had been making with the FMS toward drafting the new Métis Settlements Act. The new act would precede the transfer of title to settlement land and the protection of the land base in the Alberta Act, part of the Constitution of Canada. As for the self-government arrangements for the Métis settlements, Getty stated that "These will be enshrined in legislation. While we continue to move aggressively in this direction in Alberta, we still believe that any constitutional rights must first be defined carefully, and fully understood before they are entrenched in our Constitution. ... In Alberta's opinion, constitutional entrenchment of an undefined inherent Aboriginal right to self-government could lead to the establishment of a third order of government in Canada, possibly sovereign, or equal to both federal and provincial governments. How could a country, regardless of our good intentions, cope with that situation?"[14]

By the time participants gathered before a live national television audience at 1:30 PM on the second and final day of the conference, the conference had become nothing more than an exercise in damage control. Announcing the failure of the in-camera morning session to produce a breakthrough, Prime Minister Mulroney lamented,

> I genuinely regret that the draft amendment failed to generate the support required to make it a reality. One day we shall succeed, but this constitutional process has now come to an end. ... If in my judgment a new meeting or conference would be helpful and productive, I shall not hesitate to call one. But let us not be under any illusions. There shall be a price to be paid for our failure. I don't want anybody leaving this room or leaving this city today under any illusions about that.
>
> Unfortunately, those called upon to pay the largest share of that price shall be those least equipped to pay it, namely the Aboriginal peoples who have paid an unfair share of that price for an unfair share of time. But the concept of self-government remains alive. It remains an ideal to which many of us are committed.[15]

If the prime minister was to deliver the obituary notice for the process, it fell to Georges Erasmus, chief spokesman for the AFN, to deliver its eulogy. In a quiet and dignified manner, backed by delegates from all four Aboriginal organizations standing around him in a rare show of Aboriginal solidarity, Erasmus explained most eloquently why the "contingent" right proposal was not acceptable: "Could we take that great leap of faith and actually encourage a statement in the Constitution that we had nothing until we were given something? The answer always was the same, Mr. Prime Minister. It was always clear. It was always unequivocal. It was virtually never."[16]

The prime minister then turned to the one politician in the hall who, perhaps more than any other, had come to Ottawa to make a deal. Jim Sinclair had kept his political feelers out to the end, reviving his "sunrise clause" proposal from the 1985 conference in a last-ditch effort to forge a consensus. Regardless of the strengths of a free-standing "inherent" right to self-government in the Constitution, Sinclair, who had personally borne the full brunt of racism for much of his life, did not trust the white judiciary as an arbiter of Aboriginal rights. He had come to make a political deal that could then be written into the Constitution, but what he had found, particularly in the stance of Bill Vander Zalm and Grant Devine, was a preconceived refusal to negotiate.

Then, to the amazement of the conference and the live television audience, Sinclair exploded. He turned on the BC premier, calling it shameful that as an immigrant from a country liberated from Nazi occupation by Canadian forces including large numbers of Aboriginal soldiers, he could rise to the premiership of one of Canada's largest provinces in such a short time while refusing to "recognize the rights of our people here in this country of their origin."[17] He turned on Quebec, represented at the table by Minister of Intergovernmental Affairs Gil Rémillard, and expressed the disappointment of the Métis that Quebec would not come to their aid at the constitutional table even though the Métis had fought and died for French-language rights in western Canada. According to Sinclair, instead of giving the Métis the kind of support they needed, Quebec had come to advance its own cause.

Then he turned on the premier who had held the balance of power at the last two conferences and had used that power to block the full implementation of the federal proposal, the premier of Sinclair's own province. In response to Premier Devine's earlier complaint about provincial spending on Natives relative to net farm income in Saskatchewan, Sinclair, with the Mulroney government's farm aid package in mind, declared to a shocked Devine, "At the same time, you came to the prime minister here, and he bought an election for you for $1 billion."[18] Referring to northern Saskatchewan, Sinclair continued, "We pay twice as much ... for food as you would in the south. Yet for every bottle of wine and every bottle of whiskey that you send north of Prince Albert, you put a subsidy on that so the price of that wine is the same price in La Loche as it is in Regina. At the same time, there is no subsidy on the price of milk for our children and on the price of food for our people who are having a hard time in those communities with no jobs."[19] Referring to the lease of a vast tract of crown land to an American pulp and paper company by Devine's government, Sinclair declared, "You ask for definitions when we talk about self-government. You gave them an open-ended agreement which gave them more land than all the reserves put together in Canada. You did not ask them for a definition. You gave them one year where an 800-page document came out with not one definition but 300 definitions. That is what you got from a big company that you gave a blank cheque to."[20]

The mortified expressions on the faces of Bill Vander Zalm and Grant Devine amid the thunderous applause of Aboriginal participants said it all. Jim Sinclair had set aside constitutional niceties and brought two of Canada's premiers before a live national television audience into the realm of brass-knuckle politics. In the firebrand tradition of prairie populists, Sinclair had declared the first ministers conference process to be a monumental failure and laid responsibility squarely at the feet of two of the premiers. Sinclair had provided the catharsis to end a five-year drama of mounting frustration and broken hopes for Canada's Aboriginal peoples.

In what was probably the most charged atmosphere in the conference centre's history, Sinclair then brought the process to a close, concluding with a statement that, in the words of Liberal MP Keith Penner, "will never be forgotten in the annals of the history of this nation."

I have worked hard over the years to bring justice to my people, to sit down with governments and make deals. I have pounded on doors. I have had many guys say no. I have troubles meeting with the Prime Minister and with the Premiers. Yet, we have struggled hard to try to make a deal. We have kept our end of the bargain. We struggled with our Aboriginal brothers as to what should go on the table.

One thing I want to say, as we leave this meeting: I am glad that we stuck together on a right that is truly right for our people, right for all of Canada, and right within international law throughout the world based on human rights alone. We have the right to self-government, to self-determination and land.

The people who are here are going to continue the struggle. This is not an end. It is only the beginning. I think our leadership has made a stand now. We break new roads for those who come in the future. Do not worry, Mr. Prime Minister and Premiers of the provinces; I may be gone, but our people will be back.[21]

An angry and vocally bitter Jim Sinclair after the collapse of
negotiations at FMC '87, Ottawa, Ontario, 27 March 1987.
(CP Photo Archive)

Chapter 11

TRANSITIONS

*T*he failure of the constitutional conferences signalled a time for change in
the Métis movement at both provincial
and national levels. It also brought to life the rising
expectations of Aboriginal peoples in Canada and the
political costs of failing to meet them. Jim Sinclair had
once said that Métis people could not embrace
nationalism as long as they were impoverished and
that Métis politicians had to first address the material
needs of their followers. But the cornerstones of the
nationalist platform—a land base and self-government—had now become a material need in the minds
of many, and those Métis politicians who failed to satisfy these needs did so at their own peril.

CONSUMMATING THE
"MADE-IN-ALBERTA" AGREEMENT

In Alberta during the summer of 1987, MAA president Sam Sinclair was defeated at the polls by Larry Desmeules. As director of the Métis Urban Housing Corporation in Alberta since 1984, Desmeules had built the organization into a powerful agency as well as a strong personal political base. He had sensed from Premier Getty's comments after the 1987 conference a strong commitment to push ahead with a non-constitutional "made-in-Alberta" process on Métis issues, and Desmeules, a veteran of working within the system, had responded in kind.

In December 1987, a framework agreement between the province of Alberta and the MAA was concluded, establishing a new partnership approach to resolving Métis needs and aspirations. A joint committee consisting of the MAA president and a senior official reporting to the premier would steer the process. Sectoral subcommittees, headed by deputy ministers of various government departments and senior MAA officials, would pursue the devolution of control and funding of provincial programs and services to the MAA and its regional councils.

As part of this process, Desmeules entered into negotiations with independent service-delivery organizations, such as Métis Child and Family Services, to bring them under the umbrella of the MAA. He concluded his own memoranda of understanding with these organizations, the MAA basically absorbing them as "affiliated self-governing institutions" of the Métis people, with their boards accountable to the MAA. At the same time, Desmeules expanded the role of the MAA's own institutions, such as its economic development corporation, which moved into financial services and the provision of commercial loans to small businesses owned by Métis.

The central theme of Desmeules' administration was that, with or without a constitutional amendment on self-government, the MAA would move ahead toward its own transformation into a self-governing institution. Toward this end, Desmeules pioneered the establishment of an Alberta Métis Senate in 1989. The MAA and its regional councils appointed this group of respected individuals to act as a judiciary, resolving membership issues and disputes within the Métis organization. Desmeules also moved with the province to expand the devolution talks into a tripartite process to involve the federal government in sectoral arrangements, such as justice, that fell within its purview. Reflecting this drive toward self-government, the MAA changed its name to the Métis Nation of Alberta (MNA).

The Federation of Métis Settlements, meanwhile, moved ahead with the province after the 1987 first ministers conference to bring about changes to the legislation governing the settlements that the province had made a condition for the transfer and protection of Métis lands. In 1989, the Getty government and the FMS concluded the Alberta-Métis Settlements Accord. It established a new Métis self-government and land-holding system and a means of resolving the long-standing dispute over oil and gas revenues.

The following year, the Alberta legislature enacted four statutes to implement the terms of the accord. The Métis Settlements Act expanded the powers of existing individual settlement councils and created a new regional government, the Métis Settlements General Council (MSGC), empowered to enact laws and policies on behalf of all settlements. In effect, the legislation transformed the FMS from an Aboriginal organization into a regional government. It also established the Métis Settlements Appeal Tribunal to adjudicate disputes over membership and land allocation decisions of settlement councils and to handle other matters, such as right-of-entry orders to oil and gas companies and related compensation.

The Métis Settlements Land Protection Act granted fee simple title to Métis settlement land to the MSGC, making it the largest landowner in the province (other than the crown). It protected the land base by requiring the consent of the Métis councils and most of the people on the settlements for any alienation of settlement land. The Constitution of Alberta Amendment Act protected the land grant by prohibiting amendment or repeal of the Métis Settlements Land Protection Act or the dissolution of the MSGC without the agreement of the MSGC. It also stated the province's commitment to seek protection of the land grant in the Canadian Constitution.

The Alberta-Métis Settlements Accord had committed the parties to resolve the natural resource lawsuit launched by the Métis settlement associations in 1968. The Métis Settlements Accord Implementation Act required the province to pay $310 million to the settlements over seventeen years. The province retained subsurface rights on the settlements, but it agreed to co-manage the exploration and development of non-renewable resources on the settlements with the MSGC and settlement councils. A co-management agreement required oil and gas companies seeking to operate on the settlements to enter into development agreements with the settlement government, providing the latter with royalty and participation rights in oil and gas projects. Thus ended the lawsuit over subsurface resources launched by the Métis more than two decades earlier and consummation of the "made-in-Alberta" agreement.

JIM SINCLAIR: A FALLEN GIANT

The AMNSIS annual assembly in Batoche during July 1987 marked the return of Clément Chartier to the Métis political stage.[1] A victim of *realpolitik* within both the Métis and international indigenous movements, Chartier was now ready to confront the political machine of Jim Sinclair and finish the job that, since the political realignment of the Métis in 1983, had been left undone. The blowout at the 1987 first ministers conference had taken its toll on AMNSIS; Premier Devine, the target of Sinclair's blistering attack, had cut off the province's funding to AMNSIS and pulled out of tripartite talks. Delegates now had to decide on how the beleaguered organization would cope with the void left by the death of the constitutional process and the financial threat to AMNSIS itself.

For the pro-Sinclair delegates, now was the time for the organization to pull together. With the collapse of the self-government talks, there was no need for the Métis and non-status Indian constituencies to part ways. For the pro-Chartier delegates, now was the time for the Métis to consolidate whatever gains they had made on the organizational front in Saskatchewan, namely a revival of the pre-AMNSIS Métis Society of Saskatchewan.

In an unprecedented setback to Sinclair, the Batoche assembly adopted a resolution in favour of separating the two constituencies. A committee was established to revise the AMNSIS constitution to implement the split, and Chartier was named its chairman. From August 1987 to February 1988, his committee conducted hearings throughout Saskatchewan in advance of its report to a special AMNSIS constitutional conference of Métis to implement the split.

At a conference in Prince Albert in February 1988, Sinclair's supporters mounted a final drive to reverse the decision on splitting the membership but were rebuffed by the decision of delegates to implement the recommended changes to the AMNSIS constitution. Indignant, Sinclair and his supporters stormed out of the meeting, marking the end of Jim Sinclair's political career in the Métis movement. The conference concluded with the selection of an interim board to serve until province-wide elections could be held.

Two days after the Prince Albert conference, the interim leadership of the organization changed the AMNSIS charter to effect a change of name back to the Métis Society of Saskatchewan and to restrict membership to the Métis. True to form, Sinclair and his followers would not go down without a final fight. They promptly took legal action against the MSS, claiming an illegal takeover of AMNSIS. In March 1988, the Saskatchewan Court of Queen's Bench appointed Touche Ross to run the organization until the various issues surrounding the realignment could be resolved. In a bizarre twist, the court had handed control over what had been Canada's most powerful Métis organization to an accounting firm!

The MSS then asked the court for a referendum on the issue of separate organizations for Métis and non-status Indians. A province-wide referendum among AMNSIS members was held on 28 August 1988, with a majority voting in favour of separate representation, thereby ratifying restoration of the MSS. Sinclair, meanwhile, had established a new non-status Indian organization and asked the court for certain institutions formerly under the control of AMNSIS. In October 1988, the court awarded all institutions to the MSS, based on an understanding that it would not deny programs or services to any of the former constituents of AMNSIS.

The MSS emerged from the turmoil of the membership split with an interim board of directors governing the association and Clément Chartier representing the MSS within the MNC until elections could be held on 21 February 1989. The election represented yet another setback for Chartier, who was narrowly defeated by Jim Durocher, the veteran treasurer of AMNSIS and very much an insider in Sinclair's administration. Although they had opted for an organization without Sinclair, the Saskatchewan Métis were not yet ready to abandon the type of organization he personified.

The political demise of Jim Sinclair marked the end of an era and highlighted stark political realities that governed Aboriginal politics in Canada. It confirmed that, despite the lasting respect for the charismatic Sinclair, there would be no turning back in the drive of the Métis people toward their political destiny. Non-reinstatable Indians like Sinclair remained an issue that called for resolution, but by the Indian First Nations and Ottawa; theirs was a cross the Métis were no longer willing to bear.

The demise brought to life the personal cost of the fundamental political inequality between Aboriginal and non-Aboriginal societies in Canada. As one veteran Sinclair aide observed, had a politician with the contributions of Sinclair been white, he would have gone to the Senate or a corporate board at the end of an active political career. Aboriginal leaders, on the other hand, had nowhere to go at the end of the day and often ended up being pushed out.

In Jim Sinclair's case, he was pushed out but certainly not put down. Sinclair would go on to head off-reserve Aboriginal organizations at the provincial and national levels for most of the next two decades. And he would not be forgotten by the people he once led; the MNC would bestow its highest honour—the Order of the Métis Nation—on Sinclair for his immense contributions to the Métis cause. Catching up with Sinclair at the end of 2005, his old associate and confidant Rob Milen commented on how Sinclair, now in his seventies, was stil going strong and truly in his element. Having just provided Christmas dinner for scores of destitute Aboriginal people in Regina, Sinclair told Milen, "I started out feeding people and helping them organize to improve their lives. Forty years later, I'm still feeding them."

Yvon Dumont and Meech

In Manitoba, the collapse of the first ministers conference process only served to reinvigorate Yvon Dumont's relentless drive in the courts to uphold the Métis land claim. The federal government appealed the 1987 decision of the Manitoba Court of Queen's Bench that had dismissed Ottawa's application to strike the MMF's statement of claim. In 1988, the Manitoba Court of Appeal overturned the lower court ruling, prompting Dumont and Berger to announce their intention to appeal the decision to the Supreme Court of Canada. (On 2 March 1990, the Supreme Court would rule unanimously in favour of the MMF, upholding the ruling of the lower court to dismiss the federal government's motion and clearing the way for the Métis action to proceed to trial.)

At the MNC annual assembly in Edmonton on 16 October 1988, the boards of all member associations elected Dumont to the new post of MNC president. The restructuring fell far short of the central governing body sought by nationalists; the MNC president would be accountable to member association boards and presidents, not to the grassroots electorate. In a sign of the continuing primacy of provincial associations, the new MNC president retained his presidency of the MMF. Nevertheless, his appointment did indicate the important role that Dumont had assumed on national issues. With the collapse of the conference process, Dumont was single-handedly carrying on the court battle for Métis rights in a case that unified the descendants of the Red River Métis, the majority of whom had been dispersed across western Canada and the border states of the United States.

Like Jim Sinclair, Dumont would prove to be an adept tactician, making high-risk decisions and deals in the short term in order to fulfill a long-term strategy. In this respect, he resembled Brian Mulroney, who had impressed Dumont as a prime minister with whom the Métis could finally deal. After all, Mulroney's government, from the outset of its management of the conference process before the 1985 talks, had offered to seek a Supreme Court reference on whether the Métis fit within section 91(24) of the Constitution Act, 1867. Moreover, before the 1987 talks, the Mulroney government had proposed means of ensuring that Métis self-government negotiations and agreements could proceed unobstructed by federal-provincial jurisdictional disputes with respect to Métis.

The first test of the new MNC president's willingness to deal with Mulroney on the Constitution would surface during the national unity crisis precipitated by the attempted ratification of the Meech Lake Constitutional Accord of 3 June 1987. With the clock ticking toward the 3 June 1990 deadline for ratification, two provinces, Newfoundland and Dumont's Manitoba, were withholding their support. In Manitoba, a public consultation process and the Assembly of Manitoba Chiefs fuelled the opposition.

Coming as it did but a few months after the 1987 conference, the Meech Lake Accord had aroused widespread opposition from Aboriginal organizations, who were angered by the willingness of premiers to accommodate Quebec by way of an undefined "distinct society" clause after rejecting Aboriginal self-government before it was adequately defined. The prime minister's assurance that bringing Quebec into the constitutional fold would facilitate a future amendment on Aboriginal self-government had fallen on deaf ears—with one notable exception. Yvon Dumont believed that, with Quebec's constitutional demands accommodated and its participation in the amending process ensured, it would be possible to gather the required support for Aboriginal amendments in spite of opposition from up to three provinces, the same number that had opposed the self-government accord in the past. Moreover, Dumont believed that Meech Lake's requirement for annual constitutional conferences offered Aboriginal peoples a vehicle for getting back on the agenda during the "second round" envisaged by the accord.

On 4 April 1990, Dumont appeared before the Manitoba legislature's committee holding public hearings and stated his support for the Meech Lake Accord on behalf of the MNC and the MMF. His position would stand in sharp contrast to that of Elijah Harper, the Cree MLA from northern Manitoba whose procedural manoeuvres in the Manitoba legislature a few months later would drive the final nails into the coffin of Meech Lake.[2] It would also, according to media speculation, spell defeat for Dumont in MMF elections scheduled for the summer of 1990. Dumont would confound his critics, winning re-election as president with his largest margin of victory to date. His isolated support for Meech Lake signalled to the Mulroney government that, despite the ongoing MMF court action, Dumont and the MNC were prepared to take bold steps to improve Canada's relations with Quebec in order for the Métis to find their place in a new Canadian federation.

Chapter 12

Yvon Dumont and the Road to Charlottetown

The death of the Meech Lake Accord and the Oka crisis[1] during the summer of 1990 brought home to Canadians the depth of alienation among Québécois and Aboriginal peoples and the threat that such alienation posed to the future of the country. In a report to the Quebec National Assembly in 1991, the Belanger-Campeau Commission recommended a referendum on Quebec sovereignty by October 1992 unless the province received a new constitutional offer from Canada. The Mulroney government responded to the challenge on 24 September 1991, by tabling in Parliament a set of proposals—*Shaping Canada's Future Together*—to renew the Canadian federation by way of sweeping changes to the Constitution. In addition to addressing Quebec's demands, the federal proposal sought to address the desire of Atlantic Canada and the West for changes to federal political institutions and the Aboriginal demand for a self-government amendment. Having trumpeted Yvon Dumont's support repeatedly during the dying days of Meech Lake, the prime minister—not surprisingly—turned to Dumont and the MNC to help kick-start the new "Canada Round" of constitutional discussions.

THE "CANADA ROUND"

For MNC president Yvon Dumont and the leaders of other Aboriginal organizations, it was imperative that, if the "Canada Round" was to give Quebec its distinct society clause and the western provinces and Atlantic Canada their reformed Senate, it would have to give self-government to Aboriginal peoples. The federal proposal did provide for the entrenchment of a free-standing justiciable right to Aboriginal self-government within the Canadian federation and the description of the nature of the right in the Constitution so as to facilitate interpretation by the courts. However, the right would not be justiciable for a period of up to ten years, during which time governments would be committed to negotiating self-government agreements with Aboriginal peoples.

For Dumont and the Métis in particular, a general statement of rights, even justiciable, was insufficient if the barriers of section 91(24) and the lack of a land base were to deny the Métis people access to these rights. On this front, there was cause for concern over the federal proposal. It included a commitment to address the appropriate roles and responsibilities of governments as they related to the Métis without committing Ottawa to an assumption of constitutional responsibility. On the land base issue, it merely proposed that Aboriginal governments may possess jurisdiction over land, and this jurisdiction further depended on the requirements and circumstances of the Aboriginal group.

Métis concerns were somewhat allayed in October 1991, when Prime Minister Mulroney met with Dumont and the MNC in Winnipeg. In an impassioned speech, the prime minister pledged to work with those who were ready to move ahead on constitutional issues. Then, with words signifying a historic shift in Ottawa's relationship with the Métis people, Mulroney recognized the Métis Nation[2] and suggested that the federal government was prepared to open up a bilateral process with it.

The Mulroney–MNC summit added incentive for the Métis to work within the consultative process of the Canada Round under the stewardship of the federal minister of constitutional affairs, Joe Clark. Ottawa had funded national Aboriginal organizations to conduct parallel constitutional consultations with their constituents, and the MNC had distributed its funding among its provincial associations to establish task forces for canvassing the views of their members during the autumn of 1991. The MNC reported on the findings of these task forces to the prime minister in a document entitled *The Métis Nation on the Move*. The report identified the following issues for inclusion in the constitutional agenda: recognition of the Métis as a founding nation of Canada; a Métis land base; Métis self-government; federal assumption of responsibility for the Métis; and Métis representation in the House of Commons and in a reformed Senate.[3]

The MNC also pursued these priorities with the Special Joint Committee of the House of Commons and the Senate (the Beaudoin-Dobie Committee), conducting public hearings on the federal proposal. The MNC met four times with the committee and its subcommittee on Aboriginal issues during the period from December 1991 to February 1992, hammering away at the need for a land base and an amendment to section 91(24) of the Constitution Act, 1867, to make explicit federal jurisdiction for Métis as well as Indians and Inuit. In March 1992, the Special Joint Committee delivered its *Report on a Renewed Canada,* including a recommendation for the federal government to respond to the Métis need for land and resources, but stopped short of recommending an amendment to section 91(24).

Commencement of multilateral ministers' meetings on the Constitution during the month of March brought with it a demonstration of the improved prospects for Aboriginal self-government. The political makeup of the players at the table had changed considerably since 1987, with the Devine and Vander Zalm regimes in Saskatchewan and British Columbia replaced by NDP governments, both committed to self-government. Moreover, Canada's most populous province had elected an NDP government, and Ontario's Bob Rae was determined that Aboriginal rights be resolved in the Canada Round. Even Tory Alberta's Don Getty had come around, his fears of a third order of government in the Constitution allayed to a certain extent by the progress his government had made with the Alberta Métis on and off the settlements in the "made-in-Alberta" process.

For the Métis, prospects were enhanced by a federal government that—with many of its key ministers from western Canada—had a keen appreciation of the historical role and struggle of the Métis people. On 10 March 1992, federal constitutional affairs minister Joe Clark introduced a historic resolution in Parliament that passed unanimously, recognizing the unique and historic role of Louis Riel as a founder of Manitoba and supporting the attainment of the constitutional rights of the Métis people (see Appendix D). Clark then paid tribute to Yvon Dumont and the Métis provincial presidents seated in the gallery of the House of Commons. For Dumont, the resolution marked the culmination of a long personal struggle to rectify the vilification of the Métis patriarch and to correct history books in order to restore "the fighting spirit of the Métis people." It also marked the vindication long sought by the Métis people for their role in the founding of western Canada and their place in the Constitution.

ON THE ROAD TO CHARLOTTETOWN

The impending deadline for a Quebec referendum on sovereignty in October 1992 had set the stage for a whirlwind series of negotiations, this time to be condensed into a matter of months instead of the five-year ordeal of the first ministers conference process. Unlike other Aboriginal organizations, the MNC would not enter the multilateral talks with legions of non-Aboriginal lawyers and advisers in the background, for Yvon Dumont had assembled an all-Métis team of officials for the Canada Round of negotiations. Some were veterans of the conference process, notably his senior adviser, Clément Chartier, who had just chaired the MSS community consultations, and Marc LeClair, an Ottawa-based lawyer who had coordinated MNC's work at the last two first ministers conferences. Others were newcomers to constitutional negotiations, including Cynthia Bertolin, a lawyer from Alberta, and Remi Smith, a francophone lawyer from Manitoba who would be responsible for the translation of texts.

At a meeting of provincial Native affairs ministers in Toronto on 2 March 1992, the MNC pressed for provincial support for an amendment to section 91(24) of the Constitution Act, 1867. Most ministers agreed on federal responsibility and included this item in their final report. The MNC renewed the drive for the section 91(24) amendment at a meeting of intergovernmental affairs ministers in Ottawa on 12 March. There, at the insistence of Premier Bob Rae (also Ontario's intergovernmental affairs minister), Aboriginal leaders gained a commitment from Joe Clark for their full participation in all future constitutional discussions.

The next multilateral meeting of ministers and Aboriginal leaders started in Halifax on 8 and 9 April and finished in Ottawa on 14 April. Dumont and the MNC would not relent on the resolution of section 91(24), insisting that the Métis be placed on the same playing field as other Aboriginal peoples. The federal government indicated it was not prepared to amend section 91(24) but agreed to place it at the top of the Aboriginal agenda for the next ministers' meeting, in Edmonton on 29 and 30 April.

In Edmonton, Dumont pushed the provinces for a commitment at the table to a section 91(24) amendment. With the MNC basically filibustering until the issue was finally resolved, the federal government indicated that it would consider an amendment to section 91(24) if the provinces agreed to share in the fiscal responsibility for Métis. The meeting concluded with an agreement of the MNC, the federal government, and the provinces to establish a task force to pursue the issue further and to make an interim report to the next ministers' meeting, in Saint John.

In tackling the "nuts and bolts" of the jurisdiction question, this task force had to allay the fears of two key players. The federal government feared that an assumption of constitutional responsibility for Métis would trigger massive provincial "off-loading" of Métis-related expenditures onto itself. In addition, status Indians were vehement in their opposition to any amendment to section 91(24) to include Métis. The Indians had always feared that any expansion of the relationship between Ottawa and the Métis would be at their expense, that the total pie of Aboriginal spending by Ottawa would not get bigger but would have to be cut into smaller pieces.

At the ministers' meeting in Saint John on 6 and 7 May, the task force addressed federal, MNC, and AFN concerns by proposing four major commitments to resolve the impasse over section 91(24) and related issues.

- First, the federal government would not reduce services to Indians in response to an amendment to section 91(24).

- Second, the provinces and territories would not reduce services to Métis in response to an amendment to section 91(24).

- Third, all parties would agree to participate in negotiations regarding the provision of a land base for Métis.

- Fourth, the federal and provincial governments would agree to participate in and fund an enumeration and registration process for Métis.

The report was adopted by ministers and sent forward to the next multilateral meeting in Vancouver on 11–13 May.

By this time, Dumont and his senior advisers, including Clément Chartier and Marc LeClair, had established three strategic objectives that would shape the MNC's participation in the final multilateral meetings. First, in addition to any Aboriginal self-government amendment in the Constitution, the MNC would pursue a constitutionally binding treaty with the federal and provincial governments to remove impediments to accessing self-government rights by Métis people. Second, the MNC would pursue the long-sought separate process at the ministers' level, involving only the MNC, Ottawa, and the provinces within the Métis homeland, to conclude the treaty. And third, the MNC, not the federal government, would control the ongoing drafting of the text of this treaty.

At the ministers' meeting in Vancouver, Dumont tabled a draft treaty, which, in addition to the commitments agreed to in Saint John, encompassed a full range of roles and obligations to each other of the Métis Nation, the Government of Canada, and the provinces within the Métis homeland. He obtained an agreement to convene a special meeting of ministers to deal with it in Montreal. The meeting would be chaired by energy minister Jake Epp, who had just agreed to the prime minister's request that he assume the role of Métis interlocutor.

Epp, who represented the Manitoba riding of Provencher once held by Louis Riel, had proven to be a strong supporter of the Métis cause within the federal Conservatives and a supporter of the Métis land claim. His task force of intergovernmental affairs ministers from Ontario, Manitoba, Saskatchewan, Alberta, British Columbia, and the Northwest Territories, along with the MNC, had a mandate to deal with the draft treaty under the control of the MNC pen. After a decade of unsuccessful efforts, the MNC had finally achieved a separate constitutional process for the Métis Nation.

THE CHARLOTTETOWN ACCORD

On 20–22 May 1992, in Montreal, Epp's task force reviewed the MNC document and reported back to the multilateral ministers body that was meeting on the full range of constitutional issues. The ministers supported the majority of the elements brought forward by Epp but stopped short of recommending their incorporation as a "treaty" into section 35 (which would give it constitutional force). The ministers and the MNC did agree, though, that the commitments on Métis issues—to be named the Métis Nation Accord—would be legally binding, unlike a political accord. Consequently, the federal and appropriate provincial governments would be expected to enact special enabling legislation to bring the Métis Nation Accord into force and to make it enforceable and justiciable. With the meeting concluded, Joe Clark told Dumont that, with the Métis Nation Accord now basically accepted, he wanted the MNC to help the federal government sell its self-government amendment.

Positive feelers to the public aside, the federal government had run into difficulty with Quebec and Newfoundland over the extent of justiciability of the proposed right to self-government, by now accepted as an "inherent" right by a majority of participants. At the next multilateral meeting in Toronto, on 26–30 May, Dumont and the federal and provincial constitutional ministers agreed to the final draft of the Métis Nation Accord. On the basis of the accord, Clark indicated that he was prepared to recommend an amendment to section 91(24) to the federal cabinet. Then Dumont went to bat for the federal government.

Addressing the concerns over justiciability, he proposed that, while the inherent right of self-government should be entrenched in the Constitution, its justiciability should be delayed for a five-year period. During this period, the federal and provincial governments would be committed constitutionally to negotiate with Aboriginal peoples, with the objective of reaching agreements to implement the right. Dumont was hoping that the delay period and ample room for negotiations and agreements would break down the resistance of the hold-out provinces. On the other hand, his proposal did nothing to compromise the principles of the Aboriginal organizations; delaying the justiciability of the right to self-government would not make the right contingent on these agreements. In essence, the MNC was reviving the "sunrise clause," which Jim Sinclair had proposed in the first ministers conference process. Out of the gruelling and seemingly endless drafting sessions in Toronto,[4] a consensus began to build around the MNC proposal.

Yvon Dumont then travelled to Quebec City to meet with Premier Robert Bourassa. Theirs was a meeting of friends: Bourassa, the Québécois leader who had invested so heavily in Meech Lake and had been forced to walk a tightrope since its death; Dumont, the leader of the Métis compatriots from western Canada and the only Aboriginal leader to support Meech Lake. Despite the positive atmosphere, Dumont sensed the Quebec premier's continuing anxiety over the self-government issue, which would cast a cloud over the series of first ministers meetings during the summer.

The storm cloud would burst at the last of these meetings, in the Pearson Building in Ottawa from 18 to 22 August. There the veteran labour negotiator Brian Mulroney engineered a series of closed-door conclaves, with first ministers and Aboriginal leaders gathering in small groups to work out deal terms that could be taken back to the prime minister. Mulroney himself was sequestered with Bourassa and Newfoundland's premier, Clyde Wells, dealing with their concerns over the scope of self-government. Premier Rae had tried to allay their concerns by proposing that Aboriginal government laws would be subject to federal and provincial laws that are "essential to the preservation of peace, order, and good government in Canada," but Bourassa and Wells were also concerned about the application of self-government off a land base.

Dumont sensed that events were taking a turn for the worse, as a consensus appeared to be developing among first ministers, the AFN, and the Inuit that self-government would apply only to Aboriginal peoples on a land base, in effect excluding Métis in urban areas who were seeking their own forms of political autonomy. At one point, Dumont burst in on a meeting between Mulroney, Bourassa, and Wells and obtained a commitment from all three to work the matter out. Dumont and his advisers proceeded to find wording within an amendment that could accommodate "self-governing institutions" with sufficient authority and fiscal resources to meet the aspirations of Métis people off a land base without disrupting the jurisdictions of Ottawa and the provinces.

The fragile consensus on the Aboriginal amendments would hold. When first ministers and Aboriginal leaders gathered in Charlottetown on 27 and 28 August 1992, they gathered as political equals. Their constitutional consensus—to be known as the Charlottetown Accord—began with a new "Canada Clause" in the Constitution recognizing Aboriginal government as one of three orders of government in Canada. The justiciability of the inherent right would be delayed for a five-year period. During this period, there would be a constitutional commitment by the federal and provincial governments and the Indian, Inuit, and Métis peoples in the various regions and communities of the country to negotiate in good faith with the objective of implementing the right of self-government through agreements on jurisdiction, lands and resources, and economic and fiscal arrangements. By way of a political accord, the federal and provincial governments would commit to the principle of providing Aboriginal governments with a form of equalization payments to ensure they could provide public services at levels comparable to those available to other Canadians in the vicinity of Aboriginal communities.

The Canadian Charter of Rights and Freedoms would apply to Aboriginal governments. However, like Parliament and provincial legislatures, the legislative bodies of Aboriginal peoples could invoke the "notwithstanding clause" in section 33 of the Constitution Act, 1982, to override certain sections of the charter. The Charlottetown Accord also acceded to the long-standing demand of Aboriginal organizations that Aboriginal consent be required for future constitutional amendments directly affecting Aboriginal peoples.

The accord provided for a broad range of Aboriginal roles in public institutions, a particular concern for Métis people without a land base. It envisaged guaranteed Aboriginal representation in the new elected Senate. Aboriginal senators would have the same roles and powers of other senators plus a double majority power in certain matters materially affecting Aboriginal peoples.

With respect to guaranteed Aboriginal representation in the House of Commons, the accord called for the issue to be pursued by Parliament after it received the report of the House of Commons committee studying the recommendations of the Royal Commission on Electoral Reform.[5] While the accord did not provide for modification of the structure of the Supreme Court, it did anticipate a role for Aboriginal peoples in relation to that body, including consultations with Aboriginal peoples on Supreme Court candidates and a proposed Aboriginal Council of Elders that would make submissions to the Supreme Court when Aboriginal issues were being considered. The accord also ensured Aboriginal participation on issues affecting Aboriginal peoples in an entrenched process of first ministers conferences on constitutional matters to be held at least once a year. This would be in addition to an entrenched process of four conferences on Aboriginal constitutional matters commencing no later than 1996.

In addition to these Aboriginal constitutional amendments and political accords, a significant part of the Charlottetown Accord was devoted to the Métis Nation Accord and related constitutional amendments. The Métis Nation Accord did not lend itself to convenient sound bites such as "distinct society" or "Triple-E" Senate. It did, however, represent the most significant breakthrough at the bargaining table for the Métis people since Riel's provisional government negotiated provincehood for Manitoba.

THE MÉTIS NATION ACCORD

On 26 October 1992, Canadians rejected the Charlottetown Accord in a national referendum. For Métis people, the bitter irony of the defeat was that, despite widespread opposition to the accord, one of its key elements that did command public support was Aboriginal self-government. Having campaigned actively in support of the accord, Yvon Dumont and the MNC leadership could at least draw comfort that the Métis people had largely supported the Charlottetown consensus.

Despite its demise with Charlottetown, the Métis Nation Accord established a blueprint for state–Métis relations that would be revisited in the future. It recognized the historical contributions of the Métis and sought to strengthen their place as a distinct national community within the contemporary Canadian federation. Toward this end, it comprised a number of agreements directed toward the political, cultural, and territorial integrity of the Métis Nation.

The Métis Nation Accord set the stage for transforming Métis associations into Métis government. The signatories to the accord were to be the MNC and its provincial and territorial affiliated associations and the Governments of Canada, Ontario, Manitoba, Saskatchewan, Alberta, and British Columbia.[6] The Métis Nation Accord accepted the MNC's criteria for Métis identification or citizenship of the Métis Nation and committed Canada and the appropriate provinces to contribute resources to the Métis Nation to conduct an enumeration or census of its people in order to develop a registry or citizenship roll.

The accord committed the federal and provincial governments to negotiate self-government, lands and resources, devolution over existing programs and services, and cost-sharing arrangements with the objective of concluding tripartite agreements elaborating the relationship between the Métis Nation, Canada, and the provinces. Self-government negotiations would focus on issues of jurisdiction and economic and fiscal arrangements. For a start, Canada and the provinces agreed to transfer to Métis institutions the portion of Aboriginal programs and services then available to Métis.

As for new institutions of self-government and related programs and services to be established through self-government agreements, the federal government agreed to provide a "substantial portion" of the direct costs of Métis institutions, programs, and services. The provinces and the Métis would provide the remaining portion of the costs, the Métis share to come from existing tax dollars paid to Canada and the provinces by Métis. Canada and the provinces agreed to provide Métis institutions with transfer payments for the establishment of similar types of programs and services enjoyed by other Aboriginal peoples.

Canada and the provinces agreed to provide, where appropriate, access to lands and resources to Métis and Métis self-governing institutions. Where land was to be provided, Canada and the provinces, except Alberta, agreed to make available their fair share of crown lands for transfer to Métis self-governing institutions. The accord acknowledged that Alberta had already transferred fee simple title to 1.28 million acress of land to the Métis settlements and had committed to spend $310 million over seventeen years on the settlements pursuant to the Alberta–Métis Settlements Accord.

To facilitate this expanded role for Ottawa in the construction of Métis self-government, the Métis Nation Accord was to be accompanied by an amendment to section 91(24) of the Constitution Act, 1867, to ensure that it applied to all Aboriginal peoples. The Métis Nation Accord reaffirmed two of the commitments reached in Saint John to address federal and AFN concerns over the section 91(24) amendment. Accordingly, the federal government would not reduce funding or services to other Aboriginal peoples, nor would the provinces reduce funding for services to Métis as a result of the amendment. Another amendment to the Constitution safeguarded the legislative authority of the Government of Alberta for Métis and Métis settlement lands from the threat of court challenges based on section 91(24). As well, Parliament and the Alberta legislature would amend the Alberta Act to constitutionally protect the status of the land held in fee simple by the Métis Settlements General Council under letters patent from Alberta.

The Métis Nation Accord was to be made legally binding on Parliament and on the legislative assemblies of the provinces and an enforceable and justiciable agreement by way of federal and provincial enabling legislation. Métis ratification was to occur upon passage of a motion by a special assembly of the elected Métis representatives of the Métis Nation. The accord envisaged the enabling legislation to be passed by Parliament and the provincial legislatures after constitutional amendments were made with respect to the inherent right of self-government and section 91(24).

The MNC had made it clear from the start that the Métis Nation Accord, as the blueprint for the new relationship between the Métis Nation and Canada, should be pursued with or without a constitutional amendment on self-government. With the death of the Charlottetown Accord, the MNC reaffirmed its intention to pursue implementation of the Métis Nation Accord with willing governments and to seek constitutional protection for agreements at a later date. For the next decade, however, the constitutional fatigue—if not revulsion—of most Canadians, coupled with a change of government in Ottawa and the provincial capitals, would block any revival of constitutional reform efforts. For all its promise, the Métis Nation Accord would remain a proposal pregnant with possibility.

With the end of the Canada Round, another wave of leadership change swept over the Métis movement. The final chapter in the history of Jim Sinclair's political machine in Saskatchewan closed with the electoral defeat of his veteran lieutenant and MSS president, Jim Durocher, by Métis lawyer Gerald Morin in 1992. Tragedy struck the Métis Nation of Alberta with the sudden death of Larry Desmeules on 24 February 1993. On 4 March of that year, Yvon Dumont resigned from the presidencies of the MNC and the MMF. The next day, in an act symbolic of the role of the new nation in both the historical and the ongoing political development of western Canada, Dumont was appointed lieutenant-governor of Manitoba.

Charlottetown, Prince Edward Island, 28 August 1992: Prime Minister Mulroney gives thumbs up with MNC after consensus reached on the Charlottetown (and Métis Nation) Accord. Rear, L-R: Mark LeClair (advisor), Ron Swain (Ontario Métis Aboriginal Association), Gary Bohnet (Northwest Territories Métis Nation), Norman Evans (Pacific Métis Federation), and Gerald Morin (Métis Nation Saskatchewan). Front, L-R: Larry Desmeules (Métis Nation Alberta), Cindy Bertolin (advisor), Prime Minister Mulroney, Sheila Genaille (Métis National Council of Women), and Yvon Dumont (Manitoba Métis Federation and Métis National Council). (Collection of Marc LeClair)

THE FALLBACK
POSITION

*T*he failure of the Charlottetown Accord
and the election of a Liberal federal
government on 25 October 1993 forced
a significant shift in the strategy of Canada's Métis
leadership. With the Chrétien government preoccupied with deficit reduction and determined at all costs
to avoid any reopening of the constitutional file, the
Métis embarked on a campaign of litigation. The
impetus for this new approach came from the Métis
Society of Saskatchewan, which had revitalized since
the debilitating internal conflict surrounding the
ouster of Jim Sinclair and non-status Indians.

CRAFTING CASES

Following in the footsteps of Clément Chartier, Gerald Morin had jumped into Métis politics upon his graduation from the University of Saskatchewan Law School and admission to the Saskatchewan Bar. A native of the historic Métis community of Green Lake, Morin had played a significant role as a Chartier ally in the restoration of the MSS in 1988. In 1992, he was elected MSS president and a year later assumed the presidency of the MNC.

Having cut his teeth on the Métis Nation Accord negotiations, Morin decided to head into the courts to maintain momentum on Métis rights. In this endeavour, he would be ably assisted by his mentor. Chartier had long advocated Métis rights on a nationalist basis rather than on the narrower doctrine of Aboriginal rights and title; at the same time, as a renowned scholar and lawyer in Aboriginal and international law, he had always made it clear that the Métis did not renounce Aboriginal rights and could fall back on them in the courts in the event of an impasse in negotiations. Given his experience with the vicissitudes of Métis politics, Chartier would remain outside political office but play a central role in steering the Métis Nation into this new phase of politics with his hand firmly on the legal tiller.

For Métis nationalists, the concept of Aboriginal rights in law posed certain inherent problems and risks for the Métis people. These rights had been premised on the "prior occupation" of the land by Aboriginal peoples and the need to protect those distinct societies that had existed before contact with Europeans. Strictly applied, the "pre-contact" test would exclude the Métis as a distinct Aboriginal rights group on the grounds that they were a "post-contact" people. Their rights would then be dependent on their partial Indian ancestry and the pre-contact practices of their Indian ancestors. In effect, this would militate against their identity as a distinct Métis people and historical nation with rights derived from descent from that nation.

The scope of rights included in this concept of Aboriginal rights posed another problem for Métis nationalists. Aboriginal rights cases in the courts, reflecting the practices and customs carried over from pre-contact societies, had largely focused on subsistence activities such as hunting, fishing, and trapping. These activities were indeed an integral part of the culture and economy of many Métis communities, particularly in the north, and their subjection to provincial wildlife laws and regulations had imposed real economic hardship on many of their members. At the same time, harvesting rights such as those accorded to Indians under the treaties had demonstrated the limits afforded by the protection of the Crown. Through their provisional governments, the Métis had spurned this protection in favour of contemporary rights and powers, notably provincial status, that would have included the power of their governments to regulate resources. Could litigation end up limiting their rights to harvesting under section 35 of the Constitution?

Perhaps the greatest risk in going to the courts was the possibility of judges imposing a definition of Métis for rights entitlement purposes that clashed with that of the Métis Nation. The MNC had long argued that any criteria for identifying Métis would have to fit within the historical and territorial confines of the Métis Nation and rest on self-identification, historical Métis descent, and community acceptance. The enactment of Bill C-31[1] in 1985 had reinstated to Indian status thousands of people of mixed ancestry who had been calling themselves Métis, but there were still groups across Canada, particularly in the Atlantic provinces, and associated with the NCC successor organizations, that claimed the right to be included as Métis for constitutional purposes on the grounds of mixed ancestry. Adoption of a "pan-Canadian" definition of Métis for rights entitlement purposes by the courts could thwart the central objective of establishing the reality of the Métis Nation in Canadian law.

The foremost Métis rights litigation to date, the Dumont–MMF lawsuit,[2] avoided the limitations inherent in Aboriginal rights litigation because it was based on the recognition of extensive land rights of a clearly defined Métis political community, the Red River Métis. Moreover, the recognition had taken place in sections of the Manitoba Act, part of the Constitution of Canada, that had resulted from negotiations between Canada and a Métis government. The lawsuit challenged the constitutionality of numerous federal and provincial statutes and Orders-in-Council from the 1870s and 1880s that had deprived the Métis of those lands to which they were entitled under the Manitoba Act and highlighted the government-to-government and nation-to-nation agreement that had given birth to western Canada.

Morin and Chartier now sought a case that could establish the territorial claims and elicit the political unity of the Métis people beyond the original "postage stamp" Province of Manitoba. In the summer of 1993, the Métis Nation—Saskatchewan (formerly the MSS) decided to challenge the validity of the scrip system as a means of extinguishing the land rights of Métis of the old North-West (encompassing the rest of today's prairie provinces and portions of British Columbia and the Northwest Territories) pursuant to the terms of the Dominion Lands Act, 1879. A decision was made to initially limit the geographical scope of the litigation to northwest Saskatchewan, the region of the most recent distribution of scrip in 1906.

A statement of claim was filed in the Court of Queen's Bench in Saskatoon in March 1994 on behalf of the Métis Nation—Saskatchewan, the Métis locals in northwestern Saskatchewan, and the Métis National Council. The plaintiffs sought declarations that the scrip distribution of 1906 had not extinguished Métis rights to land and resources, harvesting rights, and the inherent right of self-government. The action was filed against the federal and Saskatchewan governments, which filed statements of defence claiming that those rights had been extinguished by the issue of scrip. Like the MMF case, the sweeping scope of *Morin v. Canada and Saskatchewan* ensured years if not decades of litigation.[3]

In the meantime, a number of individual cases were eliciting the first response of the courts to section 35 rights and their applicability to the Métis. In an Indian fishing case in 1990, *R. v. Sparrow,* the Supreme Court of Canada had decided that section 35 was to be "construed in a purposive way" and that "a generous, liberal interpretation is demanded given that the provision is to affirm aboriginal rights." The court further stated that, in order for a right to be extinguished, the intention of the Crown to extinguish such right must be "plain and clear."

In *McPherson and Christie* in 1992, a Manitoba judge found that two Métis defendants charged with hunting out of season under provincial legislation had Aboriginal hunting rights that were recognized and protected by section 35 of the Constitution Act, 1982. He declared that the provisions of the Manitoba Wildlife Act under which they had been charged were of no force and effect. On appeal in 1994, a Manitoba Court of Queen's Bench judge upheld the finding of section 35 "existing" Aboriginal hunting rights of the Métis but limited them to Métis living an Aboriginal way of life and relying on hunting for subsistence.

In 1995, Clément Chartier defended two Métis charged with violations under the Saskatchewan Fishery Regulations in provincial court in his hometown of Buffalo Narrows. In 1996, the court acquitted the defendants on the ground that they had an Aboriginal right to fish under section 35 of the Constitution Act, 1982, and that neither the Dominion Lands Act nor scrip had extinguished Métis harvesting rights. On appeal, the Court of Queen's Bench in Battleford upheld the trial judgment (*Morin and Daigneault*) in 1997. Unlike in the *McPherson and Christie* case, the decision upholding Métis Aboriginal rights was not limited to Métis living an Aboriginal way of life.

The first indication of Supreme Court of Canada thinking on Métis rights in section 35 came in an Indian fishing rights case, *R. v. Van der Peet,* in 1996. In its ruling, the court set out the "integral to their distinctive society test" for proving Aboriginal rights to be protected under section 35. The test required the claimant to prove that the activity it sought to protect was integral to its distinct society, had been practised before contact with Europeans, and had continued to be practised ever since. The court briefly addressed how this pre-contact rule would impact on Métis:

> The history of the Métis, and the reasons underlying their inclusion in the protection given by s. 35, are quite distinct from those of other aboriginal peoples in Canada. As such, the manner in which the aboriginal rights of other aboriginal peoples are defined is not necessarily determinative of the manner in which the aboriginal rights of the Métis are defined. At the time when the Court is presented with a Métis claim under s. 35 it will then, with the benefit of the arguments of counsel, a factual context and a specific Métis claim, be able to explore the question of the

purposes underlying s. 35's protection of the aboriginal rights of Métis people, and answer the question of the kinds of claims which fall within s. 35(1)'s scope when the claimants are Métis. The fact that, for other aboriginal peoples, the protection granted by s. 35 goes to the practices, customs and traditions of aboriginal peoples prior to contact, is not necessarily relevant to the answer which will be given to that question.[4]

THE INHERENT RIGHT POLICY

The process surrounding the Métis Nation Accord had raised the hopes of Métis organizations to become governments with the legal authority and financial resources to provide a full range of services to their members. It served to encourage these organizations to transition toward self-government, reforming their own governance structures to ensure greater accountability for their operations and spending. In 1993, the Métis Nation Saskatchewan declared self-government by enacting its own constitution. Accordingly, the MNS no longer operated under the corporate bylaws of the MNS secretariat but under Métis law.

Starting in 1994, the MNC separated the national office of president from the provincial office (forcing Gerald Morin to relinquish his leadership of the Saskatchewan Métis in order to retain the MNC presidency). It recast its board of directors as a cabinet and gave its members ministerial titles and responsibilities over "portfolios." The annual assembly of elected officials from each of the MNC's member associations (now known as "governing members") became the "National Assembly" that would give direction to and review the work of the cabinet and elect the MNC president.

Whether these changes would amount to more than the mere trappings of government would depend on the response of the Chrétien government to the challenge of Aboriginal self-government in Canada. In 1995, the Chrétien government unveiled a policy statement titled *Aboriginal Self-Government: The Government of Canada's Approach to Implementation of the Inherent Right and the Negotiation of Aboriginal Self-Government.* It acknowledged that, despite the failure of previous efforts to amend the Constitution to include explicit recognition of the inherent right of Aboriginal self-government, they had succeeded in building a broad measure of consensus for Aboriginal self-government. It stated that "The Government of Canada recognizes the inherent right of self-government as an existing right within section 35 of the Constitution Act, 1982."[5] It proposed to implement this inherent right by way of negotiated agreements that, where all parties to negotiations agreed, could be constitutionally protected as treaties under section 35 of the Constitution Act, 1982.

According to this inherent right policy, Ottawa would be willing to negotiate with provinces and Métis residing off a land base south of the sixtieth parallel and was prepared, with provincial agreement, to protect rights in agreements as constitutionally protected section 35 treaty rights. It endorsed the Métis view that enumeration was an "essential building block for self-government" and stated the willingness of the federal government to cost-share with provinces the enumeration of Métis who may be covered by self-government arrangements. On the crucial matter of the provision of land, the federal government was prepared to talk "but only if it is deemed necessary and complementary to the management of a federal program or service that is transferred"[6] to a Métis group.

With respect to the only Métis with a land base, the document expressed Ottawa's willingness to negotiate, alongside the Government of Alberta, self-government arrangements with the Métis settlements. Where the parties to the negotiations agreed, Ottawa was prepared to protect rights contained in self-government agreements as constitutionally protected rights under section 35 of the Constitution Act, 1982. It added that, "should lands be provided by other provinces to Métis people under similar regimes, the federal government would be prepared to negotiate similar arrangements, with the participation of the province in question."[7]

By recognizing self-government as an "existing" right within section 35, the federal policy appeared to rule out the need for further multilateral constitutional negotiations and amendments, a priority for the Constitution-averse Chrétien government. Like the "contingent" right proposed by the Mulroney government at the first ministers conferences of 1985 and 1987, the "inherent right" would take effect only after tripartite agreements had been concluded by Ottawa, the provinces, and Aboriginal peoples. The federal government, as usual, was clearly placing the onus on the provinces to do something for the Métis while it stood on the sidelines cheerleading. Without a legal requirement to negotiate, the provinces would hardly be amenable to moving in a substantive way toward establishment of a third order of government in Canada that would largely be at the expense of their diminished legislative authority in general and their ownership of public lands and natural resources in particular.

The inherent right policy, the cornerstone of the Chrétien government's approach to Aboriginal self-government, marked a decade of lost political opportunity for the MNC following the demise of the Métis Nation Accord. While recognizing contemporary rights and powers associated with self-government within the scope of section 35 Aboriginal rights, it made access to them conditional on a mechanism that was sure not to work. It took the Métis to the well but didn't allow them to drink. The inherent right policy precluded meaningful movement on Métis self-government and ensured the status quo in Canada–Métis relations under the rule of Jean Chrétien.

In practical terms, the status quo meant the federal government continued to deny jurisdictional responsibility for the Métis. The lack of a direct or government-to-government relationship between the Métis and Ottawa put the Métis at a real disadvantage relative to other Aboriginal peoples. Given their direct relationship with Ottawa, the Indians and Inuit could and would utilize their parallel processes to negotiate a variety of land claims settlements and self-government arrangements during the last decade of the twentieth century (the Nunavut Land Claims Agreement, the creation of the Nunavut Territory and government, the devolution of federal program responsibilities to First Nations governments, and the Nisga'a Treaty in British Columbia). In the absence of rights-based negotiations, there was little the MNC could do to advance the Métis political agenda other than support litigation.

The federal government continued to deny the Métis access to federal services such as health care and education available to other Aboriginal peoples.[8] Its intervention for Métis was still mostly restricted to "special programs" that could be justified as part of a broader mandate to provide Canadians with job training, regional economic development assistance, and social housing.[9] In the administration of these programs, it continued to treat the MNC and governing members as advocacy or interest groups, with all the attendant pitfalls.[10]

The inherent right policy did commit the federal government to "explore" the devolution of programs and services to Métis organizations, but the policy was permissive in nature, and most federal line departments would largely ignore it in the years ahead. Cases in point were *Gathering Strength: Canada's Aboriginal Action Plan* (1998) and the *Urban Aboriginal Strategy*, Ottawa's policy and program response to the Royal Commission on Aboriginal Peoples (RCAP). Disregarding the Métis-specific RCAP recommendations and its own commitment to provide Métis input into the design, development, and delivery of new programs and services, the federal government launched pilot projects addressing socio-economic problems of urban Aboriginal people without any support or input from the Métis.

The one area where devolution of a federal "special program" did occur was job training and employment services. Starting with an initial agreement between the MNC and the minister of human resources development in 1996, MNC governing members delivered labour market programs and services set out in Métis Human Resources Development Agreements (MHRDAs) through more than seventy-five points of delivery in urban, rural, and some remote locations from Ontario west. While each MNC governing member was responsible for the overall management of its MHRDA, decision-making to meet the training and employment needs of Métis people was based at the community level. MHRDAs represented an effective province-wide service delivery platform that gave the governing members a major role in designing, developing, and delivering an essential service to Métis throughout the homeland. Not surprisingly, it was also one of the few federal Aboriginal programs in which measurable results would be captured and direct benefits from spending tallied.

"EVOLVING" MÉTIS GOVERNMENT

Despite the constraints under which they operated, Métis organizations were becoming increasingly professional and sophisticated in their leadership and operations in the 1990s. The Ontario Métis organization, one of the "bookends" and a perennial problem in terms of representivity and strength, benefited from the return to politics of Tony Belcourt. The first elected president of the Native Council of Canada in the early 1970s, Belcourt had gone on to distinguish himself as an entrepreneur and promoter in the communications field, co-founding a film and video company with numerous award-winning products. He had also served as organizer and chairperson of Aboriginal business summits and conferences, drawing the participation of CEOs from Fortune 500 companies and generating considerable business for Aboriginal enterprises.

As the founding president of the Métis Nation of Ontario in 1994, Belcourt worked to organize Métis communities across Ontario into an effective force for the first time since the split with non-status Indians. Within the chambers of the prairie-dominated MNC, he offered forceful representation for the interests of his constituents. Most significant, he and the MNO began championing a Métis rights case in the lower courts that would eventually have far-reaching implications for the entire Métis homeland.

Following an interregnum of lacklustre leadership after the departures of Yvon Dumont, Larry Desmeules, and Jim Sinclair, the prairie associations revitalized in the second half of the 1990s. In 1997, David Chartrand was elected president of the Manitoba Métis Federation. With a career in both private- and public-sector management before entering politics, Chartrand ran a strong and competent administration and would continue to be re-elected over the next decade. Under his leadership, the MMF expanded rapidly in the range and size of services it provided to its constituents. Like Yvon Dumont, Chartrand proved tenacious in the pursuit of the MMF land claim against Canada and Manitoba, even mortgaging the MMF headquarters in Winnipeg to finance the lawsuit.

In 1998, fresh from his victory in the *Morin and Daigneault* case, Clément Chartier captured the presidency of the Métis Nation Saskatchewan and assumed the portfolio of minister for Métis rights and self-government in the MNC cabinet. In 2001, Saskatchewan became the second province in Canada to enact legislation for its Métis population, An Act to Recognize Contributions of the Métis and to Deal with Certain Métis Institutions. Proclaimed in 2002, the legislation, known as the Métis Act, recognized the historical, economic, and cultural contributions of the Métis in Canada and the leadership role of Métis institutions in providing public services to Métis people. It also placed the MNS on a stronger legal footing in its dealings with government and its own membership.

In Alberta, Audrey Poitras, a successful business owner, was elected president of the Métis Nation of Alberta in 1996, a position she would retain for the next decade. She exhorted the Métis in Alberta, particularly young people, to get education and training in order to capitalize on opportunities in the rapidly growing provincial economy and gave them the means to do so. With its network of seventeen Métis Employment Service Centres across the province, the MNA under Poitras came to be widely considered the most successful operator of any Aboriginal Human Resources Development Agreement in Canada.[11] Under her stewardship, the MNA made a shrewd investment in an oil-drilling rig business, which it eventually exchanged for shares in one of Canada's fastest-growing energy service providers, in the process creating high-paying jobs for Métis. Poitras also drove the development of Victoria Landing Provincial Métis Cultural Heritage Interpretive Centre (known as Métis Crossing) as a tourist destination.

Poitras' success in Alberta was indicative of the growing influence of women in the Métis movement. The Métis had never been divided along gender lines by federal legislation so had avoided conflicts over membership like those affecting First Nations communities. Women had long played a significant role in Métis politics at the local level, but during the 1990s they increased their representation at the regional and provincial executive levels. The MNC established a Métis Women's Secretariat in 1999 with one representative from each of the governing members. Its mandate was to promote equal participation within the Métis Nation and to ensure that the unique concerns of women were reflected within the policies, programs, and decisions of the national body.

The greatest strides toward Métis self-government during the 1990s were taken on the settlements in Alberta, where the Métis Settlements General Council and individual Métis settlements councils concentrated on implementing the four pieces of legislation accompanying the Alberta-Métis Settlements Accord of 1989. According to an assessment of the settlement system of governance in 1999,

> Given the historical and contemporary legal and political environment surrounding the assertion of Métis rights claims, the recent success of the Alberta Métis settlements in negotiating a Métis land base and delegated powers of self-government is quite a significant accomplishment. Some have criticized this accomplishment because it assumes cooperative power sharing with federal and provincial governments; adapts institutions which, at the time of their initial creation, could be viewed as undermining Métis provincial political organization; and intentionally excludes any reference to, or recognition of, Métis Aboriginal rights. Nevertheless, the Métis settlements in Alberta have

achieved what no other Métis population and most First Nations have yet to achieve: powers of local and regional government; constitutional protection of collective fee simple title to their land and the structure of regional Métis government; a significant share in, and control over, the development of natural resources on their lands; and the creation of a jointly appointed Appeals Tribunal to hear appeals arising from the administration of provincial legislation implementing this scheme.[12]

Canada's 2001 census showed a 43 per cent increase in the number of Métis between 1996 and 2001, to just under 300,000. Statistics Canada attributed about half of the growth to higher birth rates and lower death rates, the other half to the growing tendency of those previously hiding their identity to report it, due to a resurgence of pride and awareness. The limited data available for Métis depicted a young (one-third under fourteen) and predominantly urban (two-thirds) population with acute social and economic problems beyond the capacity of Métis organizations and most provinces to deal with.

In the case of the MNC's governing members, the greatest constraint on their capacity to meet the challenges of this burgeoning Métis population was the lack of a direct or government-to-government relationship with Ottawa. In fact, their sole institutional link was a federal minister with the seemingly ad hoc title of "Métis interlocutor." The administrative and fiscal regime under which they operated made it difficult to acquire the policy development, research, and planning capabilities to address Métis needs in a coordinated, cost-efficient manner. Moreover, the dysfunctional nature of Métis programming—government bureaucrats often in control of programs their departments didn't actually deliver, Métis organizations delivering programs they didn't control—made no one responsible for the results.

For Métis leadership, the solution to the lack of transparency and accountability underlying Métis programs required Ottawa and the provinces to rethink the role of their organizations: "By understanding Métis governance, it becomes clear to see how accountability to Métis people rests in these governance structures and institutions. ... They are the Métis people's chosen vehicles for the implementation of Métis self-government. ... It is a fallacy to view these structures as solely 'political organizations.' They are evolving Aboriginal governments which require access to the instruments and resources that will enable them to adequately serve their people."[13]

RENAISSANCE

Although a failure in themselves, the constitutional talks from the time of patriation to Charlottetown had succeeded in releasing a torrent of interest in identity and culture among Métis people. Political negotiations may have come to a standstill during the status quo decade of the Chrétien regime, but across the Métis homeland, a renaissance in language and the arts was fuelling the growth of Métis nationalist consciousness. Since the North-West Rebellion and the dispersion, Métis people had largely backed off from the use of Michif, the national language of the Métis that combined French nouns and Cree verbs. For much of the twentieth century, the attitude of prairie school authorities toward the use of Michif had been that " ... the best way for children to learn English was to beat Michif out of them."[14] Because Michif would not be a language choice on the Canada Census until 2001, the exact number of Michif speakers was unknown. Faced with the prospect of its ongoing decline and eventual extinction, Métis groups across the homeland mobilized to preserve and promote the use of the language.

The challenge they faced was set out at a gathering in the Métis community of Lebret in Saskatchewan's Qu'Appelle Valley: "We can get it back if we all work together. If we lose it now it will never be regained. Preserving the language is an integral part of keeping Métis heritage and culture alive. A people can't possess a culture without an understanding of their unique language."[15]

"Duck Bay Jiggers" surround Métis Second World War veteran
Leo Goulet on the beaches of Normandy, Juno Beach, France.
(Robert McDonald/MNC)

With the assistance of the MNC governing members and institutions such as the Gabriel Dumont Institute, groups began "banking" the Michif language—recording its usage, obtaining translations from those still speaking the language, and preparing learning resources for its instruction. Pemmican Publications, the publishing arm of the MMF, began publishing in Michif, with works including a dictionary and books for children. These and other resources later enabled school districts in Manitoba and Saskatchewan with large Métis enrolments to begin teaching Michif in the kindergarten to Grade 12 system.

While trying to restore their own language, the Métis were also leaving an indelible mark in the English literary world, a deliberate choice even for some who were fluent in Aboriginal languages. Following in the footsteps of nationalists and independence movements in the former European colonies in the Third World, Métis writers had decided to appropriate what they viewed as the language of oppression and turn

Dance group the Churchill River Reelers from Buffalo Narrows, Saskatchewan, at "Back to Batoche 2005." (Collection of Clément Chartier)

it into a tool of liberation. According to Métis writer, poet, and historian Emma LaRocque,[16] "I have sought to master this language so that it would no longer master me. Colonization works itself out in unpredictable ways. The fact is that English is the new Native language, literally and politically. English is the common language of Aboriginal peoples. It is English that is serving to raise the political consciousness of our community; it is English that is serving to de-colonize and to unite Aboriginal peoples. Personally, I see much poetic justice in this process."[17]

The renaissance in the arts among Métis people was driven by the autobiographical works of writers, poets, and filmmakers who brought the experience of being Métis in Canada to a broad audience. Louis Riel had prophesized that the Métis would sleep for one hundred years and that when they awoke, it would be the artists who would give them back their spirit. The artistic expression of spiritual redemption had begun with *Halfbreed* (McClelland, 1973), a description by Maria Campbell[18] of her hellfire journey through poverty, prostitution, and addiction, a journey that ended with her personal healing and return to the Métis community where she found "happiness and beauty."[19] *In Search of April Raintree* (Pemmican Publications, 1983), by Beatrice Culleton,[20] tells the story of two Métis sisters trying to cope with life in foster homes amid sexual abuse and family suicide. The novel also concludes with the protagonist overcoming barriers by accepting herself and her people. In the film *Foster Child* (for which he won the Gemini for best direction for a documentary program in 1988), Métis film director Gil Cardinal,[21] who had been placed in a foster home at the age of two, searched for his family roots and the identity of his Métis mother whose life had ended on Edmonton's skid row.

The new wave of Métis writers and poets sweeping the literary scene in the 1990s explored the difficulty of asserting and retaining Métis identity in an urban, multicultural society. Marilyn Dumont,[22] a descendant of Gabriel Dumont, poses the fundamental questions surrounding cultural survival in her poem *It Crosses My Mind*:

> It crosses my mind to wonder where we fit in this 'vertical mosaic', this colour colony; the urban pariah, the displaced and surrendered to apartment blocks, shopping malls, superstores and giant screens, are we distinct 'survivors of white noise', or merely hostages in the enemy camp and the job application asks me if I am a Canadian citizen and am I expected to mindlessly check 'yes', indifferent to skin colour and the deaths of 1885, or am I actually free to check 'no', like the *true north strong and free* and what will I know of my own kin in my old age, will they still welcome me, share their stew and tea, pass me the bannock like it's mine, will they continue to greet me in the old way, hand me

their babies as my own and send me away with gifts when I leave and what name will I know them by in these multicultural intentions, how will I know other than by shape of nose and cheekbone, colour of eyes and hair, and will it matter that we call ourselves Métis, Métisse, Mixed blood or aboriginal, will sovereignty matter or will we just slide off the level playing field turned on its side while the provincial flags slap confidently before me, echoing their self-absorbed anthem in the wind, and what is this game we've played long enough, *finders keepers/losers weepers,* so how loud and how long can the losers weep and the white noise infiltrates my day as easily as the alarm, headlines and 'Morningside' but 'Are you a Canadian citizen?', I sometimes think to answer, *yes, by coercion, yes, but no…there's more,* but no space provided to write my historical interpretation here, that *yes but no,* really only means *yes* because there are no lines for the stories between *yes* and *no* and what of the future of my eight-year-old niece, whose mother is Métis but only half as Métis as her grandmother, what will she name herself and will there come a time and can it be measured or predicted when she will stop naming herself and crossing her own mind.[23]

In *God of the Fiddle Players* by Gregory Scofield,[24] the annual "Back to Batoche" celebrations reconciles an alienated urban youth with his Métis identity.

The wilting sun catches them center stage, taking a
Well-deserved breather. Safely shielded by the big top,
Easy for me to applaud for more. An old-timer's
Favorite, my mom would say.

Surveying the dance floor, my generation is damn-near
Lost. Even me, I don't know how to promenade
Properly, let alone that quick heel-toe-on-the-spot
Step. Gyrating to a techno-beat is more my history.
Then again, who can dig roots in the city?

I have to ask a friend about being Métis, what there is
To be proud of. Because she's an elder, she says just
Watch, listen. Later we join the pilgrimage to the
Graveyard, go to the museum.

They have a special show using mannequins to
Re-enact the Northwest Resistance. Weeping openly, I
Got to meet the heroes I was ashamed of in school.

That summer, the God of the Fiddle Players visited
Batoche. I bought my first sash; wearing it proudly
Around the house, practicing the ins & outs of jigging.[25]

In *Writing the Circle*, Emma LaRocque captured the essence of Métis writing: "… Whether blunt or subtle, [it] is protest literature in that it speaks to the processes of our colonization: dispossession, objectification, marginalization, and that constant struggle for cultural survival expressed in the movement for structural and psychological self-determination."[26] In effect, Métis writers were expressing in literary form what Howard Adams had tried to achieve in his political manifesto *Prison of Grass*: resistance to the psychopathology of colonialism as it impacts on the Métis people. The message was brutally honest and powerful: In order to overcome the dire consequences of being a defeated, landless people—and in some cases to survive at all—the Métis had to achieve sovereignty as individuals before they could become sovereign as a people, asserting rights not given to them by government but inherent and inalienable.

Chapter 14

THE *POWLEY* DECISION

Breaking the impasse on Métis rights rested on the outcome of the litigation strategy that had emerged from the ashes of the Charlottetown and Métis Nation Accords. The breakthrough would occur on the eastern fringe of the Métis homeland in Sault Ste. Marie, Ontario, and involved a Métis father and son, Steve and Roddy Powley, who had been acquitted in two lower courts of unlawfully hunting a moose on the grounds that they had a constitutionally protected Aboriginal right to hunt as Métis under section 35 of the Constitution Act, 1982. Ontario had appealed the decision to the Ontario Court of Appeal, arguing that the Métis in Sault Ste. Marie did not constitute a distinct Aboriginal community, had no identity or rights separate from Indians, and that Métis harvesting rights, if they did exist, were subordinate to those of Indians. On 23 February 2001, the Ontario Court of Appeal, the highest court to have ruled on Métis rights, dismissed all of the Crown's arguments and upheld the decisions of the lower courts. On 4 October 2001, the Supreme Court of Canada granted the Crown leave to appeal. *Powley* had become the Métis rights case anticipated in its *Van der Peet* decision in 1996.

PREPARING FOR *POWLEY*

Powley acted as a catalyst for empowering the MNC to face the challenges inherent in the impending Supreme Court hearing. At the MNC's eighteenth annual assembly in Edmonton on 27 September 2002, delegates voted unanimously in favour of adopting a national definition of Métis. According to the resolution, "Métis means a person who self-identifies as Métis, is of historic Métis Nation ancestry, is distinct from other Aboriginal peoples and is accepted by the Métis Nation."

Delegates also voted unanimously to support the direct election of the MNC president by the Métis people throughout their homeland in a ballot-box election. According to MNC president Gerald Morin, "For the first time in our history, it gives our people the right to vote for the national leadership. Power to the people. We're not just saying it, we're doing it." Morin said the two decisions would provide "further momentum given that the Métis Nation will be before the Supreme Court of Canada with the *Powley* case."

Unfortunately for the MNC, it would be other legal action involving Morin that captured headlines in January 2003, when it was revealed that Morin had been arrested the previous month at an Ottawa hotel and charged with assaulting a woman while attending the Liberal Party of Canada's annual Christmas party. Upon receiving the news on 7 January 2003, the MNC board of governors asked Morin to resign. On 11 January, by unanimous decision, the board suspended Morin as MNC president and appointed MNA president Audrey Poitras as interim president. Poitras said the action was a clear message to Métis communities and the public at large that Morin's actions were unacceptable and made it impossible for him to lead the Métis Nation: "Our leadership must be held to the highest standards and values that reflect our people. We are role models to our youth and communities. We must lead by example. The board of directors reiterates that it will not condone any violence by its leadership and has zero tolerance for any violence against women within our communities and within society as a whole."[1]

On 17 March 2003, *Powley* was argued before the Supreme Court of Canada. Counsel for the Powleys consisted of Arthur Pape and Jean Teillet, a passionate defender of Métis rights and the great-grandniece of Louis Riel. Shortly before the case was heard, Teillet had stated, "We could not be in a better position to go to the Supreme Court. We won three really beautiful judgments in all the courts below. We cannot resolve all the Métis issues on the first case, but we can get a good start."[2]

As co-interveners, the MNC and its member association, the Métis Nation of Ontario (of which the Powleys were members), were represented by Clément Chartier and Jason Madden. Politics and law had become so intertwined, the stakes so high, that the MNC had dispensed with distinctions and cast the Saskatchewan

L-R: Tony Belcourt, lawyer Jean Teillet, and Steve Powley following
lower court decision on *Powley*, Sault Ste. Marie, Ontario, 1998.
(CP Photo Archive)

Métis president into court as its legal counsel. In a further interesting switch of
roles, Ian Binnie, the former associate deputy minister of justice who had cross-
examined MNC witnesses twenty years earlier during their lawsuit against Prime
Minister Trudeau, would be one of the nine justices rendering judgment on
Powley.[3] What had started out as a local Métis hunting rights case had evolved into
a drama of a people's existence, their place in the Constitution, and the obligations
of a government to deal with them, to be played out in the highest court in the
country.

"WE WON. WE WON!"

Was there a historical Métis community in Sault Ste. Marie? Was there a contemporary community? Did the Métis meet the requirements of the test for Aboriginal
rights entitlement? Did the Métis have Aboriginal rights as a distinct people, or did
these rights flow from their Indian ancestry? Could the Métis be identified for
rights entitlement purposes? These questions would shape the deliberations of the
Supreme Court of Canada as it formulated its decision on whether the Métis had
constitutionally protected harvesting rights. In essence, they spoke to the same cen-

tral issue in the legal action against Pierre Elliott Trudeau twenty years earlier, an issue that had been left unresolved as a result of the out-of-court settlement: "Who are the Métis?"

On 19 September 2003, the Supreme Court of Canada rendered its judgment on *Powley.* In response to the constitutional question before it—whether members of the Métis community in and around Sault Ste. Marie had a constitutional right to hunt for food[4]—the court answered "yes" in a unanimous decision. The Powleys and other members of the Métis community in and around Sault Ste. Marie had an Aboriginal right to hunt for food under section 35(1).

The court defined its approach to the question as follows: "The overarching interpretive principle for our legal analysis is a purposive reading of s. 35. The inclusion of the Métis in s. 35 is based on a commitment to recognizing and enhancing their survival as distinctive communities. The purpose and the promise of s. 35 is to protect practices that were historically important features of these distinctive communities and that persist in the present day as integral elements of their Métis culture."[5]

The historical evidence included in the court's analysis may have been restricted to a limited activity, geographical area, and group of people, but the factors cited had indeed shaped the rise, fall, and struggle to survive of Métis communities throughout the historical fur trade territory between the Great Lakes and the Rocky Mountains: the policy of the fur trade companies and government to discourage white agricultural settlement in order to preserve alliances with the Indians and the habitat of the fur-bearing animals; the emergence of trading communities inhabited by the offspring of European fur traders and Indian women, ethnically and culturally distinct from neighbouring Indian villages and the white towns in the east; the growth and increased domination of these communities by Métis marrying among themselves and raising successive generations of Métis; the reliance of these communities on a local resource base rather than on European imports; their ability to thrive largely unaffected by European laws and customs until government policy shifted from one of discouraging settlement to one of negotiating treaties and encouraging settlement; the transfer of effective control of Métis territory accompanied by the loss of a traditional land base and displacement to the peripheries of towns, road allowances, and Indian reserves, where the Métis continued to gain their livelihood from the resources of the land and water; and the impact of the Riel rebellions and hostile public opinion on the visibility of the Métis ("The Métis community went underground, so to speak, but it continued"[6]).

The court upheld the trial judge's key findings: of a distinctive Métis community that emerged in the upper Great Lakes region in the mid-seventeenth century and peaked around 1850; of a historical Métis community at Sault Ste. Marie, one of the oldest and most important Métis settlements in the upper Great Lakes area; of a contemporary Métis community in and around Sault Ste. Marie; and that the

Powleys were members of this Métis community that arose and still exists in and around Sault Ste. Marie. The facts were profound in their simplicity. They confirmed the existence of a people.

As for the identification of the Métis, the court found "The term 'Métis' in s. 35 does not encompass all individuals with mixed Indian and European heritage; rather, it refers to distinctive peoples who, in addition to their mixed ancestry, developed their own customs, way of life, and recognizable group identity separate from their Indian or Inuit and European forebears. Métis communities evolved and flourished prior to the entrenchment of European control, when the influence of European settlers and political institutions became pre-eminent. ... The Métis developed separate and distinct identities, not reducible to the mere fact of their mixed ancestry."[7]

As for how the rights of Métis people in section 35 should be defined, the court upheld the *Van der Peet* test for offering constitutional protection to those customs, practices, or traditions integral to a particular Aboriginal culture that have persisted over time. However, as it had stated in that case in 1996, the manner in which the Aboriginal rights of other Aboriginal peoples was defined would not necessarily determine the manner in which Métis Aboriginal rights would be defined. The court then set out the difference: "The inclusion of the Métis in s. 35 is not traceable to their pre-contact occupation of Canadian territory. The purpose of s. 35 as it relates to the Métis is therefore different from that which relates to the Indians or the Inuit. The constitutionally significant feature of the Métis is their special status as peoples that emerged between first contact and the effective imposition of European control."[8]

The court modified *Van der Peet*'s pre-contact test to reflect the distinctive history and "post-contact ethnogenesis" of the Métis:

> With this in mind, we proceed to the issue of the correct test to determine the entitlements of the Métis under s. 35 of the Constitution Act, 1982. The appropriate test must then be applied to the findings of fact of the trial judge. We accept *Van der Peet* as the template for this discussion. However, we modify the pre-contact focus of the *Van der Peet* test when the claimants are Métis to account for the important differences between Indian and Métis claims. Section 35 requires that we recognize and protect those customs and traditions that were historically important features of Métis communities prior to the time of effective European control, and that persist in the present day. This modification is required to account for the unique post-contact emergence of Métis communities, and the post-contact foundations of their aboriginal rights.[9]

Indian and Inuit rights were derived from the *pre-contact* practices and customs of their Indian and Inuit ancestors integral to their cultures that persist to this day. Métis rights were derived from the *pre-control* practices and customs of their Métis ancestors integral to Métis culture that persist to this day. Basically, the court was endorsing Métis rights based on Métis descent rather than on partial Indian ancestry: "While the fact of prior occupation grounds aboriginal rights claims for the Inuit and the Indians, the recognition of Métis rights in s. 35 is not reducible to the Métis' Indian ancestry. ... We reject the appellants' argument that Métis rights must find their origin in the pre-contact practices of the Métis aboriginal ancestors. This theory in effect would deny to Métis their full status as distinctive rights-bearing peoples whose own integral practices are entitled to constitutional protection under s. 35(1)."[10]

As for identifying Métis for rights entitlement purposes, the court emphasized that it had not been asked to provide and did not purport to establish a comprehensive definition of who is Métis for the purpose of asserting a claim under section 35. It would, however, set out the "important components of a future definition."[11] In particular, it identified three broad factors as indicia of Métis identity for the purpose of claiming Métis rights under s. 35: self-identification; ancestral connection to a historical Métis community; and acceptance by the modern community "whose continuity with the historic community provides the legal foundation for the right being claimed."[12]

The court had not endorsed a specific definition of Métis such as that of the MNC. It had even held out the possibility that the term "Métis" in section 35 could include more than one Métis people. However, by tying the definition of constitutionally protected Métis Aboriginal rights and rights holders to historical Métis communities, the Supreme Court of Canada had in effect restricted Métis section 35 rights entitlement to the territory defined by the MNC as the Métis homeland.

In a strongly worded message to governments, the court also advised, "The appellant advances a subsidiary argument for justification based on the alleged difficulty of identifying who is Métis. As discussed, the Métis identity of a particular claimant should be determined on proof of self-identification, ancestral connection and community acceptance. The development of a more systematic method of identifying Métis rights-holders for the purpose of enforcing hunting regulations is an urgent priority. That said, the difficulty of identifying members of the Métis community must not be exaggerated as a basis for defeating their rights under the Constitution of Canada."[13]

Not since recognition of the Métis in the Constitution had an event generated as much excitement in Métis communities as the *Powley* decision. The victory was particularly gratifying for Audrey Poitras, the interim MNC president who had capably guided the MNC through the months leading up to the case, and it was to

Poitras that the final verdict in *Powley* would belong: "The highest court of this land has finally done what Parliament and the provincial governments have refused to do, to deliver justice to the Métis people. To all the Métis people watching I want to say two words: "We won. We won!"[14]

THE *BLAIS* DECISION

On the same day as the *Powley* decision, the Supreme Court of Canada rendered judgment on another Métis hunting rights case, *R. v. Blais*. The case involved a Manitoba Métis convicted of hunting deer out of season. In two unsuccessful appeals in lower courts, Blais had argued that as a Métis he was immune from conviction under provincial wildlife regulations on the grounds that they infringed on his constitutional right to hunt for food under paragraph 13 of the Manitoba Natural Resources Transfer Agreement, 1930, a provision stipulating that provincial laws respecting game apply to Indians subject to the continuing right of Indians to hunt, fish, and trap for food on unoccupied crown lands. The issue for the court was whether the Métis were "Indians" under the hunting rights provision of the Manitoba NRTA. The court ruled "no" and rejected the appeal.

In ruling that the NRTA could not be read to include Métis, the court cited historical and statutory evidence to demonstrate the clear differentiation between Indians and Métis and their respective entitlements made by government and the Métis themselves from the time of the Red River Métis provisional government until the negotiation of the NRTA. The most significant point of differentiation was the status of Indians as wards of the Crown versus the independence of the Métis:

> The protection accorded by para. 13 was based on the special relationship between Indians and the Crown. Underlying this was the view that Indians required special protection and assistance. Rightly or wrongly, this view did not extend to the Métis. The Métis were considered more independent and less in need of Crown protection than their Indian neighbors. ... Shared ancestry between the Métis and the colonizing population, and the Métis' own claims to a different political status than the Indians in their Lists of Rights, contributed to this perception. The stark historic fact is that the Crown viewed its obligations to Indians, whom it considered its wards, as different from its obligations to the Métis, who were its negotiating partners in the entry of Manitoba into Confederation.[15]

While rejecting Métis hunting rights under the NRTA, the court emphasized that it was leaving open for another day the question of whether the term "Indians" in section 91(24) of the Constitution Act, 1867, included the Métis. It also stated that it was making no findings with respect to the existence of a Métis right to hunt for food in Manitoba under section 35 of the Constitution Act, 1982, because the appellant did not pursue this defence: "We do not preclude the possibility that future Métis defendants could argue for site-specific hunting rights in various areas of Manitoba under s. 35 of the Constitution Act, 1982, subject to the evidentiary requirements set forth in *Powley,* supra."[16]

Blais was the culmination of cases from pre-patriation times to gain recognition of Métis rights through an expansive definition of "Indian" in constitutional documents, building on the precedent of *Re: Eskimos* [1939], in which the Supreme Court had interpreted the term "Indian" in section 91(24) of the Constitution Act, 1867, more broadly than in the Indian Act to include the Quebec Inuit.[17] With section 35 and *Powley,* the Métis argument for hunting rights as NRTA "Indians" had been rendered obsolete. The court itself suggested that "Paragraph 13 is not the only source of the Crown's or the province's obligations toward Aboriginal peoples. Other constitutional and statutory provisions are better suited, and were actually intended, to fulfill this more wide-ranging purpose."[18]

In the absence of section 35, it is possible that a sympathetic court may have been tempted to adopt a more expansive reading of "Indian" in the NRTA to include Métis. With section 35 and *Powley,* it didn't have to. The message to the Métis was clear: pursue your constitutional rights (at least with regard to hunting) as "Métis" under the Constitution Act, 1982, rather than as constitutional "Indians."

The *Powley* and *Blais* decisions challenged the assumptions underlying the one policy that Canada has consistently pursued in its dealings with its Métis population since its purchase of the Hudson's Bay Company territory in 1869, and that is a policy of expedience. Governments have chosen to define the Métis by racial and socio-economic characteristics rather than by history and culture, subsuming them within a general population of disadvantaged Aboriginal people outside the Indian Act and then exploiting the "difficulty in identifying who the Métis are" as a pretext for inaction. When they have acted, it has been only for as long as they had to: recognizing Métis land rights in the Manitoba Act to end the provisional government in Red River, later dismissed by Sir John A. Macdonald as an "incorrect" decision once the Métis had been removed as the foremost obstacle to his westward expansion plan; including Métis in Trudeau's patriation bill to offset mounting opposition to unilateral patriation, later to be vitiated by the infamous "Chrétien letter"; and negotiating the Métis Nation Accord, part of a desperate deal-maker's bid to secure a national deal, later to be snuffed out in the ashes of the Charlottetown Accord.

With the Supreme Court confirming that the Powleys and Ernie Blais were constitutional "Métis" on the basis of their ancestral connection to and acceptance by historical Métis communities, Canada could no longer argue it didn't know who the Métis people were. Nor could it argue, as the Crown essentially did in *Powley*, that inclusion of Métis in section 35 was a mistake. The court's "purposive reading" of section 35 had caught the policy of expedience in its own contradiction: If, as the Crown was arguing, Métis Aboriginal identity and rights were grounded in their Indian ancestry, why had the Métis been included as a distinct Aboriginal people in the Constitution of Canada? The Supreme Court, faced with irrefutable evidence of the historical and contemporary existence of a people and their culture, had proceeded to reforge its tools to accommodate that reality.

Chapter 15

DEFINING THE MÉTIS HOMELAND

*P*owley had granted the Métis community of Sault Ste. Marie a constitutional exemption from the application of provincial wildlife laws. With the possibility, if not probability, that this exemption would eventually apply across the Métis homeland, the long-simmering question of jurisdiction boiled to the surface: Which governing body, if any, would legislate and regulate in matters of Métis harvesting? Métis people had always considered harvesting an inherent right and had deeply resented and resisted efforts by provincial governments to arbitrarily limit its exercise;[1] with *Powley,* their leaders intended to fill the legal void in matters of Métis harvesting with Métis-made laws and regulations. Not since the formation of Louis Riel's provisional governments in the nineteenth century (with the limited exception of the Métis settlements) had a Métis political movement been in a position to assume the legal authority of a government. Now, as then, the critical issue would be whether Canadian governments would respect that authority.

CLÉMENT CHARTIER:
"LITIGATION OR NEGOTIATION"

On 24 October 2003, in Winnipeg, delegates from the MNC member associations elected Clément Chartier by acclamation as president of the MNC. Carried in an air of inevitability, the decision marked a tribute to one man's efforts that had spanned and in a real sense shaped the Métis Nation's achievements over the previous quarter-century. Many of the political and legal milestones—reinsertion of Aboriginal rights in the patriation bill, the fight over representation at the first constitutional conference, the 1983 Constitutional Accord, the Métis Nation Accord, *Morin and Daigneault, Powley*—bore the mark of the indefatigable scholar, lawyer, politician, and Métis nationalist. The choice also paid tribute to his character and conviction, the pursuit of his principles at the cost of political office, and, in the jungles of Nicaragua, his willingness to put his life on the line for his beliefs.

Chartier wanted to channel the momentum from *Powley* into the pursuit of self-government. The court had dealt with Métis representative bodies only indirectly and within the context of defining membership for rights entitlement purposes ("As Métis communities continue to organize themselves more formally and to assert their constitutional rights, it is imperative that membership requirements become more standardized so that legitimate rights-holders can be identified"[2]) and in the implementation of the right ("In the longer term, a combination of negotiation and judicial settlement will more clearly define the contours of the Métis right to hunt"[3]). In an indication of a more formalized role for Métis governing bodies, the federal government and the provinces from Ontario westward joined the MNC in a Métis Nation Multilateral Process shortly after *Powley* to deal with Métis harvesting, access to resources, and other Métis-specific issues. The MNC, the Government of Canada, and the Government of Alberta co-chaired the process. Real government powers and authority, however, continued to elude the political institutions of the Métis Nation and posed formidable tactical challenges to the new MNC president.

Whether to pursue Métis self-government as an "existing" Aboriginal right under section 35 or through intergovernmental negotiations remained the foremost tactical challenge. Arguably, *Powley*'s site-specific, activity-specific test requirements for proving Aboriginal rights and its emphasis on traditional practices and customs could impede the affirmation of self-government rights under section 35. Chartier, for one, remained convinced that the Métis Nation Accord approach was the best way to resolve issues of self-government. However, it was premised on a legal requirement to work out the issues, something that was fundamentally missing from the inherent right policy of the Liberal government.

Chartier also had to face the challenge of the MNC's resistance to structural changes that would have to be made to prepare it for self-government. Legally speaking, the MNC had barely evolved at all in its own constitutional development since its inception in 1983. It did not have a constitution of its own but operated as a not-for-profit corporation under the federal Corporations Act and related corporate bylaws. Its structure remained confederal, somewhat analogous to a Canadian Parliament comprised of MLAs from all the provinces and a federal cabinet comprised of the prime minister and all the premiers. The most significant step taken toward consolidating the national body—the decision of the general assembly in the autumn of 2002 to mandate the direct election of the MNC president—had still not taken effect due to the high cost of holding a separate "national" election and, alternatively, the impossibility of conducting it concurrently with direct elections that were held in the provinces but on different schedules.

During 2003, the MNC's Métis Nation Constitution Commission and governing members had conducted some consultations with Métis communities across the homeland with the intention of drafting a Métis Nation Constitution for ratification by each governing member and then by the MNC general assembly. They had approached the subject cautiously, for both the MNC and its governing members had experienced difficulty with institutions or positions that had been established in an advisory or quasi-judicial capacity but had become politicized to the detriment of the decision-making process.[4] In short, institutional change, in the absence of real authority and resources required for effective self-government, had proven to be an experiment that, in the opinion of many of their leaders, the Métis organizations could ill afford.

In accepting the MNC presidency, Chartier vowed to take on the possibilities and challenges of the post-*Powley* period: "This is a turning point in our relationships with governments in Canada. The choice is clear; litigation or negotiation. We have always wanted the latter. Through negotiations, we can create a safe and respectful place for our children, communities, culture and language in Canada and build a stronger federation. Through litigation, we create uncertainty for economic development, delay the inevitable, and waste valuable resources in the courts. We hope governments see the opportunity available to them and choose negotiations with us."[5]

PURSUING *POWLEY*

In Ontario on 7 July 2004, the president of the Métis Nation of Ontario (MNO) and the province's minister of natural resources reached a four-point agreement whereby the minister agreed to recognize MNO harvester certificates in Métis traditional territories in Ontario identified by the MNO. On 6 October 2004, the minister announced that Ontario would only recognize MNO harvester certificates north of a line drawn through Sudbury, on the grounds that the province did not have proof of historical Métis communities south of the line and that further research was required to prove their existence. In spite of the MNO contention that no regional limitations had been identified in the four-point agreement when both sides had worked with a map provided by MNO for drafting terms, the province continued to charge Métis for unlawful hunting and fishing south of the line.

In Manitoba, the Manitoba Métis Federation had moved since *Powley* to establish a Métis harvesting regime, including Métis harvester identification cards, interim Métis laws of the hunt, a Métis management system, and a Métis conservation trust fund. In an address to the MMF general assembly in the fall of 2004, Premier Gary Doer pledged to uphold *Powley* in Manitoba, but it soon became apparent that the NDP government intended to limit its application to eleven historical Métis communities where the province was willing to negotiate with the MMF. Until the conclusion of these negotiations, the province would continue to charge Métis harvesters. Manitoba's conservation minister, Stan Struthers, advised Métis to buy licences from the province "so there is not the confusion out there created by harvester cards which do not have legal rights."[6] Irate MMF president David Chartrand accused the premier of betraying the Métis people and vowed to unilaterally implement *Powley* by way of the MMF's harvesting regime: "The MMF will protect all Métis Harvester Identification Cardholders hunting or fishing for food, according to the Métis Laws of the Harvest, from the illegal and arbitrary acts of the Manitoba government. Now our generation truly feels the repression our ancestors experienced during the dark times after the founding of the Métis province of Manitoba. Government broke our Treaty and trampled our Constitution."[7]

In Saskatchewan, the *R. v. Morin and Daigneault* decision in 1996 had established the constitutional right of the Métis in northwestern Saskatchewan to harvest for food. Following this decision, Saskatchewan Environment unilaterally adopted a policy that Métis living north of the Northern Administration District line in a community to which they had a long-standing connection and who were practising a traditional lifestyle could harvest for food without a licence. The *Powley* decision did not alter this policy, and the Government of Saskatchewan refused to negotiate a province-wide Métis harvesting arrangement. Because the Métis Nation Saskatchewan advised its members to use their MNS citizenship cards and continue to follow the rules set out in MNS laws and regulations, Métis were still being charged by the province.

In Alberta, on 1 October 2004, the province signed an Interim Métis Harvesting Agreement (IMHA) with the Métis Nation of Alberta (and the Métis Settlements General Council) that recognized the constitutionally protected harvesting rights of Alberta Métis on a province-wide basis. The IMHA provided for year-round harvesting for subsistence purposes only and applied to Métis harvesters who were members of MNA or eligible to be members. MNA membership cards would be accepted as proof that a person was a Métis harvester under the IMHA while the MNA pursued the development of a regulatory system for managing Métis harvesting in the province. Significantly, the Alberta government recognized the membership criteria of the MNA (the same citizenship definition adopted by all MNC affiliates) as being consistent with the "objectively verifiable" requirement set out by the Supreme Court of Canada in *Powley*.[9]

In British Columbia, the provincial government took the position that the *Powley* case had no application in the province because there were no historical Métis communities that would satisfy the *Powley* test. Its attitude was that BC Métis were essentially migrants who had drifted into the province from the Prairies; claims based on traditional customs and usage would have to be pursued elsewhere. It refused to negotiate with the Métis Nation British Columbia (MNBC) with respect to Métis harvesting and continued to charge Métis harvesters.

Ottawa's response to *Powley* was generally collaborative, perhaps not surprising given the limited extent of federal crown lands in the provinces affected by the decision. The federal cabinet adopted an Interim Policy on Métis Harvesting, treating Métis in the same manner as Indians and Inuit. It also committed funds to the MNC and its member organizations to work on *Powley* implementation, including the development of Métis identification systems and supporting intergovernmental discussions.

The varying responses of government to the *Powley* decision threatened a checkerboard of Métis harvesting rights: Alberta recognizing them on a province-wide basis, British Columbia denying them on a province-wide basis, and Ontario, Manitoba, and Saskatchewan arbitrarily dividing their provinces into zones where they did or did not apply. In order to apply their harvesting rights, laws, and regulations throughout their homeland, the Métis would be back in the courts in 2005 in Ontario, Manitoba, Saskatchewan, and British Columbia. *Powley* had represented a breakthrough in understanding the nature of Métis Aboriginal rights; the new cases would speak to the geographical scope of Métis rights.

RIGHTS-BEARING MÉTIS COMMUNITIES

The first test of governmental and judicial reaction to the *Powley* decision had actually occurred well outside the historical Métis Nation homeland. Since the patriation of the Constitution, a variety of individuals and groups in Atlantic Canada had claimed section 35 Aboriginal rights as Métis even though they did not share the history and culture of the Métis Nation. Some identified as Métis because they could not claim Indian status or live on reserves; others were Canadians who had never identified as Aboriginal but upon discovery of a distant Indian ancestor thought that was sufficient to become and claim rights as Métis. Represented at the national level by the Congress of Aboriginal Peoples (successor to the Native Council of Canada), these groups based their identity and rights on their partial Indian or Inuit ancestry rather than Métis descent.

One such mixed-blood community had organized as the Labrador Métis Nation, a group with partial Inuit ancestry who identified with Inuit culture. Immediately after the *Powley* decision was released, the Province of Newfoundland rejected their claim to harvesting rights as Métis on the grounds that they did not meet the requirements of *Powley.* In *R. v. Nichol,*[9] the Newfoundland and Labrador Provincial Court noted that, "While the Labrador Métis Association did intervene in *Powley,* there has been no decision of any Court which recognizes the distinctive and collective hallmarks of a Métis community, as seen in *Powley,* among those claiming Métis status in Labrador."[10]

R. v. Castonguay[11] was a case in New Brunswick involving a defendant charged with illegal possession of crown timber asserting a constitutional right as a Métis person to possess such timber. Judge LeBlanc of the New Brunswick Provincial Court found "there is no evidence, historical or otherwise, of a Métis community in our province,"[12] although there clearly were children of one Aboriginal parent and one European parent. He concluded that an Aboriginal genetic connection that was formed ten generations ago and has no continuity with the present cannot rise to a constitutional right.

The test of "objectively verifiable" requirements for membership in Métis rights-bearing communities set out in *Powley*—restricting section 35 Aboriginal rights to those self-identifying as Métis who could prove an ancestral connection to a historical rights-bearing Métis community and acceptance by a contemporary community that had evolved from the historical community—would prove to be an insurmountable barrier to the claims of mixed-ancestry Aboriginal people in eastern Canada. While they may have been able to prove ancestral connection to historical Indian or Inuit communities, they could not prove ancestral connection to historical Métis communities. While they may have been accepted by contemporary communities that called themselves Métis, they could not prove that these were historical Métis communities.

When applied to another region outside the Prairies, the test would produce more ambiguous results. The MNC had stated that the historical Métis homeland extended into the Peace River country in northeastern British Columbia, the only region of BC east of the Rockies and in many respects an extension of the prairie, where Métis from Lac Ste. Anne, Alberta, and before that Red River, established the community of Kelly Lake following the North-West Rebellion. West of the Rockies, Métis from the Prairies had been active in the fur trade during the nineteenth century; whether this presence rose to the level of a historical rights-bearing community in law would become the subject of the *Willison* case.

On 22 March 2005, the Provincial Court of British Columbia, in *R. v. Willison*,[13] found that a Métis charged under the British Columbia Wildlife Act with shooting a deer without a provincial hunting licence (he produced a MNBC citizenship card) had a constitutionally protected Aboriginal right to hunt for food. Evidence at the trial showed that the Métis had migrated into British Columbia with the fur trade as early as 1776 and had journeyed back and forth to Red River. Closely associated with the fur trade, they led a highly mobile lifestyle as labourers, guides, and interpreters along the Brigade Trail from Fort Kamloops south to Fort Okanagan (in today's Washington state) from 1810 until "effective European control" was established during the period between 1858 and 1864.

In referring to the role of Métis persons in that territory spanned by the fur trade Brigade Trail, Justice Stansfield accepted "that for 40 or 50 years, in connection with the British Columbia fur trade, which was a pivotal component of the evolution of British Columbia from First Nations communities exclusively to what we are calling 'European control,' the Métis were in fact 'indispensable' members of the British Columbia aboriginal/non-aboriginal economic partnerships. It may fairly be said that they 'contributed massively' to European penetration of British Columbia."[14] The judge was satisfied that a historical rights-bearing Métis community existed during this period.

On appeal, the BC Supreme Court reversed the decision of the trial judge,[15] finding that he had erred in concluding that the evidence proved the existence of a historical Métis community.[16] In the opinion of the appeal judge, a small number of Métis had entered the region as employees of the Hudson's Bay Company and had left following the decline of the fur trade. He found that the evidence did not confirm a historical Métis community with a sufficient degree of continuity and stability to support a site-specific Aboriginal right. For thousands of prairie Métis who had migrated west of the Rockies in search of opportunity since the Second World War (the core membership of one of the MNC governing members, the MNBC), *Willison* illustrated the limitations of the test requirements for rights-bearing communities. It also raised the real possibility that many of these people could meet the individual test requirements for site-specific Métis Aboriginal rights but not in the region where they actually resided.

Shortly after the *R. v. Willison* decision, two Métis Aboriginal rights cases in Saskatchewan challenged the province's policy since *R. v. Morin and Daigneault* [1996] of restricting the exercise of those rights to its Northern Administration District. On 25 April 2005, the Provincial Court of Saskatchewan in *R. v. Norton*[17] ruled on two Métis charged with fishing without a licence in the Qu'Appelle Valley in southern Saskatchewan. The judge convicted both as charged because they failed to meet the evidentiary burden set by the Supreme Court of Canada in *R. v. Sparrow* (placing the onus of proving the existence of an Aboriginal right on the person claiming it). The judge held that the defendants, who did not testify and did not produce any evidence of ancestry, had failed to prove an ancestral link to the historical Métis community or acceptance by the contemporary Métis community. At the same time, the judge rejected the crown's arguments that there was insufficient evidence to establish the existence of a historical or a contemporary rights-bearing Métis community in the area; she confirmed the existence of a historical Métis community in the Qu'Appelle Valley dating back to the late 1700s as well as a contemporary Métis rights-bearing community.

In the more definitive *R. v. Laviolette*[18] decision rendered on 15 July 2005, the Provincial Court of Saskatchewan ruled on whether a Métis from Meadow Lake,[19] a community south of the Northern Administration District, should be exempt from complying with Fishery Regulations because of an Aboriginal right to fish within the meaning of section 35(1) of the Constitution Act, 1982. The crown took the position that "Métis community" and harvesting rights had to be limited to a specific settlement and immediately surrounding area within the Northern Administration District. Historical evidence presented at the trial depicted the Métis of northwestern Saskatchewan in the century prior to the transfer of effective control to Canada as a highly mobile population with a regional consciousness shaped by trade and kinship connections along the routes of the northern boat brigades and Red River cart trails; this regional community, in turn, was linked by trade and kinship connections to a wider network of Métis communities stretching from the Red River settlement to Lac La Biche in Alberta and beyond.

Judge Kalenith found sufficient evidence to support the existence of a regional historic rights-bearing Métis community in northwestern Saskatchewan including settlements south of the Northern Administration District. He concluded that the defendant had a Métis Aboriginal right to fish for food within this traditional territory of the Métis community of northwest Saskatchewan. He also rejected the province's position that Laviolette had to prove he was living "a traditional lifestyle" in order to exercise his Aboriginal right to harvest.

In looking at the Métis people in historical terms, the courts in Saskatchewan were confirming regional, historical, rights-bearing Métis communities beyond the line arbitrarily drawn by the province for determining these rights. Moreover, despite the site-specific requirements for Métis Aboriginal rights set in *Powley*, *Laviolette* had not limited these rights to a specific town or settlement because evidence showed the historical Métis community to be a network of mobile individuals linked by kinship and trade connections over a large territory. These historical Métis communities were not isolated pockets of subsistence gatherers but part of a continuum of Métis communities spanning half a continent, an integral part of the fur trade and the early economic development of western Canada.

In validating the historical, cultural, and territorial integrity of Métis people, *Powley* and the post-*Powley* litigation acted as further catalysts in the evolution of Métis nationalism and the move to self-government. In the words of MNC president Clément Chartier, "Since the *Powley* decision, the Métis National Council has stressed that the implications of this decision are not just limited to Métis harvesting or harvesting rights for specific Métis communities that are identified as dots on a map. Our people were and continue to be a mobile people. ... I also believe that what has been undertaken at the national level on *Powley* implementation has been very helpful and important. The provincial boundaries we currently reside in are artificial to our nationhood. We must find ways to work together in the name of nationalism."[20]

DEFINING THE MÉTIS HOMELAND

Powley and the post-*Powley* litigation underscored the importance of defining the social and territorial boundaries of the Métis homeland, the territory inside which Métis constitutional rights would apply. The court cases themselves had provided some clarification: identifying historical rights-bearing Métis communities as the source and determinant of rights of contemporary Métis communities; demarcating historical Métis communities between the upper Great Lakes and the Rockies from those mixed-ancestry Aboriginal groups in eastern Canada who could not prove ancestral connection to or acceptance by historical Métis communities; and establishing a test of membership criteria for Métis rights-bearing communities that was clearly compatible with MNC's "national definition" or Métis Nation citizenship criteria. Still to be resolved were the precise boundaries of the homeland.

Since its inception, the MNC had defined the "Métis homeland" as territory comprising the three prairie provinces and "extending" into Ontario, British Columbia, the Northwest Territories, and the northern United States (i.e., North Dakota and Montana). At best, this had to be a general description, for there was no detailed map of the Métis "homeland" in the vast expanse of west-central North America. Moreover, the unique history of the Métis people—their high degree of mobility within the fur trade economy as well as their displacement, dispossession, and dispersion in the wake of the Métis land grant and scrip fiascos after 1870—ensured that the use and occupation of Métis traditional territory had changed over time.

Expedience alone would dictate that the homeland boundaries (and by extension, those of the MNC) should coincide with those of the prairie provinces. After all, Canada's "half-breed" land grant policies were largely a response to armed Métis uprisings and provisional governments on the Prairies. In a strict legal sense, the Métis were the descendants of those entitled to half-breed land grants under the Manitoba Act and scrip under the Dominion Lands Act (in fact, the MNC's original "national definition" of "Métis" had largely rested on these criteria). The boundaries of Ottawa's half-breed commissions responsible for the distribution of land grants and scrip took in the entirety of what was to become these three provinces. Moreover, the long history of Métis political organization on the Prairies—going as far back as the Depression years—did not occur anywhere else.

But as the court cases demonstrated, beyond the boundaries of the prairie provinces and half-breed commissions lay other historical, rights-bearing Métis communities such as Sault Ste. Marie. Little was known about some of the communities making up the fledgling but rapidly growing associations from Ontario and British Columbia. In fact, the prairie Métis associations still viewed the decision to include the "bookends" in the MNC back in the 1980s with ambivalence. They hoped that the Métis Nation could consolidate itself within natural boundaries rather than those imposed on it by Canadian federalism and feared the possibility of overextending the boundaries of the Métis through the admission of individuals and communities lacking the history and culture of the Métis Nation.

Ottawa's rejection of Métis land claims on the Prairies in 1981 and the exclusion of the Métis from the federal comprehensive claims process south of the sixtieth parallel had precluded a systematic delineation or mapping of traditional Métis territory, an integral part of any process to negotiate a land base. Therefore, the prairie Métis had to pursue research into Métis lands as part of their two major land claims lawsuits: the MMF lawsuit launched in 1981 to challenge the constitutionality of federal and Manitoba statutes that allegedly undermined the Métis land grants promised by the Manitoba Act, 1870, and the Métis Nation Saskatchewan and MNC lawsuit against Canada and Saskatchewan launched in 1994 to challenge the validity of scrip and its method of implementation as a means of extinguishing Métis land rights in northwestern Saskatchewan. The Métis Aboriginal Title Research Initiative at the University of Alberta under the direction of Professor Frank Tough had been undertaking much of the research into the latter claim, compiling and archiving genealogical records and scrip certificates for use in identifying traditional Métis lands and tracking the historical movement of the Métis people.

The tests set by the Supreme Court of Canada for determining Aboriginal rights and rights holders rested largely on historical evidence. *Powley* and the post-*Powley* cases had demonstrated the power of historical evidence to substantiate Métis claims in court. Even before the commencement of trials, the implications of the historical evidence behind Métis land claims were resonating in the courts: counsel for Canada in the MMF lawsuit[21] warned that a successful outcome for the Métis plaintiffs could be worth billions of dollars; in *R. v. Laliberte*,[22] Judge White of the Provincial Court of Saskatchewan commented during trial that, if necessary, he could take judicial notice of the fraud permeating the scrip process; and in *R. v. Blais* in 2003, the Supreme Court of Canada referred to the history of scrip speculation as a "sorry chapter in our nation's history."[23] The Province of Saskatchewan was identifying the scrip lawsuit as a material risk in provincial bond issues,[24] and Canadian financial institutions were becoming aware of the prominent role they had played in the scrip process.[25]

In the spring of 2005, under the auspices of the MNC, the Native Studies Department launched a new research space at the University of Alberta. The Métis Archival Project aimed to develop an MNC historical database, a source of scrip information accessible over the Internet that would serve as a documentation centre in support of Métis claims and citizenship registries. Furnished with increasingly authoritative information, Métis leaders explored the potential for filing statements of claim throughout the rest of the prairie provinces outside northwestern Saskatchewan, thereby challenging the scrip process under the Dominion Lands Acts from 1874 to 1930.

On 27 May 2005, the Manitoba Court of Queen's Bench finally committed the issue of Métis land grants under the Manitoba Act, 1870, to trial, with the court starting to hear the evidence on 3 April 2006. The MMF's amended statement of claim chronicled the negotiations between delegates of the provisional government of Red River and Sir John A. Macdonald and Sir George-Etienne Cartier, resulting in the Manitoba Act and the creation of the Province of Manitoba in 1870, followed by the confirmation of this legislation by the British Parliament in the Constitution Act, 1871. It set out the fiduciary obligations imposed on the Crown by sections 31 and 32 of the Manitoba Act, Canada's failure to fulfill its obligations under these sections, and Manitoba's interference with the granting of land to the children of Métis heads of families. The MMF claimed four principal declarations:

- that a sweeping set of federal and provincial statutes and regulations (altering the obligations set out in sections 31 and 32 of the Manitoba Act and therefore in conflict with section 6 of the Constitution Act, 1871) were ultra vires the Parliament of Canada and the legislature of Manitoba or were otherwise unconstitutional;

- that Canada failed to fulfill its obligations, properly or at all, to the Métis under sections 31 and 32 of the Manitoba Act and pursuant to the undertakings given by the Crown;

- that Manitoba unconstitutionally interfered with the fulfillment of the obligations under section 31 by enacting statutes beyond its constitutional competence by reason of the inclusion of Métis in section 91(24) of the Constitution Act, 1867, and by imposing taxes on lands referred to in section 31 of the Manitoba Act prior to the grant of those lands; and

- that a treaty had been made between Canada and the provisional government and people of Red River.

Confident MMF president David Chartrand stated that government stalling tactics over the years had given the Métis more time to locate documents backing up the claim and advised Ottawa to establish a Métis claims commission to negotiate a settlement. "We will win this case and you know it," he declared to a group of federal politicians.[26] A full quarter-century after the MMF had commenced the action against Canada and Manitoba, and almost two centuries after the first flag of the Métis Nation was unfurled on the battlefield of Seven Oaks, the issue of Canada's compliance with the terms of union it had agreed to with Louis Riel's provisional government would be put on trial.

Chapter 16

Clément Chartier and
Kelowna: The Almost Accord

*T*he swearing-in of Paul Martin as prime minister of Canada on 12 December 2003, combined with the elements of the *Powley* decision and Chartier's election as MNC president, promised an altogether new chemistry in Canada-Métis relations. Unlike Brian Mulroney and Jean Chrétien (as justice minister in 1981), who had shown a willingness to deal with the Métis only when they needed their support in national constitutional crises, Martin had developed an interest in the situation of the Métis well before coming to power. His was an interest shaped by an overriding determination to reduce the disparities between Aboriginal and non-Aboriginal Canadians; to this end, he recognized the importance to Aboriginal peoples of self-government in achieving their social, cultural, and economic development and was willing to work with their leaders in building the capacity and accountability of Aboriginal governance institutions for programs and services that would improve living conditions and opportunities.

PARTNERSHIP WITH PAUL MARTIN

Martin was also committed to applying the principles of good corporate governance to all parties in Aboriginal affairs. He placed great emphasis on tying expenditures to a results-based "accountability framework" that included clearly defined performance targets, results measurements, and outcomes. In tackling socio-economic disparities, he expected the federal government and Aboriginal leadership to commit to measuring progress according to specific indicators, sharing and building on best practices, and tracking and measuring targets constantly so that all parties in the process would be accountable to their respective constituencies. As proof of his commitment to transparency and accountability, Martin was prepared to open the books on all federal spending on Aboriginal programs and to engage himself, in an unprecedented way for a prime minister, in the process of defining and executing an action plan to improve the quality of life for Aboriginal peoples.

In Paul Martin, Clément Chartier and fellow Métis leaders sensed someone who wanted to deal with Métis governing bodies as partners rather than as targets in reducing disparities and promoting social and economic development. Chartier reasoned that if Martin was serious about dealing with the social and economic problems that his own government was highlighting, he would have to come to terms with the impact of the jurisdictional barrier on the capacity of Métis organizations (and the provinces) to deal with the problems. The prime minister's good intentions aside, the true test of his performance would be whether or not he was prepared to assume the lead role in resolving Métis issues. On this, the credibility of the Martin government would rest.

The first indication of Martin's willingness to come to terms with the Métis came in the speech from the throne on 2 February 2004. More than two decades after the Métis had last been specifically referenced in a throne speech, Martin committed his government to work with "Métis leadership and the provinces in order to find the place of the Métis in the Government of Canada's policies." The next day in the House of Commons the prime minister went further, committing his government to tackling the particular problems of the Métis and not allowing "ourselves to be caught up in the jurisdictional wrangling, passing the buck, and bypassing their needs." For Chartier, Martin's comments were telling, apparently distancing the prime minister from the pan-Aboriginal approach adopted by the Chrétien government through the Urban Aboriginal Strategy: "Our people, whether in their communities or in urban centers, are looking for Métis specific solutions, Métis specific programs and services. The pan-Aboriginal approach does not recognize the unique needs of the Métis Nation and by speaking directly to the Métis, the prime minister understands this important distinction."[1]

At a breakfast meeting in March, the prime minister, Chartier, and the leaders of the First Nations and Inuit agreed to plan collaboratively a national summit to renew the relationship between Canada and the three constitutionally recognized Aboriginal peoples. The Canada–Aboriginal Peoples Roundtable in Ottawa on 19 April 2004, broke new ground by addressing the distinct interests of the three Aboriginal peoples. The pan-Aboriginal format that had always dominated inter-governmental discussions of Aboriginal issues—with particularly adverse effects on the Métis—was scrapped in favour of specific sessions for the Métis, First Nations, and Inuit. During the prime minister's time in the Métis session, Martin committed the federal interlocutor for the Métis to move forward on entering into a framework agreement with the Métis Nation that would define the bilateral relationship and negotiations between the Government of Canada and the Métis Nation.

In a follow-up to the round table, Martin agreed to a policy retreat involving his Cabinet Committee on Aboriginal Affairs and Aboriginal leaders where, it was hoped, policy accords in the form of framework agreements would be concluded. To fully develop the issues raised at the round table and to produce collaborative outcomes for the policy retreat, a series of sectoral sessions focused on health, lifelong learning, economic opportunities, housing, negotiations, and accountability would be held over a period of six months. As in the round table, each of these sectoral sessions would have a Métis, First Nations, and Inuit breakout session, providing the Métis with the opportunity to pursue Métis-specific outcomes in each of the areas.

The calling of a federal election in June 2004 and the real possibility of a Conservative victory placed the gains of the MNC in jeopardy. Aboriginal affairs ranked much lower on the Tories' list of priorities than on that of the Martin Liberals. Moreover, the senior adviser to the Conservative leader and national campaign chair for the Conservative Party was none other than Tom Flanagan, the academic nemesis of the Métis. Flanagan had described the Métis as an "economically marginal, incohesive assortment of heterogeneous groups" and had written shortly after patriation that "the best strategy to minimize the damage caused by the thoughtless elevation of the Métis to the status of a distinct 'aboriginal' people is to emphasize the word 'existing' in section 35 of the Charter of Rights and Freedoms."[2]

On 7 June 2004, Chartier and the leaders of First Nations and Inuit people called on Conservative leader Stephen Harper to disassociate himself from the writings of Flanagan. The next day Harper responded that the Aboriginal leadership's concerns were "partisan" but that he was a "forgiving lot."[3] The MNC had always maintained a position of neutrality in federal elections in the belief that it had to work with whichever political party came into office, but on 9 June the MNC board of governors passed a resolution encouraging Métis people to vote Liberal.

Flanagan aside, Chartier's support for the Martin Liberals was premised largely on Paul Martin's personal commitment to recognize the Métis Nation through a framework agreement and a distinctions-based process that would allow the Métis to pursue Métis-specific outcomes at the bargaining table. The election of a minority Liberal government on 28 June 2004 brought on the same conundrum Chartier had faced the last time Canada had a government that was willing to negotiate with the Métis Nation: the fate of the framework agreement under the Martin Liberals, like that of the Métis Nation Accord under the Mulroney Conservatives, depended on events far beyond the control of the Métis. The challenge would be to craft a deal that could survive the fragile Martin government.

THE CANADA–MÉTIS NATION FRAMEWORK AGREEMENT

Despite its precarious position in the House of Commons, the Liberal government moved ahead with the prime minister's ambitious agenda to improve the lives of Aboriginal peoples. The day before a first ministers conference on health, 14 and 15 September 2004, in Ottawa, Aboriginal leaders participated in a special meeting on Aboriginal health with first ministers to discuss the development of an action plan to improve health services for Aboriginal peoples. The meeting exposed once again the acute disadvantage of the Métis relative to other Aboriginal peoples in intergovernmental talks as a result of section 91(24) of the Constitution Act, 1867.

Of the $700-million "Aboriginal" health investment announced by the prime minister, the Métis would derive little benefit by virtue of the long-standing policy of Health Canada to restrict Aboriginal health services to Indians and Inuit (despite the prevalence of comparable health problems among the Métis, including, by Ottawa's own admission, a Type 2 diabetes rate three to five times higher than the general population). In its news release, the Government of Canada committed to "further invest in the health services that it has historically provided to First Nations and Inuit." As for the Métis, it would "explore, with other orders of government and Métis leadership, Métis health issues."[4]

With the Health Canada stance in mind, a frustrated Chartier had written to the prime minister on the eve of the special meeting. In broad strokes, the letter set out the critical issues impacting on the health of the Métis Nation:

> Our people are suffering from a spiritual and psychological fatigue. There is a certain malaise or underlying unhealthy state being experienced by our Nation, based on the sad and unfortunate actions visited upon us by the colonial and Canadian governments historically and the continued federal government denial of our rights and our exclusion from most programs and

services provided to other Aboriginal peoples (Indians and Inuit). If we are to successfully deal with the health status of the Métis people, while dealing with the immediate and daily issues, we must also take bold forward steps to bring the Métis people and nation to a healthy state and a position equal to that of the other Aboriginal peoples.[5]

Chartier set out steps to place the Métis on a level playing field with other Aboriginal peoples in their dealings with the federal government. He outlined options for resolving the historical Métis claims to land promised under the Manitoba Act, 1870, and the Dominion Lands Acts, 1874–1930, including a judicial review, a Royal Commission on Métis Land Questions, and a Métis Nation Claims Commission (similar to the Indian Claims Commission). He then addressed the inequities in the status of the Métis at the table:

> By and large we are still treated as "organizations" while we have made substantial progress in internal governance developments. There are three constitutionally recognized peoples, with representative governmental infrastructures and processes. This reality must be taken into account. Any success in federal government-Aboriginal peoples relationships must be based on that recognition. The days of pan-Aboriginal and advocacy group representation must be abandoned. Only peoples and nations have the right of self-determination. Only such peoples and nations are capable of forming governments. As you have well recognized, we must now do business on a government to government basis.[6]

Chartier then proposed an action plan for establishing a direct relationship between the Métis Nation and the Government of Canada on a nation-to-nation and government-to-government basis. First, he recommended that the prime minister refer the issue of Métis inclusion in section 91(24) of the Constitution Act, 1867, to the Supreme Court of Canada. Second, he called for the expedited conclusion of the framework agreement then under discussion that would guide future bilateral negotiations. Third, he proposed the enactment of federal legislation, a Canada–Métis Nation Relations Act, that would recognize the MNC and its governing members as the (interim) government of the Métis Nation.

With his own ambitious action plan set out in his letter to the prime minister, Chartier could not but feel conflicted by the outcome of the special meeting on Aboriginal health. Mindful of the bad optics of Métis leadership sitting at a table where announcements of government "Aboriginal" initiatives worth hundreds of millions of dollars were being made when in fact very little of that money was being spent on their constituents, he was also encouraged by the decision of the prime minister, premiers, and Aboriginal leaders to convene a first ministers meeting dedicated to Aboriginal issues, including health, the first of its kind since the "blowout" at the 1987 conference. The reality for the Métis was that, if they went into this multilateral conference without a prior deal with the prime minister, their presence would again be largely token. The next opportunity to seal this deal would be the policy retreat of the Cabinet Committee on Aboriginal Affairs and Aboriginal leaders in Ottawa on 31 May 2005; there, it was hoped, the exhaustive policy work that the MNC had undertaken with the federal government since the round table would culminate in a policy accord formalizing a bilateral relationship with Ottawa and committing the parties to negotiate the resolution of Métis Nation issues.

A few weeks before the retreat, the MNC received some timely support when the United Nations' special rapporteur on indigenous issues, Rodolfo Stavenhagen, reported his findings on the situation of Canada's indigenous peoples to the Economic and Social Council of the international body. While acknowledging the efforts of the Martin government to close the socio-economic gap between Aboriginal and non-Aboriginal Canadians, Stavenhagen identified the inequities faced by the Métis in efforts to restore their land base: "Métis land claims have not been dealt with in any significant way, except partially in Alberta, leaving the Métis without a land and resource base and with no way of settling their grievances at the national level."[7] His report also targeted the exclusion of Métis from rights-based negotiations and self-government processes:

> While recognized in the Constitution as an Aboriginal people, the Métis have not been able to achieve recognition of their rights through modern treaties or arrangements. A number of court decisions, such as *Powley* in 2003, have affirmed certain Aboriginal rights of the Métis. RCAP (Royal Commission on Aboriginal Peoples) urges the Government of Canada to deal with Métis people, like all other Aboriginal peoples, on a nation-to-nation basis, and urges federal, provincial and territorial governments to proceed rapidly with nation recognition so that Métis nation(s) can negotiate treaties or agreements in the same manner as other Aboriginal peoples. These would specify the powers of their governments, the extent of their land base, the compensation owing to them for past injustices, their Aboriginal rights, and the nature of their fiscal arrangements with other governments.[8]

On 31 May 2005, the MNC and the Government of Canada signed the Canada–Métis Nation Framework Agreement. It marked a major shift in the relationship of the parties to rights-based negotiations in order "to engage a new partnership between Canada and the Métis Nation based on mutual respect, responsibility and sharing."[9] The agreement committed the parties to a process of negotiations over five years and covered many of the matters set out in Chartier's letter to the prime minister.

In the area of land claims and resources, the agreement sought to resolve long-outstanding issues between the Métis Nation and Canada outside of litigation. The options to be explored in this context included the funding of Métis litigation for issues that could not be resolved though negotiation. The agreement also committed the parties to work on implementing the *Powley* decision and a Métis harvesting regime.

In the area of self-government, the parties agreed to "develop and establish manageable negotiation and discussion processes ... that will address any Aboriginal and Treaty rights of the Métis, including the inherent right of self-government."[10] While the agreement did not specifically address the question of federal legislation, it did commit the parties to work toward the instalment of the same

Clément Chartier, flanked by Prime Minister Paul Martin and Federal Interlocutor Andy Scott, signs Canada–Métis Nation Framework Agreement, 31 May 2005, Ottawa, Ontario.
(Robert McDonald/MNC)

building blocks of Métis self-government that Chartier had proposed through a Canada–Métis Nation Relations Act: developing a Métis Nation Constitution; building electoral and governance capacity; providing ongoing and predictable governance financing; supporting Métis efforts relating to the identification and registration of Métis people based on their national definition of Métis for membership within the Métis Nation; and identifying federal programs and services suitable for devolution. The Canada–Métis Nation Framework Agreement allowed the parties to establish a Métis Nation multilateral process to include the provinces from Ontario westward in the discussion of issues, including land, but essentially it made work and progress on land claims resolution and self-government a bilateral matter between Canada and the MNC, unlike previous processes ("bottom-up" talks, the inherent right policy) that were dependent on tripartite support.

Establishment of the Métis Nation Registry, after decades of discussion, would be critical to the success of the social and economic development initiatives anticipated in the agreement. The 2001 Census Aboriginal Peoples Survey provided some qualitative information on the Métis for statistical purposes, but it was inherently unreliable, its information based solely on a Métis self-identification question rather than proof of an ancestral connection and community acceptance. Any serious effort to achieve "measurable results" for the Métis Nation would require a registration of its members according to MNC citizenship criteria.

The new "partnership" between Canada and the Métis Nation found its first expression in the Métis Nation Métis Human Resources Development Agreement, signed on 15 November 2005. This and similar accords to be entered into with each of the governing members extended for a period of four years Métis-specific human resources development programs and services to the Métis Nation. In accordance with the framework agreement, the accord emphasized the continued devolution of job training and employment programs to the Métis Nation; mechanisms to ensure financial and administrative accountability to the Métis communities served as well as to Canada; assistance to the MNC in capacity-building efforts; and flexibility for the MHRDA to offer training outside mandated areas in order to meet Métis priorities. The Métis Nation MHRDA represented a small but important first step for Canada and the Métis to do business on a government-to-government basis.

THE KELOWNA ACCORD

The meeting of first ministers and national Aboriginal leaders on 24 and 25 November 2005 in Kelowna, British Columbia, was held amid the fallout from the "adscam" scandal dogging the Liberal government. A no-confidence motion set for 28 November and supported by all the opposition parties was certain to bring down the minority government and force a winter election.[11] Nonetheless, a consensus had emerged that, given the problems presented and the progress made, the meeting between first ministers and Aboriginal leaders, the first of its kind since the constitutional talks, had to proceed. The agenda—health, education, housing and infrastructure, economic opportunities, and relationships and accountability—had been distilled out of the Canada–Aboriginal round table, the follow-up sectoral sessions, and the policy accords that the federal government had concluded with each of the Aboriginal peoples.

The meeting of first ministers and national Aboriginal leaders marked the first time the Métis had ever gone to an intergovernmental conference with a shopping list instead of a portfolio of positions. The MNC and its governing members were now seeking specific commitments in the action plan expected to emerge from the meeting to support their efforts to develop the social infrastructure of the Métis Nation: endowing a Métis housing authority to build new social housing; establishing a Métis health plan; expanding Métis child-care initiatives; enhancing Métis scholarship and bursary trusts; creating a Métis centre for excellence in education; and increasing investments in existing or to-be-established Métis educational institutions. They also hoped the action plan would revitalize the moribund tripartite talks that had dragged on for decades at the regional level.

The meeting concluded with the provinces, territories, and national Aboriginal leaders signing on to the prime minister's ten-year action plan for closing the gap in the quality of life between Aboriginal peoples and other Canadians. With a federal commitment of $5.1 billion for the first five years of the plan and specific five-year and ten-year targets for improvements in education, health, housing and infrastructure, and employment, the plan represented the most comprehensive and systematic effort ever undertaken in Canada to resolve the pressing social and economic problems of Aboriginal peoples. The impending fall of the Martin government may have cast a pall of uncertainty over the ultimate outcome of the conference, but Phil Fontaine, the national chief of the Assembly of First Nations, voiced the hopes of all the Aboriginal leaders when he told the media that the high-profile summit could not be ignored regardless of which party won the federal election: "The country is watching us here. The commitments that are made are significant and it's going to be very, very difficult for any government to retreat from those commitments here."[12]

The document setting out the prime minister's action plan at the conclusion of the meeting—*First Ministers and National Aboriginal Leaders: Strengthening Relationships and Closing the Gap*[13]—reflected the breakthroughs achieved by the Métis in the Canada–Métis Nation Framework Agreement. The foremost principle in guiding how the parties would work together was "respecting the unique history, traditions, cultures and rights of the Aboriginal peoples of Canada … by adopting a distinctions-based approach."[14] Half of the document was dedicated to broad commitments in the areas of health care and economic development, but provision was made for distinct First Nations, Inuit, and Métis Nation frameworks.[15] The other half of the document was dedicated to specific commitments to each of the Aboriginal peoples in the areas of intergovernmental relationships, education, and housing.

Under the "Métis" heading, the document dealt squarely with the status of the Métis and their relationship with the Government of Canada: "The rights of the Métis, as an Aboriginal people, are recognized and affirmed in section 35 of the Constitution Act, 1982. First Ministers and Métis Leaders acknowledge the special relationship between Métis and the Crown."[16] This section of the action plan committed Ottawa and the relevant provinces to work with the MNC and its governing members toward improving educational outcomes and revitalizing Métis housing through a variety of initiatives to be undertaken by strengthened Métis institutions.[17] Support was also provided for the establishment and maintenance of a Métis identification system that would facilitate the measuring of results in all program-delivery areas.

The "distinctions-based approach" would also govern implementation of the action plan at both the ministers' and first ministers' levels.[18] The action plan provided for an ongoing Métis Nation Multilateral Forum, comprising the MNC, the

MMF President David Chartrand fits Prime Minister Martin
with a gift from the Métis Nation, Kelowna, British Columbia, 24 November 2005.
(Robert McDonald/MNC)

Government of Canada, and relevant provincial governments, to monitor the progress made on first ministers' commitments to the Métis in Kelowna and report to the next meeting of first ministers and Aboriginal leaders. It also provided for the "renewal" of the regional tripartite processes involving MNC governing members at the provincial level "to better reflect the evolving relationships between Métis, the Government of Canada and relevant provincial and territorial governments based on commitments flowing from this First Ministers Meeting as well as emerging issues."[19]

Perhaps of greatest significance, the Government of Canada announced "that implementation of bilateral commitments flowing from the First Ministers Meeting will be consistent with and flow through existing Métis-federal bilateral agreements."[20] In the Canada–Métis Nation Framework Agreement, the Métis finally had a parallel bilateral process, a delivery mechanism ensuring that, regardless of the outcome of the multilateral process, rights-based negotiations would continue. For the MNC, the issue of section 91(24) had always been a smokescreen behind which a succession of prime ministers had hidden their lack of political will. In Paul Martin, they had found (and cultivated) a federal leader with the will to blow through it.

Prime Minister Martin with David Chartrand (on his right), Audrey Poitras (president of the Métis Nation of Alberta), and Clément Chartier, Kelowna, British Columbia, 24 November 2005.
(Robert McDonald/MNC)

A New Government, a "New Approach"

On 5 January 2006, the MNC encouraged Métis people to vote for the Liberals in the upcoming federal election. Its reasoning, centred on the Kelowna Accord, was straightforward: the prime minister had demonstrated leadership and commitment in tackling the issues; the Conservative Party had responded with excruciating ambiguity (its leader asserting his party's agreement "with the objectives but not with the $5 billion commitment because that commitment depends on future plans and meetings in order to refine the means to which the objective to reduce poverty will be attained"[21]). Tory finance critic Monte Solberg was somewhat more blunt in his assessment, telling a Saskatchewan radio station that "the Kelowna Agreement is something they crafted at the last moment on the back of a napkin on the eve of an election. We're not going to honour that. We will have our own plan that will help Natives a lot more than the Liberals."[22]

Amid growing fears in the Aboriginal political community about the real possibility of a Conservative majority government, MNC president Chartier took on the Tories: "Mr. Solberg conveniently ignores that over 14 months of consultations and negotiations led up to the Kelowna Agreement. Aboriginal communities and leaders from across the country were engaged. All provinces and territories have signed onto the deal. Now, the Conservative Party is unilaterally going to sabotage all this work and effort that was done in collaboration with Aboriginal peoples and replace it with their secret plan."[23]

Aboriginal organizations viewed the election of a Conservative minority government on 23 January 2006 with guarded relief since the Tories would have to work with opposition parties who supported the Kelowna Accord. At the same time, the election results forced the MNC to confront a new set of realities on the ground. The Conservative priorities of correcting the fiscal imbalance between Ottawa and the provinces and respecting provincial jurisdictions carried with them the real prospect of Ottawa's withdrawal from program spending in provincial and concurrent areas of jurisdiction and the transfer of fiscal resources, perhaps tax points, to the provinces. Accordingly, the provinces would occupy a larger part of the tax space and assume greater responsibility for social and economic development programs.

This decentralist program represented a two-edged sword for Métis aspirations. On the one hand, the Métis faced the potential loss of federal special programs upon which, despite the programs' shortcomings, they had long relied. On the other hand, movement toward decentralizing the federation could work in favour of Aboriginal governments and organizations if they, too, were at the receiving end of powers and fiscal resources from Ottawa. While balking at the price tag of the Kelowna Accord, the Tories themselves recognized that "new jurisdictional arrangements are required between aboriginal communities, provincial governments and the federal government."[24]

The surprise breakthrough of the Conservatives in Quebec, particularly in the francophone heartland of that province, demonstrated that the decentralist message of the Tories could win over allies in unexpected places. Could a decentralist regime in Ottawa facilitate enactment of Métis self-government legislation (particularly if it could be sold as a means of avoiding an expansion of Indian and Northern Affairs Canada or the creation of an equivalent Métis affairs bureaucracy within the federal government)? Could Stephen Harper prove to be the *beau risque*[25] not only for Quebec but also for Métis nationalists?

The fledgling Tory government's initial response to the Métis seemed to be positive enough. At their first meeting on 28 February 2006, president Chartier and Jim Prentice, the new minister of Indian affairs and federal interlocutor for Métis, agreed by handshake to move forward after a bitter election campaign. More specifically, they agreed that they and their officials would jointly work on an assessment of the MNC's understanding of the commitments coming out of Kelowna.

On 9 March 2006, in his first public speech since joining the cabinet, Prentice told the BC First Nations Summit in North Vancouver that Prime Minister Harper and he were supportive of the targets and objectives of the Kelowna Accord and were focused on building a sustainable plan that would achieve the Kelowna targets. He later told reporters that while the Liberals had outlined funding for five years, Kelowna required a twenty-year commitment. "We're working on building a fiscal plan around that. Stay tuned and you will see in our budget and our throne speech where the government is headed."[26]

Clearly, it was not headed in the direction of Kelowna. The Harper government's throne speech on 4 April 2006 lacked a specific section on Aboriginal peoples or any commitment to the Kelowna Accord. The government's first budget the following month confirmed the point: in contrast to the accord's five-year, $5.1-billion commitment to education, housing, health services, and economic development, of which $600 million was to have been set aside in 2006 alone, the Conservatives allocated $150 million in 2006 and $300 million in 2007. The budget document stated the government's commitment to meet the targets set in Kelowna by working with Aboriginal leaders, the provinces, and the territories "to develop a new approach with workable solutions."[27]

Why a "new approach" was needed would become an issue in itself. Monte Solberg's depiction of the accord as an election-eve payoff to Aboriginals quickly wore thin. As Clément Chartier and other national Aboriginal leaders reminded the Canadian public in a joint letter, "the Kelowna Accord was not just about money. It was about a plan that addressed government-to-government relations and began to clarify the respective responsibilities of the governments represented. It established clear targets and a process for monitoring and assessing progress, and committed the parties to future joint meetings to deal with other important issues. The plan was the result of two years of hard work to craft a consensus agreement that addresses the crushing poverty in which many Aboriginal people live."[28]

Jim Prentice, an expert on Aboriginal issues and land claims negotiations, fared little better in his efforts to discredit the Kelowna Accord. To his repeated assertions that the Martin government had not budgeted for any part of the accord's price tag, former finance minister Ralph Goodale countered that most of the $5.1 billion was new money that had been accounted for in his government's spending projections. Goodale presented to the House of Commons the testimony of Department of Finance officials that the money was "booked" in the surplus figures of the economic and fiscal update that had been presented on 14 November 2005.[29] Former Prime Minister Martin was more definitive: "We provided the money for it in the first five years and the government did not in its budget confirm that spending. The money was there and the government has waffled."[30]

Prentice then questioned whether an agreement had been reached at all, noting there was no document signed by first ministers with the title of Kelowna Accord (his press secretary referred to Kelowna as the "so-called accord"). Martin countered that "all the provinces agreed to it. Five of them with Conservative governments. It's not a partisan thing. You can't turn your back on a million people."[31]

Survival of the Kelowna Accord was of particular importance to the provinces and territories west of Ontario, home to the highest concentration of Aboriginal peoples. As BC premier Gordon Campbell told the legislature in Victoria, "That document was the product of an unprecedented government-to-government collaboration. It was agreed to by the prime minister of Canada and all premiers as an article of good faith and as a compact to restore trust, hope and confidence with Aboriginal peoples across Canada. After an 18-month, cross-Canada, collaborative effort to identify the amount for the next five years, a sum of $5 billion dollars was arrived at. The trust relationship that was the core of the Kelowna meeting demands decisive action and unflagging affirmation. As I said at the meeting, the honour of the Crown is at stake."[32]

Alberta Premier Ralph Klein weighed in with his disappointment that the Harper government appeared to be abandoning the deal: "I don't particularly like it, nor do the other premiers and territorial leaders. I liked the commitment that was given by the Liberal government to the First Nations and the Métis people. I think it went a long way to addressing some of their needs."[33]

On 29 May 2006, in Gimli, Manitoba, at a meeting with Aboriginal and territorial leaders before the commencement of the annual Western Premiers Conference, the western provinces renewed their commitment to the Kelowna Accord.

Conference host Premier Gary Doer of Manitoba said the premiers would be in a "state of suspended animation" until they learned the Harper government's long-term Aboriginal policy and expressed the hope that a united stand of the western premiers in support of the accord would change Ottawa's direction. In the meantime, the premiers intended to proceed with their commitments under the deal, Premier Campbell expressing his optimism that the federal government would eventually come to the table. In the spirit of the accord, Saskatchewan premier Lorne Calvert announced his hosting of an Aboriginal economic summit the next year as an important step forward in building economic capacity.[34]

On 2 June 2006, a Liberal MP tabled a private member's bill in the House of Commons designed to pressure the government into implementing the Kelowna Accord. What distinguished this bill from countless others destined to meet a swift death on the Commons floor was its author—Paul Martin. According to journalist Lawrence Martin, "The politician who only four months ago was the most powerful man in the country will go the route of a lowly backbencher to try to get something done. The odds of the bill passing are minute, but, to his credit, he isn't too proud to try. The cause is native people. Stephen Harper's Conservatives, Mr. Martin feels, are trying to bypass his cherished Kelowna Accord."[35]

The status of the Kelowna Accord may not have figured in the five priorities that helped to propel the Conservatives to power, but it was threatening to become the principal spoiler of the Harper government's honeymoon with the Canadian electorate. Attempts to discredit the accord had only served to highlight its strengths as a truly national consensus to make long-overdue improvements in the lives of Aboriginal people—and to highlight the Tories' lack of an alternative. The "new approach" promised by the Tories smacked of a euphemism for no policy at all. And Martin was reminding them on the floor of the House of Commons that "We have consulted long enough. We have studied enough. The time has come for the government to act."[36]

The road to Kelowna had been paved with more than good intentions. The Kelowna Accord represented a major undertaking in both social reform and fiscal accountability, a paradox in the eyes of some, but not in those of the former prime minister. As Paul Martin stated, "If I could as finance minister set the goals by which we eliminated the deficit, surely the Government of Canada can set the goals by which we can eliminate this gap between Aboriginal Canadians and other Canadians in terms of health care and education."[37]

Paul Martin had tried to apply the same discipline and principles of good corporate governance that had balanced Canada's books to the heretofore dysfunctional regime of Aboriginal program spending, requiring all parties to the Kelowna Accord not only to share objectives but also to measure and assume responsibility for the outcomes of their spending. Once removed from the crossfire of partisan politics, this approach to Aboriginal affairs should appeal to the same fiscal conservatives whose grudging respect Martin had earned as finance minister. There is reason to believe the deal will be resurrected in the future, even if, as one Aboriginal spokesperson suggested, it takes some "rebranding" to set it in motion.

What distinguished the Kelowna process from earlier efforts to accommodate Aboriginal interests within the Canadian federation was the reason behind it. The first ministers conferences of the 1980s and the Charlottetown/Métis Nation Accords had their origins in the patriation resolution and the Meech Lake Accord, vehicles of national unity that Aboriginal peoples had been forced to commandeer to get their issues on the table. The process behind the Kelowna Accord started from the time Martin assumed power and was designed to address the needs of Aboriginals and Métis exclusively.

For the Métis people, the Kelowna Accord, like the Métis Nation Accord, had demonstrated that the exercise of political will by the prime minister of Canada could remove the barrier of jurisdiction in Ottawa's relations with the Métis. Martin's embrace of the distinctions-based approach to resolving Aboriginal issues and his personal involvement in the mechanics of the process demonstrated his respect for them as Métis and his commitment to seriously deal with their issues. In their press releases officially welcoming the new Conservative government in Ottawa, more than one Métis organization paid tribute to Paul Martin as the best friend the Métis people had ever had in government.

Clément Chartier between Premiers Ralph Klein and Gary Doer (head turned), and Jean Charest (far right), reaffirm commitment to Kelowna Accord, Corner Brook, Newfoundland, 25 July 2006. (Robert McDonald/MNC)

Chapter 17

THE GLOBAL MOVEMENT

At the same time that Paul Martin's action plan was grinding to a halt under the Harper government, work on indigenous peoples' issues in international institutions was gaining serious momentum. Clément Chartier had long sought the establishment of standards and instruments for the recognition and protection of the rights of indigenous peoples in international law. These, in turn, would enable the MNC to bring pressure to bear on the Canadian government and help break the impasse on Métis land rights and self-government. Faced with a suddenly attenuated domestic agenda, Chartier intensified his involvement in the deliberations of the United Nations as well as the Organization of American States.

DECLARATION ON THE RIGHTS
OF INDIGENOUS PEOPLES

Work on the Declaration on the Rights of Indigenous Peoples by the UN Working Group on Indigenous Populations had moved at a glacial pace since 1985, not surprising given the complexity of the process—it involved more than 100 indigenous organizations as well as governments from many of the 70 countries that are home to the world's 370 million indigenous people. In 1993, the WGIP submitted a draft Declaration on the Rights of Indigenous Peoples to the Sub-Commission on the Promotion and Protection of Human Rights. In addition to adopting the self-determination clause from the *International Covenant on Civil and Political Rights*, the document set out a broad range of political, economic, social, and cultural rights of indigenous peoples, including rights to lands and resources and self-government. In 1994, the sub-commission submitted the text to the Human Rights Commission, which in 1995 established a new working group to review the draft.

This new WGIP would labour under the weight of controversy engulfing the Human Rights Commission itself. Some of the world's most notorious rights-violating states, such as Sudan and Libya, had gained membership on the commission in order to ward off criticism of their sordid human rights records. For dictators around the world, self-determination meant the right of states to repress or even exterminate their own populations. By 2005, a decade after its creation, the new WGIP had reached a consensus on only two of the forty-five articles in the declaration.

Amid international embarrassment and outrage at this debasement of the commission, UN Secretary General Kofi Annan had been forced to reform the body. On 15 March 2006, the UN General Assembly voted to replace the Human Rights Commission with a new Human Rights Council. The new body would consist of states subject to periodic review of their own human rights records (and possible suspension from the council itself) and would have the mandate to expose human rights abusers and assist member states with human rights legislation.

With the restructuring came the hope that indigenous peoples could elevate their issues within the United Nations. The new Human Rights Council would report directly to the General Assembly and meet regularly throughout the year. One of the first measures for its consideration would be a proposal to create its own enforcement mechanisms to protect indigenous peoples' rights.

Accompanying this overhaul of the UN human rights machinery was a more collaborative mood among indigenous and government representatives on the WGIP. Political ferment among the long-suppressed indigenous populations of Central and South America was influencing the outlook of the states in the region on the indigenous rights question. Government representatives from countries such as Mexico and Guatemala now had a vested interest in aligning themselves with their colleagues from northern democracies such as Norway, Denmark, and Canada in order to accommodate indigenous peoples' rights.

By the time Clément Chartier attended the Fifth Session of the Permanent Forum on Indigenous Issues at the United Nations in New York City on 18 May 2006, to review the work on the draft declaration, the WGIP had achieved more in six months than it had in the entire previous decade. Agreement had been reached on nearly two-thirds of the declaration's provisions. Momentum was gathering for the UN Human Rights Council to adopt the Declaration on the Rights of Indigenous Peoples and forward it for the consideration of the General Assembly.

The declaration would not have the legal force of a treaty that states could ratify and legally bind themselves to. It would, however, carry considerable weight in the court of public opinion and in the higher courts of North America that take international law into account in their decisions. Moreover, mechanisms within the United Nations could be applied to pressure states to comply with the declaration's provisions, the foremost being the UN Permanent Forum on Indigenous Issues and the Special Rapporteur on the Human Rights and Fundamental Freedoms of Indigenous Peoples.

AMERICAN DECLARATION ON THE RIGHTS OF INDIGENOUS PEOPLES

The Organization of American States had followed in the footsteps of the United Nations on the indigenous rights question. In 1989, the OAS General Assembly had adopted a resolution to draft an inter-American instrument on the rights of indigenous peoples. By 1997, the Inter-American Commission on Human Rights (IACHR)[1] of the OAS had prepared a Proposed American Declaration on the Rights of Indigenous Peoples.

The document declared that "indigenous peoples have the collective rights that are indispensable to the enjoyment of the individual human rights of their members."[2] It included self-determination and self-government provisions similar to those in the UN draft declaration. Notably for landless indigenous people such as the Métis, it stated that "indigenous peoples have the right to the recognition of their property and ownership rights with respect to lands, territories and resources they have historically occupied, as well as to the use of those to which they have historically had access for their traditional activities and livelihood."[3]

In 1999, the IACHR had submitted the Proposed American Declaration on the Rights of Indigenous Peoples to a meeting of government experts, the first governmental meeting of the OAS with the participation of representatives of the indigenous peoples of the hemisphere. The OAS General Assembly then established a working group of the Permanent Council to consider the draft declaration, setting the stage for formal negotiations between representatives of the member states of the OAS and indigenous organizations. A series of five negotiation sessions would be held by 2005, increasingly driven by events on the ground far beyond the hallowed halls of the OAS building in Washington, DC.

From southern Mexico to Bolivia, a shock wave of indigenous peoples' anger and militancy had been surging through the Americas. Diverse peoples with a shared experience of displacement from their traditional territories and livelihoods by outside interests (often foreign-owned agricultural, forestry, and oil and gas companies) were now seizing lands, forming their own governments, and demanding a share of resource revenues to fund social and economic development independent of their central governments. Beyond demanding political autonomy and land ownership, these movements were threatening to redraw the political map in countries with large indigenous populations or majorities, such as Guatemala, Ecuador, Peru, and Bolivia. Their political campaigns had led to the ouster of elected governments in Bolivia (2000) and Ecuador (2003), prompting renowned Peruvian author Mario Vargas Llosa to criticize them for wreaking "political and social disorder"[4] on the continent. Meanwhile, the Zapatista National Liberation Army leadership was setting up local indigenous governments in Chiapas, Mexico, and openly airing the possibility of a new independent indigenous state that would include large parts of southern Mexico and neighbouring Guatemala.

The situation of the 40 million indigenous people of the Americas was becoming a significant geopolitical and security concern for OAS member states, in particular the United States. Indigenous peoples' movements were spearheading opposition to the free-market, free-trade policies of the Bush administration and the white elites in their own countries. Bolivian writer Alvaro Garcia Linera spoke of a "mountain chain of indigenous uprisings in reaction to U.S. neoliberalism in Latin America, the most radical thing that has appeared in thirty years."[5]

In her confirmation hearings as U.S. secretary of state in January 2005, Condoleezza Rice reflected the heightened awareness of the failings of the economic reforms in Latin America to address the unique needs and aspirations of its indigenous population: "We in the United States need to associate ourselves ... with the struggle of those who are trying to overcome stratification. We can't just associate ourselves with an old order. We have to be concerned about the indigenous peoples who are trying to find their rightful place in a political and economic system. Our own history should tell us that that's an extremely important task ahead."[6]

An organization long known for its defence of the status quo, the OAS found itself under pressure to seek accommodation of indigenous peoples. In June 2005, with Clément Chartier in attendance at the OAS General Assembly in Fort Lauderdale, Florida, the foreign ministers of the Americas urged an acceleration of the working group negotiations with a view to the prompt adoption of the American Declaration on the Rights of Indigenous Peoples. On 18 December 2005, Evo Morales, an Ayamara coca farmer and radical socialist leader, was elected president of Bolivia, the first indigenous head of state of South America's poorest country since the Spanish Conquest more than 450 years earlier.

By the time Chartier arrived in the Brazilian capital of Brasilia on 18 March 2006, to represent the Métis Nation in the Caucus of the Indigenous Peoples of the Americas, the working group had made considerable headway on the draft declaration. Members had reached agreement on a number of provisions and had significantly narrowed the areas of difference in the remainder of the document. During the seventh meeting of negotiations[7] that followed the indigenous caucus, the working group targeted the critical issues of political autonomy/self-government and lands and territories that had to be resolved before the declaration could be sent to the OAS for adoption.

The importance of his work at the international level was brought home to Chartier in June 2006 when he revisited the homeland of the Miskito people in Nicaragua. Twenty years after he and Miskito guerrilla commander Brooklyn Rivera had narrowly escaped death at the hands of the Sandinista government, Chartier was welcomed by Rivera at his regional government headquarters in Puerta Cabezsa. Since the end of the Nicaraguan civil war in 1988, the Miskito had made significant progress in self-government and the economic development of their lands. Now, as Chartier and his MNC delegation were warmly received by communities such as Koom, Bilwaskarma, and Bilwi, the Miskito people could renew their friendship with the Canadian Métis leader who had brought their plight to the United Nations along with their aspirations for a land base and self-government.

THE MÉTIS NATION AND SELF-DETERMINATION

Predictably, the foremost barrier to a final consensus on the declarations of the UN and the OAS remained the application of the right of self-determination to indigenous peoples. The United States, Australia, and New Zealand were of the view that the right of self-determination under international law included, under certain circumstances, the right to secession and full independence. These countries sought to change the draft United Nations Declaration on the Rights of Indigenous Peoples to ensure that the right of self-determination could be exercised within an existing nation-state and without impacting on the political unity or territorial integrity of any state. Toward this end, the U.S. National Security Council had instructed the U.S. delegations to the working groups of the UN and the OAS to support use of the term "internal self-determination" in both declarations on indigenous rights.[8]

With the UN Human Rights Council preparing to hold a vote on the Declaration on the Rights of Indigenous People by the end of June 2006, Canada's position—which had long been supportive under previous governments—suddenly shifted. Minister of Indian Affairs Jim Prentice stated that Canada would now vote against the declaration unless it was changed. He claimed that it contained provisions that were inconsistent with the Canadian Charter of Rights and Freedoms, the Constitution Act, 1982, and Canada's land claims policies.[9]

On 29 June 2006, Canada and Russia became the only countries on the forty-seven-member UN Human Rights Council (the United States, Australia, and New Zealand being non-members) to vote against adoption of the UN Declaration on the Rights of Indigenous Peoples. By a vote of thirty in favour and two against (with twelve abstentions and three absent), the council adopted the declaration and sent it to the UN General Assembly for consideration. In explaining his country's new-found opposition, the representative of Canada cited language in the declaration that allegedly could give indigenous peoples the right of veto on land and natural resource issues or open up claims to lands already ceded.

In a letter to Jim Prentice on 31 July 2006, MNC president Clément Chartier stated that the concerns underlying "... Canada's recent and disappointing reversal of position on the UN Declaration ..." resulted from a fundamental misunderstanding of the aspirations of Canada's Aboriginal peoples, the Métis Nation in particular. He pointed out the disingenuous nature of Canada's assertion that the declaration was inconsistent with Canada's land claims policies, reminding Prentice that the Métis people had been pursuing inclusion in the federal government's comprehensive claims policy since its inception in the 1970s, without success. In fact, Chartier noted, the Métis had undertaken land claims litigation on the Prairies in order to be included in that policy.

As for the issue of self-determination, Chartier stated that the history of the Métis Nation in Canada proved that the application of this principle to indigenous populations would not threaten Canada's political unity and territorial integrity:

> The Manitoba Act and the establishment of the Province of Manitoba in 1870 resulted from the exercise of the right of self-determination by the Métis people through their provisional government under Riel. In the process, the Métis people rejected the options of negotiating statehood with the United States or the establishment of an independent Republic of the Métis Nation that had been called for earlier in the resistance to the arbitrary transfer of Rupert's Land to Canada. Prior to the 1885 Resistance in Saskatchewan, the Métis people, through their second provi-

sional government, once again sought responsible government within the Canadian federation. Our positions and proposals on self-government ever since have been designed to fit within and strengthen the Canadian federation, the most notable being the Métis Nation Accord that we developed with Prime Minister Mulroney as part of the Charlottetown Accord initiative.

... In short, the Métis people do have the right to self-determination as defined in international law but have chosen not to exercise this right in full. Our preference ... has been and continues to be to work within the Canadian federation and a process such as that set out in the Canada-Métis Nation Framework Agreement in order to achieve our objectives.[10]

With Canada, the United States, Russia, Australia, and New Zealand all stating their intention to oppose the declaration on the rights of indigenous peoples at the Sixty-First UN General Assembly in December 2006, it was unclear whether there was sufficient support at the United Nations in favour of the declaration's adoption or whether further debate and negotiation were required to reach a consensus. The stated support for the declaration from many of the 191 UN members was questionable in itself. Some had a long history of signing, then failing to adhere to human rights instruments through self-serving interpretations that rendered the rights meaningless. Others supported the draft declaration with the caveat that they had no indigenous population of their own or that their entire population was indigenous. Within this context, countries such as Canada, the United States, Australia, and New Zealand had more difficulty with the declaration precisely because they generally did adhere to the documents they signed and did recognize their indigenous populations.

In mid-November 2006, the Third Committee of the Sixty-First General Assembly took up the issue of whether to forward the declaration to the plenary session of the UN General Assembly for adoption in December. In addition to the controversial self-determination clause, the Third Committee had to deal with the concerns of several African states—which had generally not participated in the working groups over the years—that the lack of a definition of who is indigenous could cause instability in their multi-ethnic and multi-tribal states. On 28 November 2006, the Third Committee adopted by a majority vote a resolution from the southern African state of Namibia to delay consideration of the declaration by the General Assembly, possibly until the following September.

In the wake of the setback, representatives of indigenous peoples committed themselves to resolve the concerns of Namibia and other countries without weakening the rights in the declaration. A disappointed Clément Chartier, who had attended the third committee deliberations in New York City, stressed the need for future work on the declaration: "It is important that we continue to work with Indigenous peoples and the many states who are willing to champion the Declaration. It is crucial that we meet the concerns expressed so that Indigenous peoples will be welcomed into the fold of humanity as equally deserving of justice, dignity and human rights."[11]

Undoubtedly, the road ahead would not be free of obstacles, but it appeared that the international community was moving, slowly but inexorably, toward the recognition of indigenous rights and its profound implications. When adopted, the United Nations Declaration on the Rights of Indigenous Peoples and the American Declaration on the Rights of Indigenous Peoples will be the most comprehensive statements of the rights of indigenous peoples ever adopted and an unprecedented recognition of collective human rights in international law. By recognizing the right of self-determination of indigenous peoples within the countries in which they live, these declarations will make them the only peoples in the world to hold such political status.

Chapter 18

PROSPECTS FOR MÉTIS SELF-GOVERNMENT

*I*n the quarter-century since its inception, the setbacks and reversals of the MNC may have outnumbered its victories—what in Métis parlance is known as the two-step, "one step forward, two steps back"—but ultimately it will be the will and strength of the Métis as a national community rather than any process that determines its political future. In this sense, Clément Chartier and the other founders of the MNC can point with considerable pride to the achievements of the organization as an expression and instrument of Métis nationalism. Through the MNC, the Métis have succeeded in conveying their sense of unity as a people and a nation to Canada and the international community. Pointedly, in his comments at the Kelowna Conference, Prime Minister Paul Martin addressed First Nations, Inuit, and *the* Métis Nation.

History and the dictates of Canadian federalism compelled the Métis to build strong provincial associations in
order to deal effectively with provincial governments,
particularly during the decades when there was no relationship between Ottawa and the Métis. The MNC has
enabled the Métis to pursue those interests that transcend the provincial boundaries partitioning their historical homeland. Hardly the "incohesive assortment of heterogeneous groups" portrayed by their detractors, the
Métis people have re-emerged as a nation, a people with
a common history, culture, territory, and the political will
to be self-governing. Their sense of nationalism has made
and will make the MNC more than the sum of its parts.

FORMS OF MÉTIS GOVERNMENT

Any assessment of the prospects and means of accommodating Métis aspirations
for political autonomy in the future must recognize that the forms of Métis government that may emerge will vary according to the physical circumstances of and
challenges faced by the Métis people. There are basically two forms of government
available for Métis: territorial and non-territorial. The main differences between
these forms lie in the applicability and scope of their laws and regulations.

The laws of territorial government apply to everyone within the boundaries of the
territory by virtue of their residence. The laws of non-territorial government, by contrast, would apply only to those who chose to participate in its affairs; any requirement
for Métis people off a land base to submit to the authority of and receive services from
such a Métis government would infringe on their right to equality with non-
Aboriginal individuals in the same communities. The prospect of large-scale "opting
out" of self-government is slight because those meeting the Métis Nation's citizenship
criteria—based on ancestral connection to and *acceptance by* Métis communities—
would, by definition, likely want to be part of a self-governing Métis Nation.

The scope of the laws and regulations of Métis governments will vary according to
the needs of their constituents and their own capacities. Territorial governments are
responsible for many basic infrastructure needs (roads, water, sewerage, etc.) that would
not figure in the mandate of non-territorial governments since their constituents, as
residents and taxpayers of provinces and municipalities, would receive these services
from non-Métis governments. On the other hand, given their larger population base,
non-territorial governments would be responsible for matters that would generally
exceed the financial and human resources capacity of land-based governments.
Examples include the postsecondary education institutions, communications systems,

and business development services that the MNC governing members administer on a province-wide basis.

The demand for territorial forms of self-government will be strongest on the Prairies, home to most of the Métis local associations. Many are located in predominantly Métis communities or in mixed communities with significant Métis populations. Stretching north and northwest from Winnipeg through the north-central regions of Saskatchewan and Alberta and into the Peace River district, these Métis communities, despite the façade of local self-government in the form of quasi-municipal governments, are largely governed directly by provincial governments that own the surrounding land base and natural resources.

To date, two forms of territorial government, one "ethnic," the other "public, or non-ethnic," have figured in discussions affecting these communities. The foremost example of an ethnic form of territorial government is found in the regional and local governments on the Métis settlements in Alberta, the only significant Métis land base in Canada. These governments were created by and derive their legislative authority from provincial legislation. Their delegated powers include those normally associated with municipal government, but they also include certain powers—ownership and regulation of settlement lands, co-management of natural resources with the province, and administration of a dispute-resolution tribunal—normally associated with senior governments within the Canadian federation.

Provincial governments on the Prairies have suggested the possibility of accommodating Métis aspirations for self-government through a devolution of authority to public or non-ethnic forms of regional government such as Saskatchewan's Northern Administration District. The assumption has been that the Métis, by virtue of their numbers within the boundaries of these governments, could exert considerable influence over their decisions. Manitoba has explored the possibility of revising its legislation to delegate more authority to public institutions of local government in predominantly Métis areas, including the regulation of land and resource development within a certain radius of these communities, and to provide block funding for certain programs and services.

Given past experience with public forms of government, namely the original Métis-majority Province of Manitoba, Métis response has been cool. Unlike the public form of territorial government in Nunavut that the Inuit can control by virtue of a majority population living behind natural, geographical barriers, there can be no similar guarantee for the Métis population in the mid-Canada corridor with its large resource development projects and sudden influx of workers. Nor can Métis, as the situation now stands, fall back on constitutionally guaranteed land claims agreements, as can the Inuit in the remote event that they lose their majority in Nunavut.

The foremost impediment to the creation of territorial forms of Métis government is the exclusion of the Métis from the federal government's land claims resolution process. On 3 April 2006, two of Canada's most renowned land claims lawyers, Tom Berger and Jim Aldridge, commenced opening arguments in the monumental *MMF v. Attorney General of Canada and Attorney General of Manitoba*, seeking court declarations that thirty-one federal and nine provincial enactments (statutes and Orders-in-Council) affecting the Métis land rights sections of the Manitoba Act, 1870, were unconstitutional. The MMF statement of claim states that achievement of a land base for the Métis is the goal of the MMF: "In the pursuit of this goal, it would be greatly to the advantage of the Métis, in seeking to achieve a land claims agreement pursuant to subsection 35(3) of the Constitution Act, 1982, to obtain the declarations sought in this action."[1] The trial in Manitoba's Court of Queen's Bench can be seen as a way station on the long road to the Supreme Court of Canada or to an out-of-court land claims agreement that, given the precedent of contemporary claims settlements, would include the powers of self-government on Métis lands.

The demand for non-territorial forms of self-government will be strongest in the cities of western Canada. According to Canada's Standing Senate Committee on

Former MMF president John Morrisseau, between Clément Chartier and Audrey Poitras, awarded Order of the Métis Nation before commencement of *MMF v. Canada and Manitoba*, Winnipeg, 1 April 2006.
(Robert McDonald/MNC)

Aboriginal Peoples,[2] "Of the Aboriginal peoples, the Métis are the most likely to be urban residents and move frequently. Almost 70% of all Métis live in Canada's urban areas: one third of all Métis live in just five cities—Winnipeg, Edmonton, Vancouver, Calgary and Saskatoon." Figures from the 2001 Canadian Census indicate, for selected metropolitan areas, the number of people identifying themselves as Métis among the total Aboriginal identity population:

Metropolitan Area	Total Aboriginal Identity Population	Métis Single Response Identity	Per cent Métis
Winnipeg	55,755	31,395	56.3%
Edmonton	40,930	21,065	51.5%
Prince Albert	11,640	5,950	51.1%
Calgary	21,915	10,575	48.3%
Saskatoon	20,275	8,305	41.0%
Regina	15,685	5,990	38.2%
Vancouver	36,860	12,505	33.9%
Toronto	20,300	5,095	25.1%
Thunder Bay	8,200	1,795	21.9%
Average	25,729	11,408	44.3%

Tom Berger (left) and Jim Aldridge, counsel for Métis in *MMF v. Canada and Manitoba*, Winnipeg, 3 April 2006. (Robert McDonald/MNC)

The foremost impediments to the establishment of non-territorial forms of Métis government have been two misconceptions. The first is that self-government requires an ethnically exclusive land base to which the laws of the government will apply, in effect rendering the urban Métis incapable of exercising it. In fact, Canada has a long history of providing education, health, and social services to linguistic and religious minorities living in the general population (rather than on a linguistically or religiously exclusive land base) through their own institutions and, in some cases, their own legal authority.[3] In the case of religious minorities, the constitutional entrenchment of denominational school rights in the Constitution Act, 1867, forced some provincial governments to enact legislation for separate school systems, including the institutions and powers of separate school boards. These powers are extensive and include the setting of school fees and taxes (collected by municipal governments) and the responsibility for policies and procedures, financial management, and the planning, design, and delivery of education programs in accordance with provincial standards.

The second misconception mistakes the traditional mobility of the Métis people for lack of community,[4] viewing the urban Métis as migrants from rural and hinterland areas who lack the cohesion and infrastructure to handle their own affairs. This view ignores the roots of the Métis Nation in the cities of the West—many of which began as fur trade settlements with Métis majorities—where the Métis community presence has been continuous. The first Métis provisional government in Red River—in 1869, one of the largest settlements on the plains of North America west of the Mississippi and north of the Missouri, with a population of 11,400, of which 86 per cent was Métis—was, in effect, the government of today's Greater Winnipeg area.

Too often, particularly during periods when there is little engagement of their ministers with Métis leaders, federal bureaucrats, from the Privy Council Office down to regional offices responsible for implementing Urban Aboriginal Strategy (UAS) programs, tend to see and deal with the urban Métis through this "migrant" or "off-reserve" prism. Moreover, the lack of effective representation for off-reserve Indians (both status and non-status) has caused these groups to oppose the "distinctions-based approach" to program funding through First Nations and Métis Nation organizations, thereby bolstering the tendency of UAS planners to seek "pan-Aboriginal" solutions encompassing off-reserve Indians and Métis. (In the *Misquadis* case in 2003,[5] the Federal Court of Appeal upheld the judgment of the Federal Court that Human Resources Development Canada had violated the equality provisions of the Canadian Charter of Rights and Freedoms by refusing to enter into Aboriginal Human Resources Development Agreements with off-reserve Indians, such as those concluded with First Nations, the MNC, and its governing members).

Instead of channelling funding through well-established institutions under the authority of MNC governing members (for example, those involved in Métis urban housing, child and family services, educational training, and business development), the UAS has established government-appointed, pan-Aboriginal committees, clearly unaccountable to the people whom they serve. These pan-Aboriginal regional councils have treated Métis Nation urban governing bodies as third-party, non-government organizations. Not surprisingly, the federal government's own evaluation of its Urban Aboriginal Strategy acknowledges its "limited impact on the lives of urban Aboriginals" and the reluctance of Métis and First Nations organizations "to work in partnerships under the current structure."[6]

INSTITUTIONS OF MÉTIS GOVERNMENT

As the situation now stands, the Métis, unlike the First Nations and Inuit, do not (Métis settlements aside) have legally constituted governments to receive any powers that may result from a process of devolution or decentralization. While providing for an expansion of the institutional and fiscal capacity of the MNC and its governing members to deliver programs and services, the Canada-Métis Nation Framework Agreement and the Kelowna Accord stopped short of vesting them with the legislative authority of governments. In the future, the MNC and its governing members can be expected to push beyond the existing models of governance in pursuit of legal authority. Doing so will enable them to make the transition from organizations to governments of the Métis Nation. Increasingly, the focus of talks will shift from institutional and fiscal capacity to developing the jurisdictional capacities of these institutions.

The cornerstone of any federal legislation for Métis self-government, such as the "Canada-Métis Nation Relations Act" proposed by Clément Chartier in a letter to Prime Minister Paul Martin on 12 September 2004, will be a Métis Nation Constitution. This act would recognize the right of Métis people to govern themselves under a Métis Nation Constitution that would establish the principles, institutions, and powers of Métis government. The federal legislation would vest the Métis Nation Constitution with some initial powers, the foremost being identification and registration of Métis Nation members (citizens) and responsibility for the portion of federal Aboriginal programs and services currently available to Métis people. Additional powers to be vested in the Métis Nation Constitution would be derived from negotiated agreements (through processes such as the bilateral Canada-Métis Nation Framework Agreement and the multilateral Métis Nation Multilateral Forum).

The Métis Nation Constitution would establish the institutions of Métis government in Canada. Métis governments would derive their authority to legislate for and regulate the affairs of the Métis Nation from this Constitution—the source of Métis law—rather than from a delegation of powers from the federal and/or provincial governments. The "Canada-Métis Nation Relations Act" would require the federal government to facilitate the ability of these governments to fulfill their responsibilities by way of an unconditional annual grant to support their core operations, as well as transfer payments to ensure services and programs for Métis people comparable to those available to other Aboriginal peoples.

With Métis governments assuming law-making and enforcement roles, the Métis Nation Constitution will have to establish judicial bodies to adjudicate and resolve disputes arising from the exercise of powers by the MNC and its governing members or their successor bodies. The Métis Settlements Appeal Tribunal in Alberta set a precedent for this type of judiciary. One potentially contentious area in which an MNC tribunal could be expected to settle disputes would be in the identification and registration of Métis Nation members.

The MNC and its governing members would probably serve as the initial or interim governments to be established under the Métis Nation Constitution. The MNC's governing members have served as the closest thing to self-government by way of the representation, the broad range of operations, and the democratic institutions and electoral processes they have offered on a province-wide basis. The attainment of self-government powers, however, may create conditions that would challenge their ability to retain representation, as a commonality of interest develops and strengthens among communities within the provinces, potentially leading to new government structures. In the event of successful land claims litigation and negotiated agreements, residents of the affected communities will expect political representation and delivery of services from their local Métis government on the land base. Likewise, urban Métis may turn to their Métis municipal councils to provide these functions.

As the MNC is called upon to make decisions that impact directly at the grassroots level, the people affected will likely want to participate directly in the election of national representatives, almost certainly if the MNC or its successor body is vested with law-making powers. Given the distinct interests and perspectives of the residents of Métis land bases (and past experience with the Métis settlements), it is unlikely that they would agree to representation within the MNC through its governing members. More likely, they would seek direct representation within national decision-making institutions, as had Elmer Ghostkeeper in his quest for a directly elected Métis Parliament with distinct electoral constituencies for land-based communities. A similar commonality of interest may drive urban Métis groups into seeking their own direct and distinct representation within the MNC, perhaps by way of Métis urban electoral constituencies.

The Métis Nation Constitution would have to be amended to enable the electoral and institutional changes that would keep Métis governments representative, fair, and accountable for the expenditure of funds associated with their increased responsibilities. A political reorganization of the Métis Nation at the national level is a likely scenario. Should a consensus emerge in favour of the direct election of national representatives, the Métis Nation Constitution would establish a federal system of governance with a division of powers between the MNC and its governing members, each sovereign in its areas of jurisdiction. An MNC tribunal would resolve the jurisdictional disputes that inevitably will arise between the two levels of government.

Political reorganization at the national level will take a different form if the provincial associations experience a withering away of authority to local territorial and urban governments. In this scenario, a possible outcome would see responsibility for programs, services, and institutions beyond the capacity of local governments assumed by the MNC and provided on a national basis. Thus, the dream of nationalists for a Métis Parliament, cabinet, and administration in Batoche, the government of a united Métis homeland, may finally be fulfilled.

STRATEGY FOR MÉTIS SELF-GOVERNMENT

If there is one strategy that has consistently guided the Métis nationalist movement in its complex dealings with Canada during the past quarter-century, it is a singularly simple one: use whatever means are at hand to achieve the objective of a self-governing Métis Nation within the Canadian federation. Before constitutional patriation, with Aboriginal rights circumscribed by narrow judicial interpretations and, for the Métis, not recognized at all, Métis nationalists had launched a historic court battle to fulfill the promises of the Manitoba Act, the treaty between Ottawa and the Métis Nation that had given birth to western Canada. Patriation and the Aboriginal peoples' sections of the Constitution Act had opened new tracks. Section 37 would lead to Ottawa and the first ministers conferences, then to Charlottetown and the Métis Nation Accord, and finally to Kelowna. Section 35 would lead to the Supreme Court of Canada and *Powley*.

On 12 June 2006, MMF counsel began its final legal arguments in *MMF v. Attorney General of Canada and Attorney General of Manitoba*. For Clément Chartier, the case represented the opportunity for historical vindication and a way to move forward, but it was also a sobering reality. Barring an unexpected breakthrough in multilateral talks that the current government in Ottawa did not appear eager to initiate, he had to accept that the establishment of a Métis land base and self-government would probably evolve out of a patchwork of arrangements flowing from judicial intervention and subsequent intergovernmental negotiations.

Moreover, his own experience with federal governments from that of Pierre Elliott Trudeau to that of Stephen Harper had driven home the most important element of strategy when dealing with Canada: not only "getting it in writing" but also getting it guaranteed. Too many agreements or would-be agreements on self-government had fallen by the wayside with the intervention of partisan politics. The Métis need a mechanism that forces government to act. Once powers are transferred, the Métis need a guarantee that these powers will not be rescinded unilaterally. Furthermore, there is a need to entrench a claim on the public treasury to ensure that part of public revenues are reserved for Métis self-government.

There are four principal methods of constitutionalizing Métis self-government.

- The first method is by way of a constitutional amendment to create a third order of government for Aboriginal peoples, a prospect that has faded steadily since the time it was raised.

- The second and more likely method is to build self-government arrangements into land claims agreements that could be constitutionally protected as "treaties" pursuant to section 35(3) of the Constitution Act, 1982. The avenue to these agreements could run through the land claims litigation on the Prairies and efforts to resolve outstanding Métis land claims in framework agreement discussions.

- The third method is to conclude a tripartite agreement pursuant to the inherent right policy and, with the support of all the parties to the agreement, constitutionally protect it as a "treaty" under section 35(1) of the Constitution Act, 1982. The most likely provincial candidate in this process would be Alberta. In the past, it has supported a constitutional amendment to entrench Métis title to settlement lands in the Constitution of Canada. Moreover, it was the only province to recognize Métis harvesting rights on a province-wide basis after *Powley* and, unlike have-not provinces such as Manitoba and Saskatchewan, does not have to worry about a fiscal imbalance with Ottawa affecting its ability to make Métis-related expenditures.

- Failing these three methods, there is also the possibility of litigating Métis self-government as an "existing" Aboriginal right under section 35(1). On the surface, the site-specific, activity-specific test requirements for proving section 35 Aboriginal rights appear to limit or even preclude the affirmation of Métis self-government as an enforceable "existing" Aboriginal right. On the other hand, in its "purposive reading" of section 35, the Supreme Court of Canada has surmounted what has been called the foremost obstacle to the recognition of Métis rights: the refusal of the state to look at the Métis people in historical terms. Perhaps therein lies the answer.

Simply put, the Métis of Red River and the North-West spurned the protection of the Crown as a price for retaining some of their land and resource rights because it thwarted their ability to be self-governing. In the end, Canada used the Métis demand for more—that is, responsible government for the West in the form of Métis-majority provinces—as an excuse to give them less, much less. In their refusal to become wards through the paternalistic and restrictive treaty and reserve system, the Métis of the nineteenth century were not renouncing their rights as an Aboriginal people any more than Métis nationalists in twentieth-century constitutional negotiations were renouncing their rights as an Aboriginal people when they argued their case outside the context of "existing" Aboriginal and treaty rights. In the *Blais* decision, the Supreme Court of Canada found that "the stark historic fact is that the Crown viewed its obligations to Indians, whom it considered its wards, as different from its obligations to the Métis, who were its negotiating partners in the entry of Manitoba into Confederation." As a historical nation, not a tribe, the Métis were and remain in the vanguard of asserting self-government rights as an Aboriginal people in Canada.

The Supreme Court of Canada has determined that the purpose and the promise of section 35 are to protect practices that were historically important features of distinctive Métis communities and that persist in the present day as integral elements of their Métis culture. Self-government is and has always been the one practice most integral to the survival of the Métis as a distinct Aboriginal people. Proof of this persistence lies in the continuum of Métis nationalist leaders—Cuthbert Grant, Louis Riel, Gabriel Dumont, Malcolm Norris, Jim Brady, Howard Adams, Harry Daniels, John Morrisseau, Jim Sinclair, Elmer Ghostkeeper, Yvon Dumont, and Clément Chartier—and the quest to realize the destiny of the new nation in the country of its conception.

APPENDICES

APPENDIX A: THE BATTLE OF SEVEN OAKS

Would you like to hear me sing
Of a true and recent thing?
It was June nineteen, the band of Bois-Brûlés
Arrived that day,
Oh the brave warriors they!

We took three foreigners prisoners when
We came to the place called Frog, Frog Plain.
They were men who'd come from Orkney,
Who'd come, you see,
To rob our country.

Well, we were just about to unhorse
When we heard two of us give, give voice.
Two of our men cried, "Hey! Look back, look back!
The Anglo-Sack
Coming for to attack"

Now we like honourable men did act,
Sent an ambassador—yes, in fact!
"Monsieur Governor! Would you like to stay?
A moment spare—
There's something we'd like to say."

Governor, Governor, full of ire.
"Soldiers!" he cries. "Fire! Fire!"
So they fire the first and their muskets roar!
They almost kill
Our ambassador!
When we went galloping, galloping by
Governor thought that he would try
For to chase and frighten us Bois-Brûlés.
Catastrophe!
Dead on the ground he lay.

You should have seen those Englishmen—
Bois-Brûlés chasing them, chasing them.
From bluff to bluff they stumbled that day
While the Bois-Brûlés
Shouted "Hurray!"

Tell, oh tell me who made up this song?
Why it's our own poet, Pierre Falcon.
Yes, she was written, this song of praise
For the victory
We won this day.
Yes, she was written, this song of praise—
Come sing the glory
Of the Bois-Brûlés.

Source: Margaret Arnett MacLeod, comp. and ed., *Songs of Old Manitoba*. Toronto: Ryerson Press, 1959, 5–9. Translated by James Reaney.

APPENDIX B: LIST OF RIGHTS OF RIEL'S PROVISIONAL GOVERNMENT, 1870

1. That the territories heretofore known as Rupert's Land and Northwest, shall not enter into the confederation of the Dominion, except as a province, to be styled and known as the province of Assiniboia, and with all the rights and privileges common to the different provinces of the Dominion.

2. That we have two representatives in the Senate and four in the House of Commons of Canada, until such time as an increase of population entitles the province to a greater representation.

3. That the province of Assiniboia shall not be held liable at any time for any portion of the public debt of the Dominion contracted before the date the said province shall have entered the confederation, unless the said province shall have first received from the Dominion the full amount for which the said province is to be held liable.

4. That the sum of eighty thousand dollars be paid annually by the Dominion Government to the Local Legislature of the province.

5. That all properties, rights and privileges enjoyed by the people of this Province up to the date of our entering into the confederation be respected, and that the arrangement and confirmation of all customs, usages and privileges be left exclusively to the Local Legislature.

6. That during the term of five years, the province of Assiniboia shall not be subjected to any direct taxation, except such as may be imposed by the Local Legislature for municipal or local purposes.

7. That a sum of money equal to eighty cents per head of the population of this Province be paid annually by the Canadian Government to the Local Legislature of the said Province, until such time as the said population shall have increased to six hundred thousand.

8. That the Local Legislature shall have the right to determine the qualifications of members to represent this Province in the Parliament of Canada, and in the Local Legislature.

9. That in this Province, with the exception of uncivilized and unsettled Indians, every male native citizen who has attained the age of twenty-one years; and every foreigner, being a British subject, who has attained the same, and has resided three years in the province, and is a householder; and every foreigner, other than a British subject, who has resided here during the same period, being a householder and having taken the oath of allegiance, shall be entitled to vote at the election of members for the Local Legislature and for the Canadian Parliament. It being understood that this article be subject to amendment exclusively by the Local Legislature.

10. That the bargain of the Hudson's Bay Company with respect to the transfer of the government of this country to the Dominion of Canada be annulled so far as it interferes with the rights of the people of Assiniboia, and so far as it would affect our future relations with Canada.

11. That the Local Legislature of the province of Assiniboia shall have full control over all the public lands of the province, and the right to annul all acts or arrangements made or entered into with reference to the public lands of Rupert's Land and the Northwest, now called the province of Assiniboia.

12. That the Government of Canada appoint a commissioner of engineers to explore the various districts of the province of Assiniboia, and to lay before the Local Legislature a report of the mineral wealth of the province within five years from the date of our entering into confederation.

13. That treaties be concluded between Canada and the different Indian tribes of the province of Assiniboia by and with the advice and co-operation of the Local Legislature of this Province.

14. That an uninterrupted steam communication from Lake Superior to Fort Garry be guaranteed to be completed within the space of five years.

15. That all public buildings, bridges, roads, and other public works be at the cost of the Dominion treasury.

16. That the English and French languages be common in the Legislature and in the Courts, and that all public documents, as well as all acts of the Legislature, be published in both languages.

17. That whereas the French and English speaking people of Assiniboia are so equally divided as to numbers, yet so united in their interests, and so connected by commerce, family connections, and other political and social relations, that it has happily been found impossible to bring them into hostile collision, although repeated attempts have been made by designing strangers, for reasons known to themselves, to bring about so ruinous and disastrous an event.

And whereas after all the trouble and apparent dissensions of the past, the result of misunderstanding among themselves, they have, as soon as the evil agencies referred to above were removed, become as united and friendly as ever; therefore as a means to strengthen this union and friendly feeling among all classes, we deem it expedient and advisable,

That the Lieutenant-Governor, who may be appointed for the province of Assiniboia, should be familiar with both the English and French languages.

18. That the judges of the Superior Court speak the English and French languages.

19. That all debts contracted by the Provisional government of the territory of the Northwest, now called Assiniboia, in consequence of the illegal and inconsiderate measures adopted by Canadian officials to bring about a civil war in our midst, be paid out of the Dominion treasury, and that none of the members of the Provisional government, or any of those acting under them, be in any way held liable or responsible with regard to the movement or any of the actions which led to the present negotiations.

20. That in view of the present exceptional position of Assiniboia, duties upon goods imported into the province shall, except in the case of spirituous liquors, continue as at present for at least three years from the date of our entering the confederation, and for such further time as may elapse until there be uninterrupted railroad communication between Winnipeg and St. Paul, and also steam communication between Winnipeg and Lake Superior.

APPENDIX C: SECTIONS 31 AND 32 OF THE MANITOBA ACT, 1870

31. And whereas, it is expedient, toward the extinguishment of the Indian Title to the lands in the province, to appropriate a portion of such ungranted lands, to the extent of one million four hundred thousand acres thereof, for the benefit of the families of the half-breed residents, it is hereby enacted, that, under regulations to be from time to time made by the Governor General in Council, the Lieutenant-Governor shall select such lots or tracts in such parts of the province as he may deem expedient, to the extent aforesaid, and divide the same among the children of the half-breed heads of families residing in the province at the time of the said transfer to Canada, and the same shall be granted to the said children respectively, in such mode and on such conditions as to settlement and otherwise, as the Governor General in Council may from time to time determine.

32. For the quieting of titles, and assuring to the settlers in the province the peaceable possession of the lands now held by them, it is enacted as follows:

1. All grants of land in freehold made by the Hudson's Bay Company up to the eighth day of March, in the year 1869, shall, if required by the owner, be confirmed by grant from the Crown.

2. All grants of estates less than freehold in land made by the Hudson's Bay Company up to the eighth day of March aforesaid, shall, if required by the owner, be converted into an estate in freehold by grant from the Crown.

3. All titles by occupancy with the sanction and under the licence and authority of the Hudson's Bay Company up to the eighth day of March aforesaid, of land in that part of the province in which the Indian title has been extinguished, shall, if required by the owner, be converted into an estate in freehold by grant from the Crown.

4. All persons in peaceable possession of tracts of land at the time of the transfer to Canada, in those parts of the province in which the Indian title has not been extinguished, shall have the right of pre-emption of the same, on such terms and conditions as may be determined by the Governor in Council.

5. The Lieutenant-Governor is hereby authorized, under regulations to be made from time to time by the Governor General in Council, to make all such provisions for ascertaining and adjusting on fair and equitable terms, the rights of Common, and rights of cutting Hay held and enjoyed by the settlers in the province, and for the commutation of the same by grants of land from the Crown.

APPENDIX D: RESOLUTION OF THE HOUSE OF COMMONS, 10 MARCH 1992

That this House take note that:

the Métis people of Rupert's Land and the North Western Territory through democratic structures and procedures took effective steps to maintain order and protect the lives, rights and property of the people of the Red River; and,

in 1870 under the leadership of Louis Riel, the Métis of the Red River adopted a List of Rights; and,

based on the List of Rights, Louis Riel negotiated the terms of the admission of Rupert's Land and the North Western Territory into the Dominion of Canada; and,

these terms for admission form part of the Manitoba Act; and,

after negotiating Manitoba's entry into Confederation, Louis Riel was elected thrice to the House of Commons; and,

in 1885, Louis Riel paid with his life for his leadership in a movement which fought for the mainte-nance of the rights and freedoms of the Métis people; and,

the Constitution Act, 1982, recognizes and affirms the existing Aboriginal and treaty rights of the Métis; and,

since the death of Louis Riel, the Métis people have honored his memory and continued his pur-poses in their honorable striving for the implementation of those rights; and,

1. That this House recognize the unique and historic role of Louis Riel as a founder of Manitoba, and his contribution in the development of Confederation; and,

2. That this House support by its actions the true attainment, both in principle and practice, of the constitutional rights of the Métis people.

NOTES

CHAPTER 1: THE RISE AND FALL OF THE NEW NATION

Sources for map on page 6: Hudson's Bay Company Archives, B. 154/k 1; Library and Archives Canada, National Map Collection NMC0190221; R. L. Gentilcore, ed., *Historical Atlas of Canada* vol. 2 (Toronto: University of Toronto Press, 1993); D. F. Johnson, *York Boats of the Hudson's Bay Company: Canada's Inland Armada* (Calgary: Fifth House, 2006); and J. Foster, "The Plains Metis," R. B. Morrison and C. R. Wilson, eds., *Native Peoples: The Canadian Experience* (Toronto: McClelland and Stewart, 1986) 315–403.

Sources for map on page 18: F. Tough, "Activities of Metis Scrip Commissions, 1885-1924," *Atlas of Saskatchewan*, K. Fung, ed. (Saskatoon: University of Saskatchewan, 1999) 61–62; F. Tough and L. Dorion, "'the claims of the Half-breeds ... have been finally closed': A Study of Treaty Ten and Treaty Five Adhesion Scrip," for The Royal Commission on Aboriginal Peoples (1993) [Published as a RCAP Research Report on CD ROM]; F. Tough, *"As their natural resources fail": Native People and the Economic History of Northern Manitoba, 1870–1930* (Vancouver: University of British Columbia Press, 1996) 114–42; Library and Archives Canada, RG 15, Scrip applications and correspondence files; and Alberta Land Information System 1:1,000,000 digital data for current Alberta Métis Settlements.

1.   Adams 1975, 111–12.

2.   Peterson and Brown 1985, 21.

3.   In this book, the term Métis will be used generally except when it is more appropriate to use the term "half-breed" to reflect its official use by government (i.e., half-breed land grants, half-breed commissions).

4.   Such measures included seizing tallow exports and furs, imposing heavy tariffs on American imports, publicly flogging Métis free trader Louis St. Denis (1836), and censoring letters of import (1844).

5.   A schoolmaster, explorer, and lawyer, Alexander Kennedy Isbister was born at Cumberland House, Rupert's Land, in June 1822. He explored the Mackenzie River basin (1838–42) while employed by the Hudson's Bay Company (later publishing a treatise on the geology of portions of the Arctic and northwestern North America). In 1842, he left for Britain to attend university and became a schoolmaster and a prolific author of textbooks, later obtaining his LL.B. from the University of London.

In 1847, Isbister presented a petition from the Red River population to the British government, accusing the Hudson's Bay Company of abusing its privileges to the detriment of the Métis, and lobbied unsuccessfully for a judicial inquiry into the HBC monopoly. In 1857, he again challenged the HBC monopoly before the British Parliamentary Select Committee. He died in London, England, on 28 May 1883, willing a personal fortune and 5,000 books to the University of Manitoba.

6.   Morton 1957, 117.

7.   The new provisional government also created a newspaper of its own called the *New Nation*.

8.   Earlier drafts of Métis demands did provide for compensation for extinguishment of Indian title. The first list, issued in November 1869, stipulated that the Indian title to the whole territory had to be paid for at once and that, due to their relationship with the Indians, a certain portion of the money had to be paid to the Métis. It also demanded that all Métis claims to land had to be con-

ceded and that 200 acres (80 hectares) should be granted to each of their children. Letter from John Young to John A. Macdonald, 18 November 1869, Macdonald Papers, Public Archives of Canada.

9.   The Métis clearly distinguished between their political status and that of the Indians in the new province. The ninth article in their List of Rights excluded Indians from voting.

10.   Public Archives of Canada, Macdonald Papers, John A. Macdonald to John Rose, 23 February 1870.

11.   Public Archives of Canada, microfilm C-1834, vol. 9, 729–45, Joseph Howe to Lieutenant-Governor A. G. Archibald.

12.   Sanders 1979, 10.

13.   Section 6 of the British North America Act, 1871 (now known as the Constitution Act, 1871), 34 and 35 Victoria, c. 28 U.K., provides that,

Except as provided by the third section of this Act, it shall not be competent for the Parliament of Canada to alter the provisions of the last-mentioned Act of the said Parliament in so far as it relates to the Province of Manitoba, or of any other Act hereafter establishing new Provinces in the said Dominion, subject always to the right of the Legislature of the Province of Manitoba to alter from time to time the provisions of any law respecting the qualification of electors and members of the Legislative Assembly and to make laws respecting elections in the said Province.

14.   Sprague 1981, 59.

15.   An Act to Remove Doubts as to the Construction of Section 31 of the Act 33 Victoria, c. 3, and to Amend Section 108 of the Dominion Lands Act, 36 Victoria, c. 38, S.C. 1873. (Sprague 1980, 435, Appendix B: Statutory Alterations to the Manitoba Act.)

16.   Sprague 1981, 60.

17.   Sprague 1981, 57.

18.   House of Commons Debates, 6 July 1885, 3113.

19.   Sprague 1981, 65.

20.   For further insight into the impact of the rebellion on Métis communities, see Heinemann, Larry, *An Investigation into the Origins and Development of the Métis Nation, the Rights of the Métis as an Aboriginal People, and their Relationship and Dealings with the Government of Canada: Research Report of the Association of Métis and Non-Status Indians of Saskatchewan.* Regina: Gabriel Dumont Institute, 1984.

21.   Métis and Non-Status Indian Constitutional Review Commission, 1981, 7.

22.   Brown 1980, 219.

Chapter 2: In Search of Representation

1.   Mainly to protect and promote the collective (Québécois or Métis) within Canada and to preserve the language and culture of these peoples.

2.   The work was translated by E. Maguet as *Hold High Your Heads: A History of the Métis Nation in Western Canada.* Winnipeg: Pemmican Publications, 1982.

3.   Sanders 1979, 16.

4.   A precedent for this type of scheme had been established with the St. Paul des Métis colony. In 1895, the federal government leased four townships of crown land in northeastern Alberta to the Oblate fathers for the establishment of a Métis agricultural colony. The colony failed to attract a sufficient number of Métis; those off the colony heard that promises of livestock and equipment to the first settlers had not been kept. Moreover, the fierce independence of the Métis settlers clashed with the religious discipline that lay at the heart of the Oblate mission for the colony. Despite the success of some of the Métis farmers—a list from colony records shows a Diom Laboucane with 1,200 cattle; an Elzear Poitras with 400 cattle and 300 horses; and a Lawrence Garneau with 400 cattle, 135 horses, a timber berth, and a sawmill—the Oblates shifted their plans for the colony to another more pliant clientele group, French Catholics from Quebec. In 1910, Ottawa terminated the Oblate lease at the request of the fathers and threw the colony open to homesteading, prompting the departure of most of the Métis residents, who sensed the hostility of the newcomers. See F. K. Hatt, "The Land Issue and the Mobilization of the Alberta Métis in the 1930s," *The Forgotten People: Métis and Non-Status Indian Land Claims*. Ottawa: Native Council of Canada, 1979.

5.   See *Alberta: Report of the Royal Commission on the Condition of the Half Breed Population of the Province of Alberta. Sessional Paper* 72. Edmonton: Government of the Province of Alberta, 1936.

6.   Sanders 1979, 17.

7.   The province amended the Métis Population Betterment Act to make it more restrictive and paternalistic. An amendment in 1940 strengthened the power of provincial ministers over settlement affairs, in the process deleting the preamble to the original act that provided for conferences and negotiations between the province and Métis representatives. A further amendment in 1952 changed the method of selection of the chairperson of each settlement council from one of election by fellow council members to one of appointment by the branch of the government department responsible for the settlements; of the remaining four members of council, all formerly elected, only two would continue to be elected by settlement membership; the other two would be appointed by the minister.

8.   Lussier and Sealey 1978, 190.

9.   Like many radicals of this period, Adams was influenced by Franz Fanon, the black psychiatrist and revolutionary from the French island of Martinique, whose works on the psychopathology of colonialism—*Black Skin, White Masks* (1952), *A Dying Colonialism* (1959), *The Wretched of the Earth* (1961), *Toward the African Revolution* (1964)—inspired independence and national liberation movements both in European colonies and among minority groups in the First World, including the Black Power and Red Power movements in North America and, most notably, the Black Panther Party. Adams' writings would include the books: *The Education of Canadians, 1800–1867: The Roots of Separatism* (1968); *Prison of Grass: Canada from the Native Point of View* (1975); *A History of the Métis of the Northwest* (1977); and *A Tortured People: The Politics of Colonization* (1995).

10.   Adams doubled as MSS President from 1969 to 1970 while working as a professor at the University of Saskatchewan. He subsequently taught at the University of California at Davis from 1975 until his retirement in 1988. During the 1990s he taught at a number of Canadian universities, lectured across Canada and in Europe on Aboriginal issues, and founded a Métis association in Vancouver. He died there on his eightieth birthday on 8 September 2001.

11.   Ottawa could disclaim any special responsibility for Métis and non-status Indians by dealing with their problems as part of regional disparities and rural poverty. Its largest special program for the Native Council of Canada (NCC) constituents, the Rural and Native Housing Program, lumped the Métis and non-status Indians in with poor rural whites.

12.   In 1973, Arab members of the Organization of Petroleum Exporting Countries (OPEC) triggered an energy crisis by stopping oil exports to countries supporting Israel during the Yom Kippur War.

During this period, OPEC members also used their dominant position in global energy markets to force a quadrupling of world oil prices. In 1979, revolution in Iran and the overthrow of the Shah led to a sharp decline in Iranian oil production and another spike in the oil price on world markets.

13. *Calder v. British Columbia (Attorney General)*, 1973, S.C.R. 313.

14. Slobodin 1966, 12.

15. Among their publications dealing with Métis land rights were *A Social History of the Manitoba Métis* by Émile Pelletier (1974); *The Métis: Canada's Forgotten People* by Bruce Sealey and Antoine Lussier (1975); and *Exploitation of Métis Lands* by Émile Pelletier (1975).

16. The three Maritime associations were the Native Council of Prince Edward Island, the Native Council of Nova Scotia, and the New Brunswick Métis and Non-status Indian Association.

CHAPTER 3: HARRY DANIELS AND THE QUEST FOR THE CONSTITUTION

1. Quebec premier Robert Bourassa had insisted on a constitutional provision for fiscal compensation for Quebec if it chose to opt out of federal programs in the provincial jurisdictional areas of social and cultural affairs.

2. "Federalism and the Métis Nation," brief of the Native Council of Canada to the Task Force on Canadian Unity, 2 March 1978, Ottawa. In Harry W. Daniels, *We are the New Nation*, Ottawa: Native Council of Canada, 1979, 5.

3. "The Métis: Cornerstone of Canadian Confederation," brief to the Special Joint Committee of the Senate and House of Commons on the Constitution, 23 August 1978. Ottawa. In Daniels, *We are the New Nation*, 13.

4. Harry W. Daniels, "The Need for a Founding Nations Conference," *Le Devoir*, 21 August 1978, 3. In Daniels, *We are the New Nation*, 53.

5. "The Métis and Multiculturalism," brief presented to the Third Canadian Conference on Multiculturalism, 27–29 October 1978, Ottawa. In Daniels, *We are the New Nation*, 51.

6. "The Rights of Historic National Minorities," brief to the First Ministers Conference on the Constitution, 30 October–1 November 1978, Ottawa. In Daniels, *We are the New Nation*, 48.

7. Speaking to the National Conference of Chiefs on the Constitution in Ottawa on 29 April 1980, Trudeau had appealed to Quebec delegates to vote "no" in the upcoming referendum. The next day Minister of Energy Marc Lalonde assured the Indians of seats at the constitutional bargaining table to deal with issues affecting them.

8. This possibility had prompted Daniels to tell the Steering Committee of the Continuing Committee of Ministers on the Constitution on 3 December 1979, "We hear from all quarters, not only from the federal government, but almost hysterically from provincial officials, 'Who are you?', or 'Why don't you define yourselves so that we can deal with you?' These questions appear at first glance to be profound, rational, even intelligent. Now we are tempted to ask, 'Who are you?' and 'Will you please justify your existence to us?' Every oppressed people who have tried to realize their destiny or to assert their reality on the larger society which dominates them, have been put down by these simple questions."

9. The subcommittee consisted of Jean Chrétien, the minister of justice, and his provincial counterparts from Manitoba, Saskatchewan, and Alberta.

10. Métis and Non-Status Indian Constitutional Review Commission, 1981, 1 [F219]. Hatfield's

comments carried particular irony as he would go on to become a champion of Aboriginal rights among the premiers.

11. "Proposed Resolution for Joint Address to Her Majesty the Queen Respecting the Constitution of Canada," tabled in the House of Commons on 6 October 1980.

12. Named after Michael Kirby, secretary to the cabinet for federal-provincial relations, the document presented options to the government on patriation strategy. The memorandum first appeared in the press during September's First Ministers Conference on the Constitution, having been leaked by Premier Hatfield.

13. The thrust of the NIB argument was that the imperial Crown, independent of the Government of Canada or the Crown in the right of Canada, had assumed responsibilities for the Indians under the Royal Proclamation of 1763, had negotiated treaties, and therefore had obligations to the Indians that hadn't been transferred to Canada. Patriation, according to the NIB, would arbitrarily shift those obligations to Canada and would violate the principles of negotiation and consent built into the Royal Proclamation. Therefore, the NIB insisted that the British Parliament should ensure that the protections offered by the imperial Crown be entrenched in the Constitution or should refuse patriation.

Provincial Indian associations from Alberta and British Columbia would take this argument to the British courts. In turning down the Indian claims against patriation on 28 January 1982, British judges ruled that British responsibilities had been transferred to Canada through the Statute of Westminster, 1931, if not before then. At the same time, Lord Denning encouraged Canada to honour past commitments to Indians, "so long as the sun rises and the rivers flow."

14. The author of this book, then constitutional policy adviser to Daniels.

CHAPTER 4: THE PITFALLS OF PATRIATION

1. Métis and Non-Status Indian Constitutional Review Commission 1981, 24 [C1194].

2. Métis and Non-Status Indian Constitutional Review Commission 1981, 51 [F848].

3. Métis and Non-Status Indian Constitutional Review Commission 1981, 51 [F846].

4. At the press conference, Daniels released the report of his Métis and Non-Status Indian Constitutional Review Commission. A glossy, 100-page document, the report contained fifty-three recommendations for action on Aboriginal rights, including further amendments to the patriation resolution and changes in legislation and policy.

CHAPTER 5: ELMER GHOSTKEEPER AND "MÉTISISM"

1. The Alberta ombudsman condemned the raids, prompting the province to apologize to the Métis settlements, and recommended a review of the Métis Population Betterment Act.

2. The FMS and the MAA had signed their own accord in April, pledging cooperation on constitutional issues.

3. Ghostkeeper 1982, 17.

4. Dick Johnston, minister of federal and intergovernmental affairs, and Don Macrimmon, minister of Native affairs, were named to the committee.

CHAPTER 6: IN THE BEAR PIT WITH JIM SINCLAIR

1. The main items on the agenda were "Charter of Rights for the Aboriginal Peoples" and "Entrenchment of Aboriginal Title." The other items were rights of Aboriginal women; guaranteed representation of Aboriginal peoples in Parliament and provincial legislatures; an Aboriginal consent clause in the amending formula; repeal of section 42(i)(e)(f) (of particular interest to the Inuit as the section involved provincial governments in the amending formula as it affected the extension of existing provinces into the territories and the establishment of new provinces); participation in international issues; mobility rights; hunting, fishing, trapping, and gathering rights; affirmative action programs; service delivery; language and culture; family law; and ongoing process (this item aimed at determining whether governments would support an amendment guaranteeing further constitutional conferences on the rights of Aboriginal peoples).

2. In the Baker Lake case of 1980, a federal court had limited Inuit Aboriginal title to hunting and fishing rights.

CHAPTER 7: MÉTIS POLITICAL REALIGNMENT

1. Métis people, some from Red River, had played an important role in the fur trade in the interior of British Columbia since the beginning of the nineteenth century. The North-West Rebellion in 1885 contributed to a movement of Métis into the Peace River country of British Columbia, in many respects an extension of the prairie. There Métis homesteaders established communities such as Kelly Lake that remain predominantly Métis to this day. In the twentieth century, many Métis from the Prairies moved west of the Rockies in search of jobs.

During the 1970s, the BC Métis were represented by provincial Aboriginal associations dominated by the more numerous non-status Indians. Métis alienation was a recurrent theme throughout the history of the British Columbia Association of Non-Status Indians (BCANSI), later known as the United Native Nations (UNN). In 1978, the Métis of northeastern British Columbia formed the Louis Riel Métis Society, which promoted Métis participation in resource development projects. President Fred House hailed from Paddle Prairie Métis Settlement in Alberta and, through a quirk of family history, was both a nephew of and older than Elmer Ghostkeeper.

2. The proposal for guaranteed representation at this time involved a constitutional amendment to entrench the right of Métis to blocs of seats in both houses of Parliament and some provincial legislatures, the creation of Métis electoral constituencies in western Canada, and the compilation of a Métis electoral roll in each constituency. The Inuit had also voiced interest in guaranteed parliamentary representation but not the status Indians, whose emphasis on sovereignty and coexistence precluded Indian participation in what was considered to be an alien political institution.

3. CICS, Document: 830-120/027, 129.

4. CICS, Document: 830-120/027, 168.

5. From minutes of the meeting of the NCC constitutional committee.

6. The Inuit leadership seemed rather perplexed by the Métis in general since a distinct people of mixed Inuit and white origins had never emerged. Although many Inuit, including ICNI co-chairman Charlie Watt, were of mixed parentage, they identified with the Inuit culture and sought rights as part of the Inuit collectivity.

7. CICS, Document: 830-126/027, 121.

8. An infuriated McIvor warned Inuit leaders that he would oppose the repeal of section

42(l)(e), a section involving provincial governments in the amending formula as it affected the extension of existing provinces into the territories and the establishment of new provinces. This section was vociferously opposed by the two territorial governments and by the Inuit of the eastern Arctic, all of whom feared that their aspirations for provincial status could be thwarted by provinces expanding from the south. In addition to threatening to oppose the repeal of Section 42(1)(e), McIvor said he would recommend to the Province of Manitoba that it annex the eastern Arctic!

CHAPTER 8: THE MÉTIS NATION VERSUS PIERRE ELLIOTT TRUDEAU

1. Gary Gould, the NCC spokesman, drawing an analogy with Joe Clark's difficulty in holding onto his leadership, stated, "It's our version of the Conservative leadership review."

2. At his own press conference, Milen told reporters, "Things are not moving, so I've come to the conclusion that I am one of the jerks in the bureaucracy I always would have liked to have fired. So, in a sense, I am firing myself."

3. "I'm out to crush evil!" Milen once snapped, when asked by a reporter what motivated him to work at such a frenetic pace for three days without sleep.

4. Based on the notes and recollection of the meeting by Sinclair's lawyer, Rob Milen.

5. Saskatchewan Attorney General Gary Lane also supported the Métis in an interview with *Macleans* magazine (see Diebel 1983, 48).

6. A judicial remedy in the form of an order from a superior court to a government.

7. Diebel 1983, 48.

8. These hand-woven sashes, first made in Assumption, Quebec, in the eighteenth century, were often worn by voyageurs in their travels west. They were later adopted by Métis working in the fur trade and are today a Métis cultural icon. An *Assumption* sash appears on the cover of this book.

9. CICS, Document: 800-17/004, 32.

CHAPTER 9: IMPASSE

1. The Assembly of First Nations adopted the same approach under the agenda heading "Aboriginal Title and Aboriginal Rights, Treaties, and Treaty Rights."

2. The MNC proposed a tripartite enumeration committee in each of the western provinces to plan and conduct the enumeration of the Métis population according to its self-identification criteria. The enumeration process would provide for applications, their certification, an appeals process, and the compilation of a Métis registry in each province to identify those eligible to participate in the affairs of Métis self-governing institutions.

3. Letter from Clément Chartier, Chairman of MNC Constitutional Committee, to Justice Minister MacGuigan, 17 February 1984.

4. CICS, Document: 800-18/019.

5. CICS, Document: 800-18/004, 64–65.

6. Letter from Prime Minister Trudeau to Clément Chartier, Chairman of MNC Constitutional Committee, 30 April 1984.

7. The MNC proposed the following principles to be applied to a Métis land base.

> Ownership of Métis lands and resources would be vested in Métis government.

> The form of land tenure on the land base would be solely within the jurisdiction of Métis government.

> Métis lands and resources would be exempt from taxation by other levels of government.

> Lands would be transferred to Métis government through intergovernmental agreements that would be constitutionalized under section 35(3) of the Constitution Act, 1982 (CICS, Document: 830-143/001, 143).

8. Minister of Justice John Crosbie to Clément Chartier, chairman of the constitutional committee of the MNC, 1 February 1985.

CHAPTER 10: THE FIERY FRONT

1. The election of a Canadian to that post was not surprising given WCIP's heavy reliance on funding from the Canadian International Development Agency (CIDA) and the location of its head office in Ottawa. Canadian Aboriginal influence over the organization had always been strong, starting with its first president, George Manuel of British Columbia.

2. The principle was first applied in international relations by U.S. President Woodrow Wilson in his Fourteen Points of 1918. It was introduced into the framework of international law and diplomacy in the founding Charter of the United Nations in 1945.

3. MISURASATA means Miskitos, Sumus, Ramas, and Sandinistas United.

4. Their release was expedited by the fact that the peace talks that had originally drawn Chartier and the WCIP into the Nicaraguan conflict were sponsored by a group of Latin American countries headed by Colombia.

5. The Contras were a variety of U.S.-backed Nicaraguan armed opposition groups based in Honduras and Costa Rica that waged an insurgency against the Sandinista regime.

6. The AFN and the NCC both supported Chartier's suspension, one AFN delegate telling a shocked Chartier that, as a sovereign people, Canada's Indians could not countenance Chartier's violation of the sovereignty of Nicaragua.

7. CICS, Document: 830-188/004, 15.

8. According to the revised draft political accord tabled by the federal government in Ottawa at a ministers meeting on 13 March 1987, negotiations relating to self-government agreements with Métis people in identifiable communities would be conducted without regard to and without prejudice to the respective positions of the parties as to whether Métis fit within section 91(24) of the Constitution Act. In addition, where a self-government agreement was concluded, the federal government and the provincial government would introduce such legislation to implement the terms of the agreement, including any legislation required to safeguard the agreement from constitutional challenge based on section 91(24).

9. During this period, efforts could be made to define the right through negotiated agreements, failing which the right would become justiciable in the courts five years after the clause was inserted in the Constitution.

10. The federal government based its argument on the grounds that the case did not raise a justiciable issue, given that the allegedly unconstitutional legislation had been spent and that the

plaintiffs were not entitled to standing.

11. CICS, Document: 800-23/004, 43.

12. CICS, Document: 800-23/004, 114–115.

13. CICS, Document: 800-23/004, 140.

14. CICS, Document: 800-23/004, 86–87.

15. CICS, Document: 800-23/004, 190–191.

16. CICS, Document: 800-23/004, 216–217.

17. CICS, Document: 800-23/004, 225–226.

18. CICS, Document: 800-23/004, 226–227.

19. CICS, Document: 800-23/004, 228.

20. CICS, Document: 800-23/004, 227.

21. CICS, Document: 800-23/004, 228–229.

CHAPTER 11: TRANSITIONS

1. A quirk in the WCIP constitution had allowed Chartier to retain the formal title of president until the expiration of his term in 1987. He continued to make public appearances as WCIP president and pursue the same uncompromising stance on the rights of indigenous peoples that had led to his de facto ouster from WCIP the year before.

2. Holding an eagle feather, Harper stood in the Manitoba legislature and said no to a request for unanimous consent to waive the requirement for notice that was needed to introduce the constitutional resolution, thereby ensuring it would not be considered before the deadline set for ratification of the 1987 Constitutional Accord (Meech Lake Accord).

CHAPTER 12: YVON DUMONT AND THE ROAD TO CHARLOTTETOWN

1. The land dispute between the Mohawk community of Kanesatake and the town of Oka lasted from 11 March to 26 September 1990 and involved an armed standoff between Mohawk militants and Canadian Forces. Other Mohawks at Kahnawake blockaded the Mercier Bridge between the Island of Montreal and the South Shore suburbs at the point it passed through their reserve, creating enormous traffic jams.

2. The Mulroney-MNC summit provided further impetus to the prairie-centred MNC to extend its representation to the outlying regions of the historical Métis homeland. The "bookend" organizations from Ontario and British Columbia that had been brought into the fold during the first ministers conference process had failed to establish themselves as credible and truly representative bodies and, on account of their weakness, had proven susceptible to manipulation by Jim Sinclair in his factional feuds with the nationalists. The prairie associations had taken steps to limit the influence of the "bookends" within the MNC's decision-making councils and to encourage more effective representation for the outlying regions.

The day before the summit, the Ontario Métis and Aboriginal Association (OMAA) had agreed to constitutional representation under the MNC, replacing the Northwestern Ontario Métis

Federation, which had withered away since the death of Paddy McGuire. OMAA brought with it a broader base of Métis 'representation from across northern Ontario. The Pacific Métis Federation (PMF) had gained admission to the MNC after the 1987 conference, replacing the Louis Riel Métis Association of British Columbia, which had drawn its membership from northeastern BC communities near the Alberta border. The PMF had been organized on a province-wide basis, offering representation both to historical Métis communities and to the large number of Métis who had migrated west of the Rockies in search of economic opportunities since the Second World War. It had adopted a province-wide ballot box system of democratic elections.

The Métis Nation Northwest Territories (MNNT) had also concluded an accord with the MNC for constitutional representation before the summit. Founded in the 1970s, the organization had stayed out of the MNC during the first ministers conference process despite the close historical and cultural ties of many of its members to the prairie Métis, concerned that the MNC's position on a distinct Métis land base could jeopardize the inclusion of its members alongside the Dene in the land claim settlement based on Aboriginal title in the Mackenzie District. Since the 1987 conference, however, the claims process in the North had fragmented, and the Métis association had to focus on safeguarding Métis interests. It had also come under pressure from Red River Métis locals, such as Fort Smith, to join the MNC. With the participation of the MNNT and by extension the southern Mackenzie District, the MNC would represent the entire historical Métis homeland in the next round of constitutional negotiations.

3.   The MNC had originally proposed the inclusion of guaranteed parliamentary representation in the agenda of the first ministers conference process but dropped the item when it failed to generate support from the other Aboriginal delegations. The MNC recommended establishment of Métis electoral districts to the Royal Commission on Electoral Reform and Party Financing in 1991, and the recommendations of this commission would figure in the Charlottetown Accord.

4.   Clément Chartier recalls that during one gruelling drafting session lasting into the early morning hours, he, as the sole MNC drafting official present, tried to stay awake by counting the lawyers in the AFN delegation—there were nineteen of them.

5.   The commission recommended a process for guaranteed representation of Aboriginal peoples in the House of Commons through the creation of Aboriginal electoral districts that would overlay general electoral districts.

6.   In deference to Alberta's Métis settlements, not part of the MNC's formal structure, the accord recognized the Métis Settlements General Council as having the sole right to negotiate agreements on behalf of its constituents.

CHAPTER 13: THE FALLBACK POSITION

1.   Bill-31, An Act to Amend the Indian Act, 28 June 1985.

2.   The lawsuit had been continuing its tortuous route through the provincial courts since the Supreme Court of Canada had refused to allow the case to be struck in 1990. Subsequently, the federal government went to court with a demand for particulars, arguing that the MMF specify "with respect to each enactment, each and every Métis person to whom it is alleged an interest in land was not conveyed as promised" and "each and every Métis person whose interest in land already conveyed to him or her is alleged to have been stripped from him or her as the case may be." The MMF, for its part, would amend its statement of claim to assert federal jurisdiction for Métis, the conclusion of a treaty between Canada and the provisional government in the Red River Colony, and a breach of the Crown's fiduciary obligations to the Métis arising from sections 31 and 32 of the Manitoba Act.

3. The statement of claim would be followed by years of research into the scrip process toward verification of the claims by a University of Alberta research unit (Métis Aboriginal Title Research Initiative X or MatriX) under the direction of Professor Frank Tough. It would also mobilize the prairie Métis associations into joint action on developing further research and litigation options with respect to the issues raised in the lawsuit and their application to other parts of the prairie provinces. Clément Chartier, president of the Métis Nation—Saskatchewan, would spearhead the establishment of a Prairie Métis Leaders Forum to coordinate work on these issues at both the political and the technical levels. Composed of the elected boards of the Prairie Métis provincial governing bodies, the forum would hold its first meeting in Saskatoon in January 2002, followed by semi-annual meetings thereafter.

4. *R. v. Van der Peet* 1996, paragraph 67.

5. *Aboriginal Self-Government: The Government of Canada's Approach to Implementation of the Inherent Right and the Negotiation of Aboriginal Self-Government* 1995, 3.

6. Ibid., 14.

7. Ibid., 15.

8. MNC governing members, with the support of the provinces, had built up some capacity to deliver services in these areas through a variety of institutions: in health care, the Métis Addictions Council of Saskatchewan and the Métis Nation of Ontario Long Term Care Initiative; in education, the Gabriel Dumont Institute in Saskatchewan and the Louis Riel Institute in Manitoba; and in child and family welfare, Métis Child and Family Services agencies in Alberta and Manitoba. They had also been able to supplement these efforts with some sporadic federal assistance to run bursary programs and health projects (which they had to bid on as contractors).

9. The MNC governing members had actually built up their strongest capacity in these federal special programs areas, but the lack of protection for these programs (unlike on-reserve programs) amid the fiscal austerity of the decade would take its toll. Métis capital corporations, despite a proven track record in providing small-business financing and advisory services to Métis entrepreneurs, had been unable to meet the growing demand for their services due to the failure of Industry Canada to recapitalize these institutions. The decision of the Chrétien government in 1993 to withdraw from social housing—ceasing new commitments under Canada Mortgage and Housing Corporation (CMHC) social housing and transferring its social housing portfolio to the provinces—had deprived Métis housing corporations of the ability to meet the soaring demand for urban and rural housing units. Based on CMHC data, Métis households on the Prairies accounted for 50 per cent of off-reserve Aboriginal households in core housing need in 2001. More than 20,000 Métis households were in core need, about one in every five. Métis people on waiting lists for urban Native nonprofit housing units in Winnipeg number in the thousands.

10. Lacking the ultimate budgetary authority and predictable financing of government, Métis organizations often worked on short-term projects, funded by different federal departments, each unaware of what the other was doing. Priorities were set by the bureaucrats allocating the funds. Funding was inconsistent and erratic—in most cases inadequate for the task at hand, in other cases impossible to spend within the timeframe provided—creating constant cash flow problems. Management was difficult, if not chaotic, given the need to produce activity and financial reports on a variety of schedules throughout the year.

11. In 2005, Poitras signed a $52-million agreement with Canada to provide assistance to more than 6,000 Métis clients annually.

12. Bell and Métis Settlements Appeal Tribunal 1999, 5–6.

13. Métis National Council 2005, 3.

14. LaRose 2000. Interview with Michif language restorationist Bruce Flamont.

15. LaRose 2000.

16. Emma LaRocque was born in a one-room log cabin near a trapline in 1949 and grew up in a small Métis community in northeastern Alberta. She received a PhD in history and English from the University of Manitoba, where she has been a professor in the department of Native Studies since 1977. She has written extensively as a poet, social and literary critic, and historian. Recent publications include: "When 'The Wild West' is Me: Re-viewing Cowboys and Indians" in *Challenging Frontiers: The Canadian West,* 2004; "Native Identity and the Métis: Otepayimsuak Peoples" in *A Passion for Identity: An Introduction to Canadian Studies* (4th edition), 2001; and nine of her poems in *Native Poetry in Canada: A Contemporary Anthology,* 2001.

17. LaRoque 1990, xxvi.

18. Born in northern Saskatchewan in 1940, Maria Campbell wrote *Halfbreed* to deal with anger, despair, and the pressure to return to a life on the streets as a prostitute and drug addict. The book continues to be one of the most widely taught texts in Canadian literature. Campbell went on to a distinguished career as a writer, playwright, theatre producer, and filmmaker. She has written four children's books and *Stories of the Road Allowance People* (1995) her version of traditional Métis tales. From 1985 to 1997, she operated her own film and video production company, writing and directing seven documentaries and producing the first Aboriginal television series, *My Partners, My People.* Her stage play *Flight* was the first all-Aboriginal theatre production in Canada. She followed that with six more plays, which she wrote, directed, and produced. Campbell is an assistant professor at the University of Saskatchewan.

19. Campbell 1973, 2.

20. Beatrice Mosionier (formerly Culleton) was born in St. Boniface, Manitoba, in 1949. She based her first novel, *In Search of April Raintree,* largely on her life experience, having grown up in foster homes and experienced the suicide of two of her sisters. Mosionier has also written books for children and has scripted *Walker* (1991), a short film for the National Film Board.

21. Filmmaker Gil Cardinal was born in Edmonton in 1950. He has directed more than thirty documentaries and television dramas with Aboriginal themes. A graduate of the Northern Alberta Institute of Technology, Cardinal began his career as a studio cameraman with Access TV in Edmonton, where he eventually became a senior producer. He left Access in 1980 to become active with the National Film Board as a freelance director, researcher, writer, and editor. His NFB films include *Children of Alcohol* (1983), *Hotwalker* (1985), the internationally acclaimed *Foster Child* (1987), *The Spirit Within* (1990), and *David with F.A.S.* (1997). In 1998, he directed the CBC miniseries *Big Bear,* for which he was nominated for a second Gemini. He has also directed numerous episodes of the television program *North of 60.*

22. Born in Olds, Alberta, in 1955, Marilyn Dumont worked in video production with the National Film Board for three years before completing an MFA in creative writing at the University of British Columbia. Her first book of poetry, *A Really Good Brown Girl* (1966), won the 1997 Gerald Lampert Memorial Award from the League of Canadian Poets for the best first collection of poetry by a Canadian poet.

23. Dumont 1996.

24. Gregory Scofield was born in Maple Ridge, BC, in 1966. He attended the Gabriel Dumont Institute in 1985 and began writing in 1988 after returning to the West Coast. His first book of poetry, *The Gathering: Stones for the Medicine Wheel,* was published in 1993 followed by three more books in the same decade: *Native Canadiana: Songs from the Urban Rez* (1996); *Sakihtowin-maskihkiy ekwa peyak-nikamowin/Love Medicine and One Song* (1997); and *I Knew*

Two Métis Women (1999), a tribute to his mother and aunt. His autobiography, *Thunder Through My Veins: Memoirs of a Métis Childhood*, was published in 1999.

25. Scofield 2001, 335.

26. LaRoque 1990, xviii.

CHAPTER 14: THE *POWLEY* DECISION

1. MNC press release, 12 January 2003.

2. Megan Easton, "The Family Business," *University of Toronto Magazine*, (winter 2003).

In the article, Teillet recalls how, growing up in St. Vital, Manitoba, where Riel had spent part of his childhood, she got kicked out of her elementary school class at the age of nine for challenging the teacher's history lesson on her great-grand-uncle. "My teacher said that Riel was some kind of madman, and she presented a version of history that was absolutely disgusting. I never have been shy and I don't know what I said to her, but it probably wasn't very nice."

At the end of high school, she was torn between pursuing a degree in dance and law school, eventually opting for dance. "I basically decided that you can be a lawyer when you're 40 but you can't be a dancer when you're 40." She entered the field of modern dance, dancing professionally in Toronto and eventually combining performing with writing, teaching, choreography, and directing. She ended up pursuing her second career choice, graduating from the University of Toronto Faculty of Law in 1994 and practicing law with the firm of Pape and Salter. She was also one of the founders of the Métis Nation of Ontario. In 2002, she won the Law Society of Upper Canada's first Lincoln Alexander Award both for her legal successes and for her contributions to the Aboriginal community as a teacher and mentor.

3. Binnie was appointed to the Supreme Court of Canada in 1998. Another veteran of the first ministers conference process hearing *Powley* was Frank Iacobucci, deputy minister of justice and deputy attorney general for Canada from 1985 to 1988, who was appointed to the Supreme Court in 1991.

4. The actual wording read: "Are ss. 46 and 47(1) of the Game and Fish Act, R.S.O., 1990, c. G.1, as they read on October 22, 1993, of no force or effect with respect to the respondents, being Métis, in the circumstances of this case, by reason of their aboriginal rights under s. 35 of the Constitution Act, 1982?"

5. *R. v. Powley* 2003, paragraph 13.

6. Ibid., paragraph 27.

7. Ibid., paragraph 10.

8. Ibid., paragraph 17.

9. Ibid., paragraph 18.

10. Ibid., paragraph 38.

11. Ibid., paragraph 30.

12. Ibid., paragraph 33.

13. Ibid., paragraph 49.

14. "Ontario Métis Given Right to Hunt," *CBC News*, 19 September 2003.

15. *R. v. Blais* 2003, paragraph 33.

16. Ibid., paragraph 42.

17. The furthest the Métis had gone in this respect was with the case of *Grumbo*, a Métis charged with unlawful possession of wildlife in 1994 under the Wildlife Act in Saskatchewan. Counsel for the defendant, Clément Chartier, argued that Grumbo as a Métis was an "Indian" within the meaning of the NRTA. The trial judge found that Grumbo was not an Indian for NRTA purposes and convicted him. On appeal, the Court of Queen's Bench quashed the conviction on the grounds that the Crown had failed to establish that Grumbo was *not* an Indian. The Queen's Bench judge ruled that, if there was any doubt, it should be resolved in favour of the accused.

During the period between the Queen's Bench decision on 2 August 1996, and 14 May 1998, the Métis throughout Saskatchewan had the right to hunt. On the latter date, however, the Saskatchewan Court of Appeal overturned the Queen's Bench judgment. A majority held that there was a preliminary issue to be determined before the court could rule on whether Métis were "Indians" for NRTA purposes, and that was whether the Métis had existing Aboriginal title or harvesting rights prior to the enactment of the NRTA. They ordered a new trial, keeping the door open to argue Métis hunting rights as NRTA "Indians," but the door closed with *Blais*.

18. *R.v. Blais*, paragraph 26.

Chapter 15: Defining the Métis Homeland

1. Years before *Powley*, some MNC member associations had established their own governance systems for harvesting that, despite lack of recognition from provincial authorities, had guided the harvesting activities of their members. In 1994, the Métis Nation Saskatchewan had enacted its own Wildlife and Conservation Act and accompanying regulations and had been advising its members to use MNS citizenship cards for identification purposes for the harvest. The Métis Nation of Ontario had a harvesting policy in place since 1995 and had been issuing harvester certificates for harvesting within traditional Métis territory, such as the Sault Ste. Marie district that became the focus of *Powley*.

2. *R. v. Powley* 2003, paragraph 2.

3. Ibid., paragraph 50.

4. In the case of the MNC, a dispute had arisen over a decision by the honorary governor of the Métis Nation to seek office provincially despite a restriction to the contrary in his terms of office. The prairie Métis leaders dominating the board of governors were also reluctant to proceed with major institutional change until the homeland boundaries were set.

5. MNC press release, 24 October 2003.

6. *Winnipeg Free Press*, 23 October 2004.

7. MMF press release, 22 October 2004.

8. "Interim Métis Harvesting Agreements, Fact Sheet," Alberta Aboriginal Affairs and Northern Development.

9. *R. v. Nichol* 2005 N.J. no. 315 was a case largely unrelated to Aboriginal rights in which the defendants argued that their right to fish for cod as Newfoundlanders trumped the federal government's authority to regulate the inshore fishery.

10. Ibid., paragraph 74, note 4.

11. *R. v. Castonguay* 2003, NBPC 16. The judge determined that the criteria for membership in a Métis rights-bearing community as set out in *Powley* would apply to this case, which was heard after lower-court decisions on *Powley* had been upheld by the Ontario Court of Appeal but before the final appeal was heard by the Supreme Court of Canada. The decision was upheld by the Court of Queen's Bench of New Brunswick (2003 NBQB 325).

12. *R. v. Castonguay* 2003, paragraph 77.

13. *R. v. Willison* 2005, BCPC 0131.

14. Ibid., paragraph 85.

15. *R. v. Willison*, rev'd 2006 BCSC 985.

16. The trial judge also addressed the issue of identifying who is within the rights-bearing group and efforts by the Métis National Council and its constituent organizations to compile a centralized registry of Métis rights bearers based on their definition or citizenship criteria for Métis (paragraph 113). He concluded,

> Provided that persons meet the membership criteria set out in *Powley* and the 'national definition of Métis' as established by the Métis National Council, I do not believe it to be necessary to establish that every member of the local Métis community can demonstrate a personal ancestral connection to the particular Métis persons who formed the British Columbia ancestral community. ... But the Métis National Council requirement that historic Métis nation ancestry be demonstrated, and the genealogical compendium of Métis families which was Exhibit 9 in the trial, together serve to remind us that there are real and meaningful pre-conditions to demonstrating membership in the rights-bearing community; inevitably there will be a limited number of persons who can do so.

17. *R. v. Norton* 2005, SKPC 46.

18. *R. v. Laviolette* 2005, SKPC 70.

19. Counsel for the accused consisted of MNC President Clément Chartier, Jason Madden, and Jean Teillet.

20. Chartier 2005.

21. On 7 February 2002, in yet another twist in the tortuous path of the case, the Court of Queen's Bench of Manitoba granted a postponement of the case but not the indefinite postponement requested by governments (2002 MBQB 52). The court noted that the MMF had amended its statement of claim to add numerous statutes and Orders-in-Council to those originally impugned as being ultra vires or unconstitutional.

22. Provincial Court of Saskatchewan, April 1996.

23. *R. v. Blais* 2003, paragraph 34.

24. In a prospectus dated 7 October 2004, to borrow US$1 billion, the Province of Saskatchewan noted as material litigation that

> There is an action by Métis Nation of Saskatchewan (the "Métis") against the Province and Canada claiming approximately 145,000 square kilometers of land in northwestern Saskatchewan, as well as claiming additional unspecified damages, based on a claim of unextinguished aboriginal title.

There have been no pretrial negotiations, and the action has not yet proceeded to trial and likely will not for another two to four years. The
Province's counsel is of the opinion that the claim has little chance of success since Métis claims to aboriginal title were extinguished by federal government action in the early 1900s and the Métis also cannot show the
exclusive possession of the lands necessary for a claim to aboriginal title.
Even if the claim is successful, the Province's counsel is of the opinion the
land involved would not be more than a small fraction of the land claimed,
and certainly not more than 10%. Based on past settlements with Indian
Bands, it is anticipated that the cost of any final judgment would be shared
approximately equally between the Province and Canada, although
Canada will likely argue that this is exclusively a provincial responsibility.

Province of Saskatchewan, Prospectus US$1,000,000,000 Euro Medium Term Note, Arranger
Credit Suisse First Boston, 7 October 2004, 34.

25. A study undertaken by the Aboriginal Banking section of the Royal Bank of Canada in 1997,
by Kelley Lendsay and Wanda Wuttunee, *Historical Economic Perspectives of Aboriginal Peoples:
Cycles of Balance and Partnership,* noted that "most of the 1.4 million acres, set aside by the
Manitoba Act for the Métis slid into the hands of chartered banks via the scrip transactions" (see
section II [c][4] "Métis Scrip"). It also noted that in the distribution and delivery of 26,000
northwestern Métis scrip notes, 52 per cent of the notes ended up with chartered banks, 17 per
cent with private institutions and large speculators, 12 per cent with small speculators, and 11
per cent with the Métis.

26. *Winnipeg Free Press,* 27 May 2005.

Chapter 16: Clément Chartier and Kelowna: The Almost Accord

1. MNC press release, 3 February 2004.

2. Flanagan 1983, 314.

3. MNC News Release, "Mr Harper, We Do Not Need 'Forgiveness' for Being Concerned About
the Future of Our People Under a Conservative regime," Ottawa, 10 June 2004.

4. "Improving Aboriginal Health: First Ministers and Aboriginal Leaders Meeting,"
Government of Canada News Release, Special Meeting of First Minister and Aboriginal Leaders,
Ottawa, Ontario, 13 September 2004.

5. Letter from Clément Chartier, president of the Métis National Council, to Prime Minister
Paul Martin, dated 12 September 2004.

6. Ibid.

7. Stavenhagen 2004, 13.

8. Ibid., 9–10.

9. Métis Nation Framework Agreement between Her Majesty the Queen in Right of Canada
and the Métis National Council, 31 May 2005, 2.

10. Ibid.

11. The balance of power position of the NDP in the House of Commons proved to be a two-
edged sword for the national Aboriginal organizations. Ottawa's revitalized commitment to

Aboriginal housing could largely be credited to the NDP's decision to spare the Liberals from defeat on a budget bill on 26 April 2005, in return for increased social spending in areas including Aboriginal housing. But the public backlash against the Liberals with the release of the first-phase report of the Gomery Inquiry on 1 November 2005 sealed the fate of the Liberal-NDP alliance and drove the NDP into the arms of the other opposition parties, who supported the no-confidence motion.

12. Canadian Press, 25 November 2005.

13. Government of Canada, *First Ministers and National Aboriginal Leaders: Strengthening Relationships and Closing the Gap*, Kelowna, BC, 24–25 November 2005.

14. Ibid., 2.

15. Within the area of health, the MNC and its governing members would participate in developing and implementing the Blueprint on Aboriginal Health, sharing in new federal funding (beyond that committed at the special meeting of first ministers and Aboriginal leaders in 2004) directed to initiatives in areas such as nutrition and food security, diabetes prevention and treatment, public health, continuing care, mental health, suicide, and addictions. They would also participate in economic development initiatives to build economic infrastructure, including broadband connectivity, training and skills development, and apprenticeships, and to promote resource and business development opportunities.

16. *First Ministers and National Aboriginal Leaders: Strengthening Relationships and Closing the Gap*, 16.

17. The action plan committed Ottawa and the relevant provinces to work with the Métis to improve educational outcomes within public education systems through kindergarten to grade 12 (K–12), innovation supports such as stay-in-school programs, literacy initiatives, mentoring and role model programs, and in-school cultural programs. It provided for the establishment of a Métis Nation Centre of Excellence in Education and Innovation to develop educational materials and resources. It also offered support for those programs related to K–12 and transitions delivered by existing Métis educational institutions (the Gabriel Dumont Institute in Saskatchewan and the Louis Riel Institute in Manitoba) and for the development of new Métis educational institutions. The bursaries managed by the MNC's governing members would be enlarged to fund the postsecondary education of Métis students.

In partnering with the Métis governing bodies to revitalize Métis housing, Ottawa and the relevant provinces committed to investments in new Métis housing and in the ongoing maintenance of existing Métis-delivered social/subsidized housing. A Métis Nation Housing Institute would be established to support capacity development for existing Métis housing agencies and new Métis social/subsidized housing and to serve as a think-tank for housing solutions.

18. Monitoring and assessment of progress would be conducted annually at the ministerial level, at a two-day meeting that included distinct First Nations, Inuit, and Métis forums involving the respective Aboriginal leaders and federal and provincial ministers. The format would also apply to the next meeting of first ministers and Aboriginal leaders in two to three years to measure progress.

19. *First Ministers and National Aboriginal Leaders: Strengthening Relationships and Closing the Gap*, 17.

20. Ibid.

21. Letter from Stephen Harper, Leader of the Opposition, to President of Congress of Aboriginal People, dated 10 January 2006.

22. Interview with CJWW Radio, Saskatoon, 9 January 2006.

23. Canada Newswire Group, Ottawa, 10 January 2006.

24. Letter from Stephen Harper, Leader of the Opposition, to President of Congress of Aboriginal People, 10 January 2006.

25. The so-called *beau risque* was a strategy adopted by Parti Québécois premier René Lévesque to see whether a political solution short of separation was possible with Canada. The strategy was the underlying reason for PQ support for Brian Mulroney in the 1984 federal election and proved crucial to the Tory sweep in Quebec and the attainment of a majority government.

26. Mark Hume, "Prentice Makes No Promises But Is Praised at Summit," *Globe and Mail*, 10 March 2006.

27. Government of Canada, *The Budget Speech 2006, Chapter 3, Families and Communities: Helping Aboriginal Communities*, Ottawa: Department of Finance, 2 May 2006.

28. *National Post*, 29 May 2006.

29. Anita Neville, Liberal MP and Indian affairs critic, "Indian Affairs Minister Jim Prentice Must Retract His Statements," press release, 31 May 2006.

30. Elizabeth Thompson, "Scrapping Kelowna Accord Would Be 'Immoral': Paul Martin," Montreal *Gazette*, 2 June 2006.

31. Lawrence Martin, "Miles to Go before Martin Sleeps," *Globe and Mail*, 1 June 2006.

32. Canadian Press, 4 May 2006.

33. Canadian Press, 3 May 2006.

34. *CBC News*, 29 May 2006.

35. Lawrence Martin, "Miles to Go Before Martin Sleeps," *Globe and Mail*, 1 June 2006.

36. "Martin Urges Tories to Support Kelowna Accord," *CBC News*, 2 June 2006.

37. Elizabeth Thompson, "Scrapping Kelowna Accord Would Be 'Immoral': Paul Martin," Montreal *Gazette*, 2 June 2006.

CHAPTER 17: THE GLOBAL MOVEMENT

1. The IACHR had conducted on-site visits and general reports on the situation of indigenous peoples, including the Miskito situation in Nicaragua about the time of Chartier's clandestine mission in 1985–86.

2. *Proposed American Declaration on the Rights of Indigenous Peoples*, Article II (2).

3. Ibid., Article XVIII (2). Another provision of particular importance to landless people is Article XVIII (7): "Indigenous peoples have the right to the restitution of the lands, territories and resources which they have traditionally owned or otherwise occupied or used, and which have been confiscated, occupied, used or damaged, or when restitution is not possible, the right to compensation on a basis not less favorable than the standard of international law."

4. Vargas Llosa's remarks were made at a seminar in Colombia and published on 11 November 2003, by the Ecuadorian daily *El Universo*.

5. Tom Hayden, "Bolivia's Indian Revolt," *Nation*, 21 June 2004.

6. Jerry Reynolds, "OAS Goes Another Round on Indigenous Rights Negotiations," *Indian*

Country Today, 11 February 2005.

7.   The sixth meeting of the working group, the first away from the Washington, DC, headquarters of the OAS, was held in Antigua, Guatemala, in October 2005. Dr. Paul Chartrand, a Métis professor of law at the University of Saskatchewan, represented the MNC in the meeting of the indigenous caucus prior to the working group sessions.

8.   On 18 January 2001, the U.S. National Security Council had advised the U.S. delegations in both the UN and the OAS to use the following definition:

> Indigenous peoples have a right of internal self-determination. By virtue of that right, they may negotiate their political status within the framework of the existing nation-state and are free to pursue their economic, social, and cultural development. Indigenous peoples, in exercising their right of internal self-determination, have the internal right to autonomy or self-government in matters relating to their local affairs, including determination of membership, culture, language, religion, education, information, media, health, housing, employment, social welfare, maintenance of community safety, family relations, economic activities, lands and resources management, environment and entry by non-members, as well as ways and means for financing these autonomous functions. (U.S. National Security Council, "Position on Indigenous Peoples," 18 January 2001, point 3.)

In May 2006, the United States joined with Australia and New Zealand in reaffirming its opposition to the original self-determination clause in the draft United Nations Declaration on the Rights of Indigenous Peoples on the grounds that it was inconsistent with international law.

9.   "Canada Opposes UN Aboriginal Treaty," *CBC News,* 20 June 2006.

10.   Letter from MNC President Clément Chartier to Jim Prentice, Federal Interlocutor for Métis, 31 July 2006.

11.   MNC Press Release, "Métis National Council Statement on the Decision of the General Assembly Third Committee on Delaying Adoption of the United Nations Declaration," Ottawa, 29 November 2006.

Chapter 18: Prospects for Métis Self-Government

1.   Amended Statement of Claim, 12 November 2004, *Manitoba Métis Federation v. Attorney General of Canada and Attorney General of Manitoba,* Manitoba Queen's Bench, 4.

2.   Standing Senate Committee on Aboriginal Peoples 2003, 12.

3.   Among these institutions are school boards, hospital authorities, and family services agencies.

4.   According to the final report on urban aboriginal youth by the Standing Senate Committee on Aboriginal Peoples, "For young Métis, if they live in a city, their chances of living in a lone-parent family are double that of their rural counterparts. Their chances of remaining in one place are much less than other Aboriginal peoples: one-fifth of all Métis moved in the year previous of the 2001 Census." 2003, 12.

5.   *Ardoch Algonquin First Nation v. Canada (Attorney General),* 2003, FCA 473.

6.   Privy Council of Canada evaluation report commissioned to Goss Gilroy Inc. in 2002 and obtained through the Access to Information Act.

REFERENCES

BOOKS, REPORTS, AND ARTICLES

Adams, Howard. *Prison of Grass: Canada from the Native Point of View.* Toronto: New Press, 1975.

Bell, Catherine E., and the Métis Settlements Appeal Tribunal. *Contemporary Métis Justice: The Settlement Way.* Saskatoon: Native Law Centre, University of Saskatchewan, 1999.

Brown, Jennifer S. H. *Strangers in Blood: Fur Trade Company Families in Indian Country.* Vancouver: UBC Press, 1980.

Campbell, Maria. *Halfbreed.* Toronto: McClelland & Stewart, 1973.

Chartier, Clément. "State of the Nation Address." Métis National Council General Assembly, Calgary, Alberta, 19 March 2005.

Culleton, Beatrice. *In Search of April Raintree.* Winnipeg: Pemmican Publications, 1983.

Daniels, Harry W. *We are the New Nation: Nous Sommes La Nouvelle Nation.* Ottawa: Native Council of Canada, 1979.

Daniels, Harry W., ed. *The Forgotten People: Métis and non-status Indian Land Claims.* Ottawa: Native Council of Canada, 1979.

de Trémaudan, Auguste Henri. *Histoire de la Nation Métisse dans l'Ouest Canadien.* Montreal: Albert Lévesque, 1936.

Diebel, Linda. "A Confrontation on the White Man's Turf", *Macleans,* 21 March 1983: 46–50.

Dumont, Marilyn. *A Really Good Brown Girl.* London: Brick Books, 1996.

Flanagan, Thomas. 1983. "The Case Against Métis Aboriginal Rights". *Canadian Public Policy,* IX:3 : 314–325.

Ghostkeeper, Elmer, ed. *Métisism: A Canadian Identity.* Edmonton: Alberta Federation of Métis Settlement Associations, 1982.

Government of Canada. *Shaping Canada's Future Together: Proposals.* Ottawa: Supply and Services, 1991.

Hatt, F. K. "The Land Issue and the Mobilization of the Alberta Métis in the 1930s." In *The Forgotten People: Métis and non-status Indian Land Claims.* Ottawa: Native Council of Canada, 1979.

LaRoque, Emma. "Preface: Or, Here Are Our Voices Who Will Hear?" *Writing the Circle.* Ed. Jeanne Perreault and Sylvia Vance. Edmonton: NeWest, 1990.

Lussier, Antoine S., and D. Bruce Sealey. *The Other Natives, the-les Métis: Vol. 2, 1885–1978.* Winnipeg: Manitoba Métis Federation Press; Éditions Bois-Brûlé, 1978.

Métis and Non-Status Indian Constitutional Review Commission. *Native People and the Constitution of Canada: The Report of the Métis and Non-Status Indian Constitutional Review Commission.* Ottawa: Native Council of Canada, 1981.

Métis National Council. "Accountability Policy Paper." Canada-Aboriginal Peoples Roundtable, Ottawa, Ontario, 25–26 January 2005.

———. *The Métis Nation on the Move*. Ottawa: Métis National Council, 1992.

Morton, W. L. *Manitoba: A History*. Toronto: University of Toronto Press, 1957.

Native Council of Canada. *A Statement of Claim Based on Aboriginal Title of Métis and Non-Status Indians*. Ottawa: Native Council of Canada, 1980.

Pelletier, Émile. *A Social History of the Manitoba Métis*. Winnipeg: Manitoba Métis Federation Press, 1974.

———. *Exploitation of Métis Lands*. Winnipeg: Manitoba Métis Federation Press, 1975.

Peterson, Jacqueline, and Jennifer Brown, eds. *The New Peoples: Being and Becoming Métis in North America*. Lincoln, Nebraska: University of Nebraska Press, 1985.

Royal Commission on Aboriginal Peoples. *Aboriginal Self-Government: Legal and Constitutional Issues*. Ottawa: Royal Commission on Aboriginal Peoples, 1995.

———. *Report of the Royal Commission on Aboriginal Peoples: Volume 2. Restructuring the Relationship*. Ottawa: Canada Communications Group, 1996.

Sanders, Douglas. "Métis Rights in the Prairie Provinces and the Northwest Territories: A Legal Interpretation." In *The Forgotten People: Métis and Non-Status Indian Land Claims*. Ottawa: Native Council of Canada, 1979.

Scofield, Gregory. "God of the Fiddle Players" from *The Gathering*. Vancouver: Polestar Book Publishers, 1993.

Sealey, Bruce, and Antoine Lussier. *The Métis: Canada's Forgotten People*. Winnipeg: Manitoba Métis Federation Press, 1975.

Slobodin, Richard. *Métis of the Mackenzie District*. Ottawa: Canadian Research Centre for Anthropology, St. Paul University, 1966.

Special Joint Committee of the Senate and the House of Commons on a Renewed Canada (Beaudoin-Dobbie). *A Renewed Canada: The Report of the Special Joint Committee of the Senate and the House of Commons on a Renewed Canada*. Ottawa: Queen's Printer, 1992.

Sprague, D. N. "Government Lawlessness in the Administration of Manitoba Land Claims, 1870–1887." *Manitoba Law Journal* vol. 10 (1980): 415–441.

———. "The Métis People and the Manitoba Act." In *Native People and the Constitution of Canada: The Report of the Métis and Non-Status Indian Constitutional Review Commission*, 52–68. Ottawa: Native Council of Canada, 1981

Stanley, G. F. G., *The Birth of Western Canada*. Toronto: University of Toronto Press, 1961.

Standing Senate Committee on Aboriginal Peoples. "*Urban Aboriginal Youth: An Action Plan for Change.*" 2003.

Stavenhagen, Rodolfo. *Indigenous Issues: Report of the Special Rapporteur on the Situation of Human Rights and Fundamental Freedoms of Indigenous Peoples (Addendum: Mission to Canada)*. Geneva: Commission on Human Rights, Economic and Social Council, United Nations, 2004.

TRANSCRIPTS

Canadian Intergovernmental Conference Secretariat (CICS)

Document: 830-120/027. 1983. Verbatim Transcript 31 January–1 February. *Federal-Provincial Meeting of Ministers on Aboriginal Constitutional Matters*. Ottawa.

Document: 830-126/027. 1983. Verbatim Transcript 28 February–1 March. *Federal-Provincial Meeting of Ministers on Aboriginal Constitutional Matters*. Ottawa.

Document: 800-17/004. 1983. Verbatim Transcript 15–16 March. *First Ministers' Conference on Aboriginal Constitutional Matters*. Ottawa.

Document: 830-143/001. 1984. Verbatim Transcript 13–14 February. *Federal-Provincial Meeting of Ministers on Aboriginal Constitutional Matters*.Toronto.

Document: 800-18/019. 1984. Métis National Council. "Draft Constitutional Accords on Métis Self-Identification and Enumeration." 8–9 March. *First Ministers' Conference on Aboriginal Constitutional Matters*. Ottawa.

Document: 800-18/004. 1984. Verbatim Transcript 8–9 March. *First Ministers' Conference on Aboriginal Constitutional Matters*. Ottawa.

Document: 800-20/013. 1985. Government of Canada. "Proposed 1985 Accord Relating to the Aboriginal Peoples of Canada." Tabled 2 April. *First Ministers' Conference on Aboriginal Constitutional Matters*. Ottawa.

Document: 830-188/004. 1985. Verbatim Transcript 5–6 June. *Federal-Provincial Meeting of Ministers on Aboriginal Constitutional Matters*. Toronto.

Document: 800-23/004. 1987. Verbatim Transcript 26–27 March. *First Ministers' Conference on Aboriginal Constitutional Matters*. Ottawa.

LEGAL CASES

Re: Eskimos, S.C.R. 104 (1939).

Calder v. British Columbia (Attorney General), S.C.R. 313 (1973).

Hamlet of Baker Lake v. Minister of Indian Affairs and Northern Development, 1 F.C.518 (T.D.) (1980).

Manitoba Métis Federation v. Attorney General of Canada and Attorney General of Manitoba (Q.B. File No. CI81).

Dumont v. Canada (Attorney General), 1 S.C.R. 279 (1990).

R. v. Sparrow, 1 S.C.R. 1075 (1990).

R. v. McPherson, 4 C.N.L.R. 145 (1992); 2 C.N.L.R. 137 (Man. QB) (1994).

Morin v. Canada & Saskatchewan (Q.B. File No. 619-1994).

R. v. Van der Peet, 2 S.C.R (1996).

R. v. Grumbo, 3 C.N.L.R. 122 (Sask. Q.B.) (1996); 3 C.N.L.R 172 (Sask C.A.) (1998)

R. v. Morin & Daigneault, 3 C.N.L.R. 157 (Sask Prov Ct) (1996); aff'd 1 C.N.L.R 182 (Sask. QB) (1998).

R. v. Castonguay, NBPC 16; (2003 NBQB 325) (2003).

R. v. Powley, 2 S.C.R. 207, 2003 SCC 43 (2003).

R. v. Blais, 2 S.C.R. 236, 2003 SCC 44 (2003).

R. v. Nichol, N.J. no. 315 (2005).

R. v. Willison, BCPC 0131 (2005).

R. v. Norton, SKPC 46 (2005).

R. v. Laviolette, SKPC 70 (2005).

CONSTITUTIONAL AMENDMENTS

Constitution Act, 1982
PART II
RIGHTS OF THE ABORIGINAL PEOPLES OF CANADA

35. (1) The existing aboriginal and treaty rights of the aboriginal peoples of Canada are hereby recognized and affirmed.

(2) In this Act, "aboriginal peoples of Canada" includes the Indian, Inuit, and Métis peoples of Canada.

(3) For greater certainty, in subsection (1) "treaty rights" includes rights that now exist by way of land claims agreements or may be so acquired.

(4) Notwithstanding any other provision of this Act, the aboriginal and treaty rights referred to in subsection (1) are guaranteed equally to male and female persons.

35.1 The government of Canada and the provincial governments are committed to the principal that, before any amendment is made to Class 24 of section 91 of the "Constitution Act, 1867", to section 25 of this Act or to this Part,

> (*a*) a constitutional conference that includes in its agenda an item relating to the proposed amendment, composed of the Prime Minister of Canada and the first ministers of the provinces, will be convened by the Prime Minister of Canada; and

> (*b*) the Prime Minister of Canada will invite representatives of the aboriginal peoples of Canada to participate in the discussions on that item.

PART IV.1

CONSTITUTIONAL CONFERENCES

37.1 (1) In addition to the conference convened in March 1983, at least two constitutional conferences composed of the Prime Minister of Canada and the first ministers of the provinces shall be convened by the Prime Minister of Canada, the first within three years after April 17, 1982 and the second within five years after that date.

(2) Each conference convened under subsection (1) shall have included in its agenda matters that directly affect the aboriginal peoples of Canada, and the Prime Minister of Canada shall invite representatives of those peoples to participate in the discussions on those matters.

AGREEMENTS

Constitutional Accord on Aboriginal Rights, Ottawa, 16 March 1983.

Alberta-Métis Settlements Accord, 1 July 1989.

Interim Métis Harvesting Agreement Between Her Majesty the Queen in Right of the Province of Alberta and the Métis Nation of Alberta Association, 28 September 2004.

Métis Nation Framework Agreement between Her Majesty the Queen in Right of Canada and the Métis National Council, 31 May 2005.

Métis Nation Accord on Human Resources Development Between Her Majesty the Queen in Right of Canada and the Métis National Council, 15 November 2005.

AGREEMENTS-IN-PRINCIPLE

Consensus Report on the Constitution (1992) (Charlottetown Accord), 28 August 1992.

Métis Nation Accord, 7 October 1992.

First Ministers and National Aboriginal Leaders: Strengthening Relationships and Closing the Gap (Kelowna Accord), 24–25 November 2005.

PROPOSED INTERNATIONAL DECLARATIONS

Proposed American Declaration on the Rights of Indigenous Peoples (Organization of American States)

United Nations Declaration on the Rights of Indigenous Peoples

POLICY STATEMENTS

The Government of Canada's Approach to Implementation of the Inherent Right and the Negotiation of Aboriginal Self-Government. Ottawa: Indian Affairs and Northern Development, 1995.

Gathering Strength: Canada's Aboriginal Action Plan. Ottawa: Indian Affairs and Northern Development, 1997.

ACKNOWLEDGEMENTS

I wish to thank two truly inimitable personalities, Vic Valentine and the late Harry Daniels, for getting me involved in the Métis movement thirty years ago. I also wish to acknowledge and express my sincere appreciation to the Métis leaders who encouraged and assisted me in my efforts to chronicle the evolution of the Métis nationalist movement—Yvon Dumont and Ferdinand Guiboche in Manitoba, Jim Sinclair in Saskatchewan, and Elmer Ghostkeeper in Alberta. My foremost debt in this respect is owed to Clément Chartier, whose tireless efforts to achieve Métis self-government at home and Indigenous peoples' recognition in international law shaped so much of my story, and without whose encouragement and insight this book would never have been done. I also wish to thank the contemporary leaders of the Métis movement—Audrey Poitras, David Chartrand, Tony Belcourt, and Bruce Dumont—for assisting me in bringing the book up to date; they are taking the drive toward self-determination and self-government to a level far beyond our expectations during the years explored in *Quiet Revolution West*.

I wish to acknowledge two friends and colleagues who provided me with invaluable advice and insight over the years: Marc LeClair and Rob Milen. I also benefitted greatly from individuals in the academic world, most notably Douglas Sanders from the UBC Law Faculty, a brilliant mind, great guy, and foremost unsung hero in the understanding and recognition of Aboriginal and Métis rights in Canadian law; and Doug Sprague, a historian who dared to think "outside the box." David Hawkes and the Institute of Intergovernmental Relations of Queen's University provided me with an excellent opportunity to explore the theoretical dimensions of the Métis self-government question in the mid-1980s and I am indebted to them. Thanks, as well, to Armand Ruffo of Carleton University, a pioneer in the role of Aboriginal writers in Canadian literature, who shared with me his insight into the role of the Métis in this burgeoning field, and to my editor, Dallas Harrison, for his helpful comments and suggestions.

In *Quiet Revolution West*, I have tried to capture many of the key events, issues, and personalities of the Métis nationalist movement. I would, however, be remiss if I did not state that a significant part of the story lies with hundreds of other committed Métis individuals—educators, artists, linguists, community organizers and activists, field workers, professionals, entrepreneurs—who are fulfilling Louis Riel's vision of a Métis Nation reawakening a century after his death and martyrdom. They are an integral part of the quiet revolution in the Métis homeland in western Canada.

Index

FIFTH
HOUSE

About Fifth House

Fifth House Publishers, a Fitzhenry & Whiteside company, is a proudly western-Canadian press. Our publishing specialty is non-fiction as we believe that every community must possess a positive understanding of its worth and place if it is to remain vital and progressive. Fifth House is committed to "bringing the West to the rest" by publishing books about the land and people who make this region unique. Our books are selected for their quality and contribution to the understanding of western-Canadian (and Canadian) history, culture, and environment.

Look for the following Fifth House titles at your local bookstore:

The Amazing Death of Calf Shirt and Other Blackfoot Stories, Hugh A. Dempsey

Buffalo Days and Nights, Peter Erasmus

Chief Smallboy: The Pursuit of Freedom, Gary Botting

Earth Elder Stories, Alexander Wolfe

Finding My Talk: How Fourteen Canadian Native Women Reclaimed their Lives after Residential School, Agnes Grant

Firewater: The Impact of the Whisky Trade on the Blackfoot Nation, Hugh A. Dempsey

Just Another Indian: A Serial Killer and Canada's Indifference, Warren Goulding

Loyal till Death: Indians and the North-West Rebellion, Blair Stonechild and Bill Waiser

People of the Blood: A Decade-long Photographic Journey on a Canadian Reserve, George Webber

Prison of Grass: Canada from a Native Point of View, Howard Adams

The Rez Sisters, Tomson Highway

Silent Words, Ruby Slipperjack

Toronto at Dreamer's Rock and Education is Our Right: Two One-Act Plays, Drew Hayden Taylor

The World is Our Witness: The Historic Journey of the Nisga'a into Canada, Tom Molloy with Donald Ward

York Boats of the Hudson's Bay Company: Canada's Inland Armada, Dennis F. Johnson